A barn

B front garden

C house

D patio

E dining area

F raised vegetable beds

G garden shed and staghorn sumac

H cabin and toolshed

I bluestem meadow

J copper beech

K red-twig dogwoods

L crabapples

M apple trees

N compost

O winterberry and viburnum

P water garden

Q *Miscanthus* 'Giganteus' bed

R far shrub borders

S *Aesculus parviflora*

A Way to Garden

A HANDS-ON PRIMER FOR EVERY SEASON

Margaret Roach

TIMBER PRESS
Portland, Oregon

Page 1: Ostrich fern fronds unfurl in spring and mingle with dwarf white pine needles and candles.
Frontispiece: The fallen flowers of an old rhododendron make a pool of lavender beneath its gnarled trunks.
Opposite: The far shrub borders in fall are a pollinator- and wildlife-friendly mix of fruiting shrubs, conifers, and ground covers.

Published in 2019 by Timber Press, Inc.

The Haseltine Building
133 S.W. Second Avenue, Suite 450
Portland, Oregon 97204-3527
timberpress.com

Printed in China

Text design by Laura Shaw
Cover design by Hillary Caudle
Endpaper illustration by Mia Nolting

ISBN 978-1-60469-877-0

Catalog records for this book are available from the Library of Congress and the British Library.

> "Show me your garden, and I shall tell you who you are."
>
> —Alfred Austin
>
> For amazing Grace, herself a bold example of the life cycle at work

Contents

Preface

M Y HOW TIMES HAVE CHANGED. Though at first thought, the idea of rekindling a 21-year-old garden book might not seem like a task as radical or needed as, say, redoing one of the same vintage about computers, it turns out otherwise. Yes, we still use shovels (if not Word 6.0; I'm now pecking away on version 16.16.2).

Yes, the horticultural operating system still begins with "green side up," though I did recently gift a friend some paperwhite narcissus to force, forgetting to state what seemed to me the obvious. I got a call a few weeks later asking why white spaghetti was sprouting from the pot.

And one more yes, before we get to all the nos. Were they alive, my money's on the likelihood that Alice B. Toklas and Gertrude Stein would still be discussing the most perennial of evergreen garden topics:

The story goes that Toklas once asked Stein what she saw when she closed her eyes.

"Weeds," Stein replied.

Me, too; now and forever, I forecast that the gardener shall forevermore have plants growing in the wrong place, ad infinitum, ad nauseam. *Help*!

Much else has been upended, I came to realize as I dug in to revise the book. No, mere updates would not do, Margaret. The catalog sources at the back of the first edition are now mostly fond memories of old friends long gone from the business. (Their progeny live on in my garden, and I still unearth the occasional old plastic label, the printing so faded as to be nearly illegible.)

Some "it" plants of that moment that everyone grew (or wanted to, if only they could secure a piece) are now known thugs, and I, like gardeners everywhere, will spend the rest of my days hoicking them out, sometimes losing the battle. Their tenacity is an in-our-faces, perennial reminder of inadvertent environmental wrongdoing—of cultivating what proved to become invasives.

Plants that were rare—a dramatic variegated- or gold-leaf version some savvy gardener identified from a sport, perhaps—stayed that way a relatively long while. The ramp up to wider distribution was once upon a time dictated by the math of the plant's inclination to set seed

A female green frog perches on the lip of a water- and *Azolla*-filled trough she has claimed as home.

Frogs and birds and poppy
pods: Indoors and out,
elements of the natural
world are ever-present at
my house.

(opposite) *Rodgersia
podophylla* sends up creamy
plumes in early June, but
its bold foliage is the main
attraction from emergence
till hard frost.

A spring peeper, *Pseudacris crucifer*, rests on a leaf of European wild ginger (*Asarum europaeum*) outside the kitchen door.

or provide ample divisions or cuttings. As tissue culture laboratories have proliferated, and the secrets of micropropagation, or cloning, for more species unlocked, the pace for many plants has likewise accelerated. Advancements in other methods of mass production, like of wholesale baby plants called liners or plugs, has evolved, too, in ever more mechanized greenhouse facilities. You barely have time to gloat over being among the first to have something special, before it confronts you en masse at the big-box store.

I knew, and grew, some native plants back then—notably winterberry hollies and asters—but our current collective consciousness about the role of natives, about habitat gardening and pollinator gardening, had not taken hold. Today native status is even printed on plant labels (though often imprecisely, since few things are native to the entire nation). The word "nativar," for a cultivar of a native plant with showier attributes or a different habit than the straight species, has been added to the vocabulary.

Ticks were familiar, but those tiny arachnids hadn't yet traumatized a chunk of the nation. Our longtime No. 1 annual, the impatiens, hadn't been assaulted by a devastating fungus-like disease called impatiens downy mildew, and a related species of DM hadn't yet attacked beloved basil. (As I type this, news is just out that the impatiens genome "sequence and assembly" has been cracked, a critical step in developing a strategy to breed in resistance someday to DM.)

And so many introduced forest pests have increased their pressure: The ever-wider encroachment of hemlock woolly adelgid, as one example, saw to it in these ensuing years that I would not dare plant *Tsuga*. Instead I mourn former stands of what was a foundation species of the northeastern forests I live surrounded by.

Even the earthworm has evolved from being regarded as a gardener's (and farmer's) best friend to a leading suspect in environmental havoc. I didn't even know years back that there

were no native earthworms in the northern United States—that they were all introduced species (including many kinds in warmer regions). And nobody knew just how destructive some of the latest imports, notably jumping worms from Asia in the genera *Amynthas* and *Metaphire*, would prove to gardens, yes, but to forest ecologies most terrifyingly, as they impoverish soil and interrupt the process of succession in parts of the Great Lakes Forest, the Great Smoky Mountains, and New England. We will be hearing more about them regularly, I forecast.

Need I mention that the gardener's other once-reliable companion, the weather, doesn't seem very friendly or familiar at all, either, as the climate shifts? The expected meteorological pacing of each space of a season is no longer, and all the time we face extremes that are ever more perplexing to manage around.

As unsettling to keen gardeners (and to a greater degree, farmers) has been consolidation of the seed industry, as seed genetics became regarded as intellectual property—something to patent and own. The number of players has shrunk to a few giants, and their focus is on money-makers—genetically engineered agribusiness crops, yes, and also classically bred hybrids suited to large-scale farming because of their uniformity, perhaps, or inclination to ripen all at once for ease of harvest. Some heirloom home-garden seeds that didn't have such

The now-muscular trunk of a European copper beech was just a youngster when planted decades ago on the hillside above the house.

13

The fist-size buds of Asian biennial *Angelica gigas* foretell big, wine-colored, umbel-shaped blooms.

profit potential got neglected, but, blessedly, counterforces have risen up to protect and reinvigorate some of them.

I didn't know years back that my garden would become a laboratory for data collection. Though I was interested in science—something the garden opened up for me in a way no high school teacher ever had—I was not yet one of what are now millions of citizen scientists who today record backyard observations, adding my bird counts and moth counts and more to giant databases that scientists can use for research (but could not compile without us).

In the old text of the book, I could hear the first hints of the gardener, and person, I would become. I met a Margaret who was, as I am now, devoted to organic practices, and already proselytizing. I also met one-time friends, plants that starred in the first edition but have since

gone—not because they all died, but because my enthusiasms shifted. For example, once mad for silver, I'm now all about the gold (leaves, that is).

A younger Margaret shared joyful anecdotes of interactions with the first birds she came to know, and an apparent delight at a growing number of beneficial insects, too, as her deepening sense of connection to the bigger picture took hold. Missing in the original book were amphibian adventure stories, as their populations in the garden have multiplied to almost comical proportion, and I have undergone the metamorphosis into She Who Lives with Frogs. I likewise failed then to celebrate my reptilian brethren—to trumpet how important it is to make snakes at home in an organic garden. There is good reason for that last oversight: I was not yet a *recovering* ophidiophobiac. Quite to the contrary.

Today, I describe my approach to gardening as "horticultural how-to and 'woo-woo'"—a blend of stuff you need to memorize, like how deep to plant a daffodil bulb, and stuff you need to feel when you witness a seed germinating, for instance, and just surrender to (like getting over a fear of snakes, and instead of screaming, thanking them for eating slugs and mice). I was glad I could hear both how-to and woo-woo notes in the old Margaret, and my nowadays constant invocation to strive for a 365-day garden was evident, if not labeled yet as such. I guess I am still me (or always was?).

One more thing, or actually two, have not changed even a little. First, *I garden because I cannot help myself.* I hope that you may feel that calling.

Most of all: this book is still titled *A Way to Garden* because it is not the only way, just my way. It's the one way I have gradually sorted out despite all the shifts in trends and technology and even the taxonomic order of things, as tried-and-true plants were renamed (and sometimes then unrenamed for dizzying good measure). Whatever pest or predicament is thrown at me, onward I do dig, and most of all: weed. Perhaps mine is a way to garden that will work for you, too. I hope so.

Introduction

A GARDEN WITHOUT A GARDENER is a jungle waiting to happen. But a gardener without a plot to till is likewise a very sorry sight. This book is about both sides of the equation: the delicious organism that gardener and garden, once united, quickly become, as they ride the peaks and abysses of what the weather and life dish out. In this, the 21st-anniversary edition, the book is also about what happens when you stay in one place and keep digging holes, as I have.

This is a basic garden book, but then again it is not so basic. It supplies guidance to those looking for the way to succeed with tomatoes or prune a hydrangea, but it also shares guidance from the other side of the equation: advice and insight I have gotten in return from my plants.

By becoming a gardener, I accidentally—blessedly—landed myself in a fusion of science lab and Buddhist retreat, a place of nonstop learning and of contemplation, where there is life buzzing to the maximum and also the deepest stillness. It is from this combined chemistry that my horticultural how-to and "woo-woo" motto derives.

On the second half of that equation, I think of my garden and myself as the two main components of the same organism—like the *Jerry McGuire* character played by Tom Cruise, who finally professed to exhausted Renee Zellweger, "You complete me" (though I did not resist surrender anywhere near as long). That perspective makes me think about the gardening year in a way that may, at first, seem a bit unfamiliar, or even odd. I imagine the garden year as roughly parallel to the six seasons of my own life, from conception through birth and on to youth, adulthood, senescence, and finally death and afterlife. Moving from phase to phase takes months or years (if all goes well) in the case of a human; in the garden, it's all packed into a single year, and then starts over, and over, even long after the gardener is gone.

In my system, each phase is roughly equivalent to two months. For example, Conception is January and February, a time when we are conceiving of the garden by planning on paper and ordering seeds. I've tried to cover each subject within the section of the book corresponding to the time of year when the information would be most useful—so preventing spindly seedlings is discussed in Birth (March and April), and sowing the fall vegetable garden is covered in Adulthood (July and August). By the time we get to Death and Afterlife, it is November and

A woolly bear caterpillar of the Isabella tiger moth curls up in an abandoned bird's nest.

17

Above the backyard water garden, a female green frog speaks her piece to the vintage Indonesian bust of Buddha.

The pollen-laden male catkins of the black pussy willow, *Salix gracilistyla* 'Melanostachys', start reddish, evolve to pink, and then to black.

On the hillside in autumn, native little bluestem and goldenrod are backed by a copper beech and a grouping of *Metasequoia glyptostroboides* 'Gold Rush'.

December, and we gather up the year's debris and make compost (one form of eternal life I feel certain of), and carefully store away saved seeds (another way that next year's garden rises up out of the one gone by).

I find this anthropomorphic view of the garden comforting, a handle to hold when trying to remember what to do when reviewing the incessant chores list. It also reminds me that this gardening stuff is not just a hobby, like building model airplanes or stamp-collecting. The medium is alive, and always changing, and no, you are never really in charge for a second, no matter how straight your rows nor sturdy your staking. Something larger is always at work, something no mere hand of a gardener can control.

How I Came to Garden

I came to the garden in my twenties, at a time when things were not going so well in the people parts of life.

My new friends, the plants, helped me through a long spell facing an impossible responsibility: how to ethically, sensitively care for a parent who would never get well but would live a very long time. Each quart pot of some unknown growing thing (at this stage, even common names were Greek to me, and botanical Latin was unthinkable) gave me a reason to rouse myself for another day. The young plants needed me, and I them, since unlike my failing mother, they showed promise, and possibility.

Now, when I conjure in my mind's eye the garden that I made in those five or so years before she could no longer live at home, I laugh. Set around the house I grew up in and returned to in crisis after a decade's absence, in suburban Queens County in New York City, the nascent garden was, as my late father had always labeled agreeably eccentric people, a real pip. At the feet of the aged privet hedge, I tried determinedly to coax a carpet of *Lobelia erinus*, the sprawling lobelia with dark blue flowers normally used as an annual in hanging baskets. There was virtually no spare soil around the privet's roots, but I was insistent on a blue swath the length of the hedge-row, and used the strongest, sharpest trowel in the garage to gouge out tiny pockets to stuff the transplants into. A chisel and crowbar might have made planting easier.

I was incredulous when the lobelia refused to grow. The little plastic labels imprinted with the pretty picture said this plant required "part shade," and that's what I provided. It didn't mention that one cubic inch of loose soil wasn't enough for any plant, or that root competition from a 50-year-old hedge probably wasn't lobelia's cup of manure tea, either.

The hedge continued in its role as test kitchen when I took saw and loppers to it in my first attempt at "Rejuvenation of An Aging Shrub"—the next foundational lesson I tackled in my impromptu home-study course in horticulture. My self-taught unit in "Annuals as Ground Covers" hadn't gone so well—the lobelia didn't even make it a month, let alone become a blooming carpet—but I was undeterred. Caring for the dying had put me in a state of perpetual motion, and gardening was my personal occupational therapy, my sedative. (Many years later, when I shared this anecdote in a lecture, an insightful audience member pointed out that I was experiencing horticultural therapy. Yes.)

A jumble of houseplants and other tender things summer outdoors in the shady paved area leading to the kitchen door.

Looking up into the field from the backyard in fall, the view is past the water garden all the way to the copper beech.

Even in monochrome, masked by snow, the garden is alive in sensuous curves and shadow play. This view is uphill past the water garden and the hidden Buddha.

A collection of pineapple lilies, or *Eucomis*, began in recent years with *E. bicolor*.

Another class in the experimental curriculum that never ends might have been called "Sculptural Plants." For a strippy bed cut out of a steep hillside beside the driveway, I'd chosen a palette of hens and chicks (*Sempervivum*) and red-hot pokers (*Kniphofia*), and who knows why. But how I loved this peculiar, even pitiful pairing—the lurid orange-and-yellow pokers jutting upward from the succulents. Perhaps I thought the hens and chicks needed a rooster, and there is something vaguely birdlike about the red-hot pokers, and unarguably masculine. How ugly my combination was. How proud it made me to see them grow.

True 365-day garden plants in the backyard include a gold Hinoki cypress (right) and an espaliered Asian pear against the house.

Ostrich fern croziers push up as another spring begins.

In May, a jumble of hellebores and spring ephemerals surround a little gate upcycled from a vintage protective window grate.

By June, the spot is a mass of foliar textures, including *Astilboides* and variegated *Hosta* 'Sagae'.

The area slides into fall, helped by a big *Hydrangea paniculata* and a backdrop of yellow foliage from *Aralia spinosa*.

The front entry area in June is richly decked out, as the kousa dogwood and bigroot geranium and everything else are all happening.

Or take my first significant encounter with perennials and with propagation, enduring evidence of which is still inscribed in pencil inside the back cover of my first gardening book, *The Victory Garden* by James Underwood Crockett. Once I calculated how much it would cost at $3.99 or $5.99 a pot (vintage prices!) to actually plant even a modest border, I apparently decided to grow my own from seed. Between the color flower headshots in his book and those in the delightfully gaudy Thompson and Morgan seed catalog of the day, I'd drafted a list of a dozen must-have perennials. "Leave no color unturned" apparently was my motto. You may wish to put on your sunglasses to dare conjuring it, even in your mind's eye: maroon-and-gold *Gaillardia*; lavender Canterbury bells (*Campanula*); white balloon flower (*Platycodon*); reddish pink *Dianthus*; fuchsia bee balm (*Monarda*); hot red Maltese cross (*Lychnis chalcedonica*); red and yellow columbines (*Aquilegia canadensis*); pink foxglove (*Digitalis*); multicolored lupines (*Lupinus*); pale blue perennial flax (*Linum perenne*); pansies (not even a perennial, but what did I know?), and fire-engine-red painted daisies (*Pyrethrum*). *Ugh.* To this day, not a single garden pot or bed of mine has included one of those plants, nor *Lobelia* and *Kniphofia*—proof that the trauma, although suppressed, remains imprinted on my psyche.

I ordered them all and began collecting yogurt cups, milk cartons, and other castoffs for seedling pots. There was, of course, no spot in the house suitable to support a thousand plant-lets that wouldn't be ready for the open ground for half a year. And what did I know about achieving a long bloom season, or even about the plants' habits or needs? I had been drawn in by all those postage-stamp-size catalog pictures of one luscious flower each, and headlines like "Extra-Large Exotic Blooms Will Be the Envy of Your Neighbors—and So Easy to Grow!"

I did it all wrong: wrong plants, wrong propagation setup, and I even started every seed in every packet—as if I could use 100 or 80 or 300 of something. In those days, results didn't really matter. I was hooked on the hopefulness: the sense that there was something worth waiting

In winter, the birdbath (filled with sedums and mosses in season) is like a giant's birdbath meringue pie

Vintage children's blocks and other paraphernalia add interest in the living room.

Crypsis: A stick caterpillar, the larval form of some geometrid moth, hides in plain sight on a bottlebrush buckeye twig.

for—another spring, perhaps, or more ripe tomatoes than the year before. I loved those spindly seedlings fiercely, and from them learned my first lessons in the life (and unfortunately, death) cycles of plants.

Today, new plants at the nursery or in catalogs sometimes tug at me to take them home and love them, but that's no longer really it. What's *it* is coming upon a twig in the massive old bottlebrush buckeye that isn't a twig at all, but a stick caterpillar, disguised by the genius of crypsis to blend in with its environment, defying predators and munching unnoticed. What's *it* is all the insects who have evolved to take on the coloration of or even the appearance of bees—hover flies (syrphids), and some beetles like the locust borer, and even the clear-winged sphinx moth—again to say "don't eat me," because a mouthful of bee is apparently not a popular menu item. What's *it* are the birds who caught on early that I offered more diversity on my land than the cornfields across the way, and became regular visitors, egging me on to learn about native plants, succession of bloom, and therefore an extended supply of delicious insects, seeds, and fruit, so that I might in turn be accompanied on my rounds by their songs, their distinctive behaviors, their flashes of color.

We have grown up together, the garden and I, and now we approach growing old together, too, with bits falling off here and there on both of us, and others not working quite so smoothly. It is about 40 years since I tortured that first flat of lobelia. These days, in the garden I have had for more than three decades in the Hudson Valley, a couple of hours' drive north of that first experiment, I try to be kinder, with respect for what the world has given me (and I never grow seedlings without a proper light source). What follows are some of the lessons I've learned so far—regarding plants, processes, tricks, and most of all, a lifetime supply of wonder—to nudge you beyond approaching gardening as merely outdoor decorating, and to enrich the seasons of your garden and your life.

Conception

JANUARY & FEBRUARY

A NEW CYCLE, A NEW SEASON

"**I LAY NO CLAIM** either to literal ability, or to botanical knowledge, or even to the best practical methods of cultivation," a woman of great gardening wisdom once began an essay, and that was fine for her to say because it was humility, pure and simple. But if I tell you that in my case these same claims do indeed hold true, you can trust it. I mean, a painting of modest Gertrude Jekyll's well-worn gardening boots hangs in the upper-crusty Tate Gallery in London; somehow I doubt that my sorry L.L. Bean specials will ever make their way to anywhere but the local dump.

But what I do share with Jekyll—regarded as most responsible for the renaissance of classic garden design in the twentieth century, whose writings I could read and read again—and I trust with you, too, is a wonder at the very existence of plants.

How can it be that they have such intricate beauty: have you ever seen the clever paintings that live inside a flower? How is it that so many garden plants can disappear come winter and then, from nowhere, reappear in spring, unbeaten by having "lived" like Birds Eye vegetables in the earth's own freezer, month after frozen month?

How can it be that a border of daffodils blooms each spring in the woods above my rural home, though the people whose house they once adorned are decades gone? And why does a tomato smell great, and its foliage just smell, and why aren't every plant's leaves—the centers of photosynthesis—the color green? It is this natural curiosity, coupled with the need to touch and smell and otherwise get to know these living things, that counts first and foremost, all manner of scientific degrees notwithstanding.

I want to tell you where this instinct of botanical wonder came from, at least in my case, about the zinnias my Grandma Marion cut and stuffed into the Fiestaware bowls of water, flowers that picked up the brightest flecks in the old linoleum of that kitchen painted, walls and ceiling and cabinets, in yellow high gloss.

I want to tell you everything, to talk to you about the image of the iron padded chaise beneath the old, contorted wisteria at Grandma's, too. They plopped me on that chaise for my birthday photo, while all around me, wisteria pods fell to the upholstery canvas and the slate patio beneath. Manna from heaven. Happy Birthday, Margaret. Welcome to the garden.

Digging down deeper into the psychological subsoil will take some time. All I can tell you now are fragments like that one; flashes of memory, moments of recognition. All I can say for certain is that it is gardening that I love more than anything else I've ever found, and here is a simple example of the reason why:

Just the other night I reached into the freezer for a large container of "tomato junk," a hodgepodge I use as the stock of my winter diet. It is a commingling of whatever edible was still standing and producing when frost closed the last season down—tomatoes, beans, parsley, kale, and squash. There, like a reddish brick of ice in my hand, and then a few hours later in its next incarnation as the base of lentil soup, my garden was with me again.

Gertrude Jekyll, in uncharacteristic immodesty, called herself a "garden-artist," but do not look in this place for any such lofty figure. Simply, I like two things very much: the smell of freshly washed laundry, and the smell of warming earth that is hit by a rain shower (properly called petrichor). Hence down deep I am part washerwoman, part ditchdigger, and thankfully it is a true symbiosis. The former helps undo the filthiness the latter wreaks on the hands.

No, neither my garden boots nor my garden are the stuff that art is made of, a fact for which I am only partly apologetic. My garden is where I can be myself—perhaps the only place besides the pay-by-the-hour couch that invites me to be so, in fact. This is where I think big, where I overdo it, where I don't turn inward and downward but really stretch myself—damn the insecurities.

In the untidy maze of garden this wintery weekend, the zinnias will be waiting, dried and shrunken to a dilapidated state of brown, contorted by months of cold days and nights as Grandma's wisteria was by age. I did not cut my zinnias to fill the bowls my ancestor did, at least not in the season's final month. In my kitchen, the bowls hold shallots and garlic, a 'Blue Hubbard' and a 'Buttercup' squash, all destined for the winter kettle. My zinnias, doornail dead, and nearby the coneflowers and rudbeckias and all, have a higher final purpose.

To the birds, each dried seed head is a minifeeder, and as the sun comes up on these frigid mornings, I am content to sit and watch the goldfinches having at it, bursting from one botanical snack bar to another with zeal such as I only feel when . . . to tell the truth, I never get quite that energetic anymore.

My bird feeding, next to my gardening, is what amuses my friends most, though frankly I see nothing funny in it. I know, when other gardeners' checking balances are finally spared the growing season's near-daily drains for pots and plants and seeds, there I am in my woolens, hurtling up to the Agway farm store, possessed by a mantra of "seed sale, seed sale, seed sale." When others are clipping supermarket coupons to spare the household budget, I am urging the birds to "eat, eat, eat," in hopes of moving one hole closer on the Birdseed Club punch card to that as yet elusive free 20-pound bag.

"We are building a habitat," an old friend used to needle, impersonating my voice and using my very words, as we'd dig yet another hole for a berry-bearing shrub or drive yet another feeder pole into the good earth. But underneath the kidding he knew it is the magical intertwining of things that gets to me—we feed the birds in the lean times, they eat our bad bugs, and thus there's a harvest.

And the bottom line is that is what I am doing when I am gardening: building a habitat. It is a place for me, and for my friends, and for our friends the birds and bugs, and yes, even the blubbery woodchuck who rambles down the hillside from time to time in fairer months, in search of a refill for his sagging belly.

Lately, it has been the place for a hungry stray farm cat, too, a truly wild creature, and when I throw a little stone close by to chase him from beneath my sacred feeders, I feel a twinge of sorrow, for after all, he is just trying to join in the cycle, too.

A vivid winter sky, with the moon still up and a tracery of fresh snow on the trees, makes for a beautiful day in the garden.

Studying the Catalogs

The cheapest gardening education can be had in the pages of plant and seed catalogs. If you are not welcoming the New Year in possession of a pile on the bedside table and another on the dining table, make it the first resolution to order some now.

Seed catalogs used to flood my post office box as the holidays were waning, followed by bulb and plant ones. Now there is a race for vendors to get the printed seed offerings, at least, in the mail and online as early as Thanksgiving. Therefore, thoughts on how I choose among which seed companies to frequent—because not all seed is created equal, either genetically or ethically—are covered in the section called Death and Afterlife (which covers November and December). Realistically, though, I think we mostly still do our orders around this time, so following are a few general guidelines.

When I first paged through a garden catalog, seed and plant merchants didn't have websites. Today I place my orders online, but only after marking up my stack of competing catalogs, talking to myself all the while about how many kinds of peas is too many (the number goes up every year), or whether I already have a particular pineapple lily (*Eucomis*) that looks so sexy in a photo. I long ago lost track of the labels on some of them, so I excuse myself a binge or two in the name of potential newcomers.

At the start, I got just two catalogs. As soon as I placed an order, the number in my mailbox soared. Many were worthless, but I knew I was getting somewhere when I could discern which—when I could tell the real gardeners behind the best from the mass marketers behind the rest. Read up about your would-be merchants.

At the start of one's gardening life, a good catalog will be one that's full of color photos, like baby's first books. By a few years in, if all is going well, I dare you: Screw up the courage to shop from—or at least peruse—a couple of nonillustrated listings, too, many of which these days are online-only. Before the internet, these were abundant, and I remember the total plant nerds behind them who felt like pen pals, each with a specialty and a passion for the unusual—the 9 varieties of chives (who knew there was anything but just "chives"?) and 44 mints at Well-Sweep Herb Farm, alongside hundreds of other things. Most of my old list-publishing friends are gone, but I see that J. L. Hudson, Seedsman, is (like Well-Sweep) still at it, and each of the 15-ish aquilegia and 16 acacia sounds equally charming, amid seeds for trees, native wildflowers, and who knows what wonders.

Plant societies often have seed exchanges, where members can order (or donate) seed. Browsing the American Primula Society or North American Rock Garden Society lists might awaken your collector spirit and up your game. Or try reading the websites of specialty wholesalers, like Landcraft Environments or Iseli Nursery. You cannot order, but go to your garden center prepared to ask for better tender things for seasonal containers or specimen conifers, respectively.

Nonillustrated catalogs make you really read the entry and see whether a plant will thrive in your region's conditions, rather than get you all excited by a color close-up of a flower that won't work. The people behind hardcore catalogs are typically connoisseurs, so you'll be selecting from among more unusual plants. Most important: These lists require you to sharpen your Latin skills, which anyone intending to make gardening a habit must accomplish. Common

A young rose-breasted grosbeak, nestled in a giant leaf of *Petasites hybridus*, observes the backyard goings-on.

names aren't useful; they're imprecise and may vary, according to local tradition, and are not even unique. Did you want false indigo the perennial (*Baptisia australis*) or false indigo the small tree (*Amorpha fruticosa*)? They're hardly interchangeable.

Read the fine print—especially with seed sources. Seeds aren't an average mail-order product, since who else ships live embryos (well, I suppose some poultry suppliers do—but how often do you order those?). We scan the listings for irresistible attributes like a very big (or small) sunflower, or an unusual color of chard (think 'Bright Lights' mix or orange-stemmed 'Oriole')—or practical ones like adaptability, in a Northern (short-season) tomato, or cucurbits with built-in downy mildew resistance in the Southeast, perhaps.

Consider catalogs the textbooks of your ongoing correspondence course in horticulture. A dozen or two will do, if they're the right ones. Subscribe today.

Early, Middle, Late

Repeat after me: early, middle, late. That's the secret. When you are passionate about a particular plant, whether lilacs, daffodils, hydrangeas, tulips, *you name it*, don't include one variety in your order (nor cart home just one from the nursery). Read the labels or descriptions carefully,

or do homework first, then choose some that are early, others that bloom in the middle of that plant's flowering cycle, and still others that are late. (Bulb catalogs make this easier than the other catalogs may.) Selecting some early, middle, and late lilacs, for instance, would mean you'll have one or the other to enjoy for many weeks, not all at once for just ten days. With *Narcissus* you could stretch it to a couple of months; with *Hemerocallis* to nearly a summer. Now what's our mantra?

Look Out the Window: Design 101

I'll admit that humility, and sometimes even downright humiliation, have been regular elements of my horticultural epiphanies, especially when it comes to garden design. I suppose it all fits, since the root of the word humility comes from the soil: from the Latin *humus*, for earth or ground. A good soil is rich in the partially decayed, formerly living plant and animal material called humus, and I find myself brought to my knees in contact with it regularly, both figuratively and in real life.

The afternoon I learned the most important design lesson of all was one such grounding moment. Glenn Withey, an accomplished designer friend, was visiting from Seattle; he and I were starting supper, standing at the stove, which faces east through two windows that flank the range. Soup, not shock and awe, was on the menu—or so I thought.

Without missing a beat of his whisk, he asked: "Do you like looking at the door of your car every day, Margaret?"

Because that's what we were staring at, just beyond the glass: the passenger side of my car, parked in the driveway, which way back then continued all the way up alongside the house.

Garden design begins with going inside and looking out the window: out the bedroom window in springtime, looking west.

The same bedroom window view in August, when giant cannas totally obscure the patio.

What I was getting my first glimpse of: When undertaken most intelligently, home-garden design is an inside-out exercise. Garden Design 101, Lesson 1: Always go inside and look out the window before digging a single hole or otherwise committing to what goes where (including figuring out what needs to just go away in the name of the greater good).

The following Monday morning, a contractor was retained to erase that last little gravel stretch so that I could look out for the rest of my days at garden, not automobile. The Loebner

Looking uphill to the south in summer.

The pots and water troughs sit on pavers in the entry by the kitchen door.

magnolia called 'Ballerina', which I'd had the sense to plant years before just beyond the far edge of the former driveway, would become the start of my new unobstructed view.

It must seem obvious in that example that something had to give—that I should not sentence myself to car door penance. I also know that moving a driveway isn't always a solution. I was willing to walk another 50 feet from where I'd have to park instead. Even if I hadn't been able or willing to make the change, though, Glenn's inside-out insight changed everything in the way I saw what I was doing—or meant to be doing—as I set about to make a garden, and thankfully he didn't stop there.

A series of subsequent exercises followed, some involving bamboo poles and colorful flagging tape. He demonstrated that even when the situation is subtler, what we see from inside is quite a different perspective than the same spot viewed from outdoors.

Go ahead and try it: Site a planned grouping of shrubs or a new tree where you think it works best, using bamboos of different heights to represent each one (unless you've brought home the actual plants). Then go inside and see whether you've created a picture you can admire from spots where you'll be spending much more time. Real gardeners don't spend a lot of outdoor hours lying on a chaise admiring their handiwork. When we are outside, we are weeding, dividing, transplanting, mulching, edging, mowing—and repeat.

Together Glenn and I looked out other key windows, with an eye to improving axial views and positioning well-placed pictures to enjoy in every season. Besides ideas for specific plant-by-plant positioning, we looked at the overall size and shape of each bed, too; many looked skimpy from the indoor vantage point, and today are much more substantial islands whose shapes and heft I prefer.

We observed the light at various times of day, and talked about how by comparison it moves across the place in other seasons, so that I would not deprive myself of its best dramatic effects. Instead, I could site some good subjects for backlighting, like ornamental grasses or a red cutleaf Japanese maple—and avoid the costly mistake of placing tall-growing conifers where they would interrupt views or block that beautiful light.

To further enliven a favored westerly gaze, we positioned stakes repeatedly here and there along both sides of the journey from house to property edge. Each stake represented a gold-leaf shrub, like a bouncing ball of yellow that would hit several spots and then land for good in one larger gleaming specimen at the far extreme.

The ghost bramble, *Rubus cockburnianus*, became one such subject, along with the golden cutleaf staghorn sumac (*Rhus typhina* 'Bailtiger', marketed as Tiger Eyes), *Spiraea thunbergii* 'Ogon', and the prostrate yew called *Taxus baccata* 'Repandens Aurea'. The final moment: a big old *Physocarpus opulifolius* 'Dart's Gold', or ninebark.

Looking out the window informs many decisions, like where a winter garden might go (no, not in the out-of-sight far reaches, but perhaps on axis from the chair by the fire). One note on placing winter plants: Remember that deciduous things between the house and spots you're considering will have dropped their leaves, extending your uninterrupted view farther than in the growing season. Dramatic moments, like a large island of winterberry hollies (*Ilex verticillata*) or a specimen tree with extravagant bark and dramatic silhouette, can be enjoyed from a considerable distance in the quieter months. Sited maybe 10 feet beyond a key downstairs window, even a single specimen dwarf conifer (I'm thinking *Abies nordmanniana* 'Golden Spreader'), or a clump of a red-twig dogwood like 'Bailhalo' (sold as Ivory Halo) with variegated leaves then brilliant red winter stems, is a beacon 365 days a year.

On the other extreme of scale, I've selfishly started placing my "hummingbird plants" closer in to the windows, so that I can actually see those tiny birds in action. For them (and myself) I always cultivate a stand of tall verbena (*Verbena bonariensis*) and flowering tobacco (*Nicotiana mutabilis*, *N. sylvestris*, and others) right on the patio, which draw butterflies, too, and

A perfectly hardy
southeastern native
honeysuckle, *Lonicera
sempervirens*, twines around
the back porch post to
entice hummingbirds where
I can see them.

For fullest enjoyment of
small visitors like the giant
swallowtail butterfly or
hummingbirds, treats like
Verbena bonariensis are
placed within window view.

my back porch post is encircled with *Lonicera sempervirens*, my favorite honeysuckle (and one they likewise adore).

One final garden design bonus tip, having nothing to do with windows but with foot traffic: Alongside the former last bit of driveway now turned into path flanked by beds, I am careful to use plants that look good over many months of the year. Not every guest will get to see the garden from indoors from the best seats and windows in the house, but anyone who approaches (including me, over and again, day in and out) deserves a proper welcome.

Planning, on Paper or Otherwise

Teachers—whether at horticulture lectures and classes or in books—always said the same thing: Put it all down on paper before you plant, even before you purchase a single seed packet or a single pot of anything. I quickly came to wonder if I would ever really be any good as a gardener, because try as I might, I simply could not force myself to map out planting plans ahead of time. Shop the nurseries, yes. Order by mail, definitely. But figure out in advance what I planned to do with most of it? Never.

Planning on paper in winter is about as satisfying as eating a February-issue tomato. In January or February, I am as impatient for the payoff—the real thing—as a child whining from the back seat on a long car trip: "Are we there yet?" No amount of paper and crayons (or even a grown-up notebook and pen) will quiet me.

That doesn't mean I don't make notes, and more specifically lists—lists of several kinds, including the obvious to-do list that evolves over each day and week of each season, as things are added and others ticked off. It is always at the ready, on my clipboard.

A second list is a kind of trickier to-do reminder than just "weed tomato bed" or "edge front path." It's a list of projects I want to tackle, and am pondering, like: "rethink front bed by *Juniperus virginiana*," or "island of *Vaccinium* or native *Viburnum* above meadow area?" Many entries end with a question mark, since I'm ruminating.

I refer to this list during catalog-shopping season, hoping to match specific plant possibilities and firm up my imaginings, and if that happens I pace off the space before deciding whether it's 3 highbush blueberries or 11 that are needed, and then maybe what goes under them. This isn't literally planning on paper—as in drawing a detailed planting plan for a bed—but it works for me.

The last kind of plan I do make—again a list—is of what edibles I intend to grow from seed. When to start seed for what is covered elsewhere, but this third list is about what the "what" is in the first place. I confess that with a pile of seed catalogs beside me, the answer to the question, "What seeds can't I live without?" becomes, "I simply must have everything."

To try to get real and filter "everything" down to "doable," I list what I enjoy eating most often and most of all, which may still be too many things to fit in my available space. Yes, I like eggplant, and jalapeño peppers—but I only use each a couple of times a summer, and could probably buy them and devote that space otherwise. To keep narrowing, I mark which are available as organic produce locally for a reasonable price. This is where zucchini, for example, may not rate much (or any) precious garden space compared to sowing a teepee covered in the heirloom pole bean 'Aunt Ada's Italian' that is the secret ingredient in my vegetable soup.

Some crops just aren't available, or in comparable quality, as homegrown—like peas, for instance, which I have never regretted making room for both spring and fall. Lettuce never gets stricken from the list, either, because it doesn't take much space and grows fast and is best very fresh (not having been in a bin, or worse a plastic box) and can cost $8-plus a pound organic at my food co-op. Your list will differ, but the thinking to get there is the same.

I do some cold math calculations, too. To purchase three crates of plum tomatoes from my neighboring organic farmers for my year's supply of tomato sauce and vegetable soup would cost about $100 to $120. Do I have space instead for maybe eight tomato plants (total cost $5 in seed, some bagged fresh germinating mix, and a lot of TLC)? I like to have winter squash as close to year-round as possible. Let's say I devote a big bed to growing 25 or 30 fruits of an average 5 pounds apiece at $1.79 to $2.49 retail—at least $225 worth of squash, and probably much more. Worth it.

This kind of thinking informs why I give garlic a big space October through July. Have you seen the price of organic garlic at the market? Plus: once you get enough of a crop built up you can save your own "seed garlic" from year to year and be garlic-independent.

Maybe lists will work for you, too, whether instead of or to supplement more detailed planning. I probably should have taken that landscape design class at the botanical garden all those years ago, and if you aren't so stuck in your ways already, that's something to investigate. Put it on the list.

Journals: Writing It All Down

In recent years, prodded by my sister (a writing teacher), I offered a class online that I called "Garden Writing for Everyone." I told prospective students: Gardening, and writing, are the two interwoven threads that have shaped my adult life. I cannot imagine being without either; each is far more than a mere career component, but more of a life practice. I heartily recommend digging into both, even if simply for your own sanity and joy—or at the simplest level, for record-keeping—in the privacy of a garden journal, and not for publication.

I encourage each of us to give voice in at least the most basic way to what comes up—whether tulips, or a sense of intimate connectedness—when we head outside. Why take the time to write it all down? When I write something down, it really sinks in, aiding memory. With all the layers that the garden has to offer—not just the what-blooms-when notations that might inspire future plant combinations if one was eventually transplanted beside the other, but also the slightly more woo-woo stuff—that's really valuable.

Like the catalogs, your garden journal offers free gardening lessons, gleaned from your own adventures, and something else no other publication will: highly localized cultural information, geared precisely to this spot. Here is where we learn what is and is not possible, if only we write it down, and pay attention.

When I began gardening, a sturdy notebook was the standard issue, but a computer is a fine place to store garden records, too, though far less romantic. It will never become dog-eared by

Deciding what rates precious space in the raised bed vegetable garden takes some advance planning.

muddy fingers, or grow too wide to close because of all the flowers and leaves pressed inside. If you prefer the digital medium, there are apps for garden journaling, or start a blog with one of the free programs such as WordPress.com and journal there. What's critical is to create an information storage system and use it—and again, hopefully also make it a repository of observations that are a bit more on the inspirational side.

Most important to record are bloom dates (start and finish), to identify what plants might make good partners. Planting dates and the precise names will be helpful. Note where you got each plant—print and save order confirmation emails, to paste or copy into your notebook— and record where each permanent one was placed. This latter detail will be especially helpful when you find yet another label in the middle of the lawn, or in the compost heap, and have to try to figure out which epimedium or daffodil it belonged to.

I record sightings of bird comings and goings in the citizen-science database eBird.org—like an online checklist—a project of Cornell Lab of Ornithology and Audubon. For those wishing to contribute other natural history data, the Nature's Notebook program of the USA National Phenology Network would be happy to have you, and you'll become a sharper observer by observing and recording the timing of plant (and animal) phenophases—the switch between phases such as from dormant buds to bud break to flowering to setting seed.

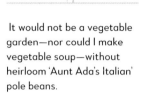

It would not be a vegetable garden—nor could I make vegetable soup—without heirloom 'Aunt Ada's Italian' pole beans.

In my earliest journals, I had a page each month for self-criticism of a sort, a multi-column list whose categories simply read: Rescue, Remove, and Ugh. The plants under the first heading are judged as worthy ones, but deserve a better home than I had given them; they're getting too much or too little light, moisture, space. The Remove list is not so clear; will I dig it out and compost it, or find the plant a new home in my yard or someone else's? The Ugh list is obvious.

One problem: You'll get so swept up in sowing and weeding and edging and dividing (hopefully) that you'll forget. Promise to at least take pictures weekly all year. Organize them by date in a computer or cloud photo management program or even just post them to Instagram—whatever it takes so that you can see the evolution by scrolling or swiping through, and be reminded what happened when in your corner of the world.

Zones and Other Considerations

Half the nation's 80 million or so gardeners found themselves officially declared a half-zone warmer in January 2012, when the U.S. Department of Agriculture updated its Plant Hardiness Zone Map for the first time since 1990. No, the new map was not technically a confirmation of a trend toward global warming—a different data set is used than in those longer range calculations—but simply a more accurate picture of America's growing conditions.

Ever more sophisticated computers enabled the sharper take, particularly in tricky mountainous areas or those near bodies of water, which can cause sharp variations despite close adjacencies.

The 2012 map draws on data from 1976 to 2005, specifically 30-year averages of what are essentially extreme events—minimum winter temperatures. Climatologists studying climate change, by comparison, look for trends in overall average temperatures over a 50- to 100-year period. I was one of the 50 percent who changed zones, to 5B from 5A, which means my zone gets down to about −10 to −15°F (each full zone is 10°F winter minimum). However, I feel like I am in Zone All Bets Are Off lately, as I suspect others also do, with ever more unexpected weather patterns.

Nursery plants and catalog listings are typically marked with the USDA hardiness range, but there is a limit to how much you can rely on that alone to determine what you can and cannot grow—and to what degree of perfection, or at least satisfaction. Use the numbers as a guideline, but then let the garden tell you, instead. I'm not recklessly leaving any Zone 8- or 10-rated plants outdoors in winter, but I've been growing many supposedly Zone 6 plants even before my zone was officially 5B—and have killed plenty of Zone 4 or 5 plants.

Winter low temperature is just one factor. Place a bone-hardy plant in a poorly draining spot, so that it is effectively standing in an icy sump, and you will kill it. A plant deprived of adequate soil moisture leading up to winter is also ill-prepared for coming through the cold weather well. Don't confuse such havoc with lack of hardiness.

Moisture of another kind, in the form of humidity, can be a blessing or curse. In winter, high relative humidity means less moisture is lost from foliage, dormant buds, and even twigs, minimizing damage as the temperature drops. But a low-humidity wintertime blast, perhaps accompanied by wind, will be tough going, especially for conifers and broad-leaf evergreens (rhododendrons, for instance, or mountain laurel, boxwood, or holly), maybe causing desiccation and even dieback.

Other elements in the hardiness equation may include the duration of extreme cold spells—momentary, or tenacious—and whether there is insulating snow cover. How long ago the plant was installed and how well rooted-in it is can make a difference. Repeated dramatic freeze-thaws can be a major killer of newly planted things. Whatever is said on that nursery label, even the hardiest will die if heaved from the ground.

Another one I'm attributing more damage and losses in woody plants to lately, with the unhinged "new normal" of the seasons: whether the plant had a chance to properly harden off the previous fall. Ideally, the fall season is a gradual cooling-down phase; plants slow gradually toward dormancy as days shorten and temperatures drop. If the first deep freeze comes very early, or the fall is exceptionally warm, it may catch those plants unprepared and render some tissue vulnerable. Fertilizing after about July here or even pruning too late could also have been the culprit, by causing the plant to send up succulent new growth that wasn't stress-ready.

Though a relief to us, sunny late-winter days can bring havoc. Imagine standing out there in the bright sun all day—particularly on the south side of a building with the extra reflected heat that warms your tissues—and then, when darkness falls, having the temperature plummet. Leaves like a broadleaf evergreen's are most susceptible, since they may heat up to 10 or 20 degrees higher than the rest of the plant, then feel the drop at night the worst of all.

This is also when overwintered flower buds that are just starting to swell (ones on mophead, or *macrophylla*, hydrangeas, for instance, and the earliest blooming magnolias), literally get nipped in the bud, and the gardener assumes the plant isn't hardy, or at least its flowers aren't. Wrong, or at least maybe wrong.

Buds on plants sited on the southern side of a building are especially vulnerable to being awakened a little too early, then killed if a late frost follows unseasonably warm weather. It's great to have the first magnolia on the block to bloom, which the protected location yields, but in volatile years you may have no flowers at all. The same plant on the north or east side, out of intense direct sun, would stay asleep a little longer, perhaps until the weather settled, and might miss the rollercoaster.

My basic approach to zones is: Educate yourself, but then never fear trying a plant that's one zone less hardy than your location. Don't buy 20 of something marginal as a test, but do try a couple, preferably in different locations. Try again a second year. And if you fail twice but still covet the plant, pot one up and enjoy it that way.

Taxonomy Lite

It all sounds like *Plantus unknowniensis* at the start, but botanical Latin is the mother tongue of gardening, and must be reckoned with. Besides being the only precise way of asking for what you want, it's often actually quite informative—once you get the hang of it.

The genus name, which comes first, is expressed as Latin in an italicized word starting with an uppercase letter. A genus is a group of related species—such as *Helianthus*, the sunflowers. (The plural of genus is a surprise: genera, not genuses.) It is not always obvious what the genus name derives from, unless you speak Latin, know the history of botanical exploration, or possess some other equally arcane skills. Many genera are named for the explorer who discovered them (*Davidia*, for instance, after Pere David) or someone they were meant to honor (*Franklinia*, for Ben Franklin, or *Dahlia*, for a botanist called Dahl); others are simply Latin words for what they look like (*Aster* means star).

The species name, or specific epithet, which follows the genus to form each two-part name, or Latin binomial, is lowercase and expressed in italics. A species is a group of individuals that are closely enough related to interbreed (two distinct species in the same genus typically won't, with exceptions). Often, the species name tells us something extra about the plant's background or appearance:

Some species names reflect their discoverer (*Magnolia wilsonii*, after English plant collector E. H. Wilson, or *Prunus sargentii*, for Charles Sargent, first director of the Arnold Arboretum). Or they might reveal the person they were meant to honor. Physician and botanist George Engelmann, instrumental in identifying native plants of western North America, had a native spruce, pine, oak, and even a prickly pear cactus named for him with the specific epithet *engelmannii*.

The plant's place of origin can also be invoked. Some that come up again and again include *virginiana* (of Virginia, or the area roughly equivalent to the early colonies), or *occidentalis* (western), or *japonica* (Japan).

Physical appearance is another common possibility: *argentea* (silver), *aurea* (gold), *lanata* (fuzzy), and *nana* (dwarf) are common examples.

Some are easier than others, and even hint at their English translations, like *prostratus* and *horizontalis*, for growing horizontally, or *columnaris* (for another growth habit altogether), and *decidua*, for deciduous, or *variegata* for variegated—but don't get too excited. I'm afraid memorization is the key.

Hosta 'Sagae' (syn. *Hosta fluctuans* 'Variegata') is, as its name would imply, variegated, and also big and lush.

A third word is sometimes used to identify a cultivar, short for cultivated variety This version of the plant, usually an asexually propagated one or clone, is known only in cultivation, and was selected out of the average population of the straight species for some unusual feature. It might have variegated leaves, or different-colored or double flowers, or a weeping habit. This third word is usually expressed in English (Roman letters) inside single quotes, and begins with an uppercase letter, as in *Pinus strobus* 'Pendula', a semidwarf eastern white pine cultivar with weeping, trailing branches.

There is always more to learn A disheartening fact is that even for those who have been memorizing plant names for years, things change. Taxonomists are insistent on getting everything just right, down to the last chromosome, and keep re-examining plants under higher-powered microscopes or other methods, pollen granule by pollen granule, and regrouping them.

Some familiar garden coleuses, for instance, were for a moment no longer *Coleus blumei*, but *Solenostemon scutellarioides*; then they became *Plectranthus scutellarioides*. Perhaps the biggest shock of all was when *Chrysanthemum* ceased to be what we knew it as. *Dendranthema* and other genera became the new homes to the chrysanthemum's former members for a while; then the common florist's type and some others got switched back again in 1999. If you were hooked on their shorthand common name during that chaotic time, sorry, because mum wasn't the word . . . well, at least not for a moment or two.

Though they have undergone various name changes in my years as a gardener, I still call these favorite foliage annuals coleus, and always will.

The place to get the latest lowdown on who goes where is the ICNCP, or International Code for the Nomenclature for Cultivated Plants. Typically the latest edition is not available to the public online, however, so instead I search The Plant List (theplantlist.org), a collaboration between esteemed botanical organizations including the Royal Botanic Gardens Kew, Missouri Botanical Garden, New York Botanical Garden, and the Royal Botanic Garden Edinburgh. The Encyclopedia of Life (eol.org) also includes taxonomic notes for many plant entries, sometimes with a bit of the history of past name changes.

I think it's important to know the correct nomenclature, but as a gardener, being ever so precise can have its limitations. In catalogs, reference books, and certainly in the aisles at the garden center, the renamed plants will probably still be where they were, and are likely to stay put for years. I didn't ask for a flat of *Solenostemon* during that temporary uprising, and even now I don't ask for *Plectranthus* (which would likely have me directed to the robust and more sideways-growing ones I like to use as trailers in my biggest summer pot designs, like silvery *P. argentatus*). I stuck with *Coleus*.

Say What? Speaking Latin

The worst part of basic botanical Latin is worries about proper pronunciation. I only wish that someone had told me 20 years earlier that any pronunciation was fine—and light-years better than imprecise common names. Botanical Latin, it turns out, isn't a real spoken language at all, not the mother tongue of ancient Rome, but a system of nomenclature (or naming) invented by Carl von Linné, also known as Linnaeus, in 1753.

How do you pronounce the words of a language that doesn't belong to any one nation or people, exactly? Any way you like, I think, and I have that on good authority. The preeminent botanist William T. Stearn, in his classic 1966 manual *Botanical Latin,* gave us the O.K. when he wrote: "Botanical Latin is essentially a written language, but the scientific names of plants often occur in speech. How they are pronounced really matters little provided they sound pleasant and are understood by all."

Indeed, what's important is that you learn the words and let them help you to find the desired plant. As a bonus, certain botanical Latin words also reveal a plant's characteristics. This is particularly true among the species names, the second word in each binomial, which modifies the genus. What follows is a sampling, in most cases expressed with a -us ending (-a and -um are also used when the gender of the subject being modified is appropriate):

COLOR

Yellow may be expressed with *flavus* (a pale version), *luteus,* and *citrinus* (lemon-colored). **Red** is *rubrum*; rosy pink is *roseus*. **Purple** is simple: just say *purpureus*. If it's very dark, it might be *atropurpureus*. **White** is *albus*; **black** is *nigrum*. **Silver** is expressed as *argenteus*; **gold** is *aureus*. **Green,** when it's noted, might be *viridis* (or *sempervirens* in the case of **evergreen**). **Shades of blue** include *azureus* (a sky-blue color) and *caeruleus* (somewhat darker).

GROWTH HABIT

If a plant is **graceful** or **slender,** it might be designated *gracilis*. If globe-shaped, *globosus* might be more appropriate. A **pyramid?** Maybe *pyramidalis*. A **shrubby** plant might be labeled *fructicosus* or *frutescens*. **Upright** and **columnar?** Look for the words *fastigiatus* or *columnaris*. Downright **narrow,** with nearly parallel sides: *linearis*.

A **dwarf** plant might be *nanus* or *pumilus*; a **creeping** one, *repens*; one **flat** on the ground, *prostratus* or *procumbens*. If it spreads in a **straggly** manner, *divaricatus* is a possibility. If instead the plant **climbs,** it could be called *scandens*.

SURFACE TEXTURE OR PATTERN

Pleated leaves might be indicated by the word *plicatus*. **Woolly** ones are often labeled *lanatus*. *Mollis* means **soft** (because the plant is covered with soft hairs); *glaucus* (as in some blue-leaved hostas) means **glaucous,** coated in what's called bloom—a fine waxy, powdery coating. If the surface **glistens,** it could be called *fulgens*. If it's **spiny,** *spinosus* is a more appropriate epithet.

Variegated leaves or flowers are sometimes labeled *variegatus,* but might also be called *pictus* (which means **painted,** and is used to indicate bright coloration of other kinds, too). **Spots** might be indicated by the word *punctatus*.

Inodorus means a plant has **no fragrance**. *Aromaticus* and *fragans* mean that it does, but so do *pungens* (**pungent**), *odoratus* (**sweet-smelling**), and *foetidus* (**fetid**, or stinking).

BLOOM TIMES

Some epithets, such as *praecox*, mean simply **early**. Seasonal interest in **spring** is expressed by *vernalis*; **summer** by *aestivalis*; **fall** by *autumnalis*, and **winter** by *hyemalis*.

HABITAT OF ORIGIN

Plants from **wet places** are often called *palustris* (or *aquaticus*, if they actually live in water). Those from **rocky areas** may bear the specific epithet *saxatilis*. If **sand** was in their background, *arenarius* is the word. **Woodland** denizens may be *sylvaticus* or *sylvestris*; those from **above the treeline** are *alpinus*.

Hybrid, Heirloom, or Both?

What I have realized in recent years is that "hybrid or heirloom?" isn't an either-or debate but rather a false construct, as if one could not ethically elect to grow both (as I do). I long thought I was not a hybrid person, but an open-pollinated (OP) type, and I often "vote" this way with my seed-shopping dollars for sentimental reasons, and as a nod to helping preserve the plant's genetic imprint into the future. I also like to save seed from some varieties, and OPs—whether 50-plus-year-old nonhybrids referred to as heirlooms or newer modern OPs, which may become the heirlooms of tomorrow—will come true to type if grown properly (sometimes isolation distances must be observed). Hybrid seed doesn't; you need to order more, or be O.K. with an unpredictable next generation.

But none of that makes hybrids bad. Gregor Mendel made hybrids; nature has done it herself by moving pollen around. Hybrids have saved me in more than one tough season, when I have been growing a hybrid bred for particular disease-resistance—something some heirlooms may not have. If you have ever had an outbreak of early blight in the tomato patch, a fungal infection that can cause the plants to lose leaves from the bottom up, or verticillium wilt, which can occur in a cold, wet, season with susceptible varieties, you will understand.

Speaking of tomatoes, my two musts—the cherry tomato called 'Sun Gold' and highly disease-resistant 'Juliet', which produces grape-like clusters of 2¼-inch fruit that I make sauce from—are both hybrids, growing alongside various heirloom beauties.

I like to read all the fine print when seed shopping because sometimes, in either OPs or hybrids, it's some unexpected quality that breeders or other seed stewards of that variety have made possible—a quality I didn't know I was looking for. By guiding the genetics of open-pollinated varieties through selection, favoring certain naturally occurring traits over

The highly disease-resistant small hybrid tomato called 'Juliet', borne in grape-like clusters, is my go-to for tomato sauce.

others, a bean that's easier to locate, and pick, amid all those leaves has been created—such as purple-podded 'Blue Coco' (a pole type and pre-1775 French heirloom) or bush 'Royal Burgundy'. Cucumbers, too, can be elusive under lush foliage, but OP 'H-19 Little Leaf' has what its name implies (and more visible cukes), plus it sets fruit without pollination and can be left under a row cover all season, if cucumber beetles are an issue.

Through active hybridizing work—classical breeding like Mendel did by providing a human hand in cross-pollination, not laboratory-style gene splicing that creates transgenic hybrids or GMOs—traits from different parents are married. A hybridizer might aim to create a cucumber resistant to a range of diseases—or a broccoli that heads up and can all be harvested at once, the kind of uniformity that farmers, in particular, rely on. While I may like a broccoli that produces a little bit at a time over many weeks (like 'Piracicaba'), it would be unmanageable to harvest an acre of it repeatedly for market.

Look beyond the photos, and even beyond the labels of merely OP or hybrid (often listed as F1) and see all of what each variety has to offer.

Seed Viability versus Vigor

The seed catalogs are here, and I'm getting organized. Step 1: taking inventory of what's on hand. But how many of the seeds I have left over are still not just viable, but also have sufficient vigor to perform well, start to finish? That's the sort of advanced question I'm asking after a little episode with a packet of leftover collard seeds that I was feeling glad to have on hand—a feeling that quickly changed to dismay a couple of weeks into their sorry time outdoors.

When taking inventory, first I refer to the general guidelines for how long seeds last, summarized generally in the chart provided on the following page. I do a germination test of any packets older than a year (assuming there are enough seeds left). Being low-tech old-school, I simply line up 10 seeds on a double thickness of moist paper towel, fold it over, and put it in a sealed plastic bag in a warm spot in my house. I check inside the bag, starting after two or three days, taking note of how many seeds sprout after how many days, hoping to see perhaps that eight or more have done so and in a timely manner—and also basically in unison with their siblings, not staggered days and days apart. Temperature and type of seed affects how long a good result will take—carrots or parsley make you wait longer than a radish or a bean.

The collards in question, which were in their third year with me, sailed right through; virtually all germinated concurrently. But when the other seeds from that same packet were direct-sown in the garden, things were different: They came up, yes, but then just stood there, like miniatures, never developing.

Germination tests predict viability (the ability to germinate), but cannot accurately predict vigor—the seeds' potential for uniform, fast germination and subsequent development in real outdoor conditions. Life in the field isn't the same as life in a piece of moist paper toweling indoors, or in the germination chamber of a seed-company lab.

As viability declines, damage to the seed—a reduction in its vigor—accumulates gradually, until eventually the seed dies. Like my unfortunate collards were on their way to doing.

If I'd had a second packet of fresher collard seeds on hand, and tested it at the same time as the three-year-old one, I might have seen some differences (emphasis on *might*, since I am not a trained plant physiologist). Perhaps the roots of the older seeds would have been less developed, even stubby or nonexistent, or the cotyledon (the first leaves) might have been in some way visibly deformed, with one missing, or overall the tiny plants on that paper towel might have looked more crooked or scrawnier than those from the fresher lot.

There's no home test for vigor, though several kinds are used in agriculture, where this critical subject is the focus of continuing fine-tuning. But knowing a little more than I did about vigor when I failed with those deceptively high-germinating collards serves several purposes for me, and that's why I mention it. It makes me think about storing leftover seed more carefully, and about replacing seed more frequently, not pushing it. Also—small comfort, but something at least—it makes me realize that collard failure wasn't something I did wrong in the planting or aftercare. Try as they might, those seeds just didn't have it in them to go all the way. I'm now clear on this lesson: Just because seed germinates, doesn't mean that it will thrive.

Remember: The viability chart assumes that you're storing properly dried seed in optimal cool, dry conditions—and that it's seed that developed on its parent plant under optimal conditions in the first place, including good conditions close to harvest time, when wet heat and humidity can diminish its eventual staying power.

Seed Viability Chart

HOW LONG DO SEEDS LAST? (ESTIMATED VIABILITY)

	Fedco	Johnny's	Virginia Tech	Iowa St. IPM
beans	2–3 years	2–4 years	3 years	3 years
beets	3–5 years	2–5 years	4 years	4 years
brassicas	3–5 years	3–5 years	3–5 years*	5 years**
carrots	2–3 years	3–4 years	3 years	3 years
celery	2–3 years	3–5 years	3 years	
chard	3–5 years	2–5 years		
corn	2–3 years	1–3 years	2 years	2 years
cucumber	5–10 years	3–6 years	5 years	5 years
eggplant	2–3 years	4–5 years	4 years	
lettuce	2–3 years	1–6 years	6 years	5 years
leek	2 years	2–3 years	2 years	
melon (muskmelon)	5–10 years	3–6 years	5 years	5 years
melon (watermelon)	5–10 years	4–5 years	4 years	4 years
onion	1 year	1–2 years	1 year	1 year
parsnips		1–3 years	1 year	
parsley		1–4 years	1 year	
peas	2–3 years	2–4 years	3 years	3 years
peppers	2–3 years	2–5 years	2 years	2 years
radish	3–5 years	4–5 years	5 years	5 years
spinach	2–3 years	1–5 year	3 years	5 years
squash/pumpkin	2–5 years	3–6 years	4 years	4 years
tomato	5–10 years	3–7 years	4 years	4 years

*kale 4, Brussels sprouts 4, cabbage 4, broccoli 3, collards 5
**broccoli, cabbage, cauliflower 5

Onions (and their cousins the leeks) are the first seeds I sow in February, in hopes of having a good harvest to store come fall.

First Sowing: Onions and Leeks

It is too early for tomatoes, but not for leeks and onions—my official first indoor seeding of each new growing season. Each such crop needing an indoor head start in my Northern location will grow under lights in flats or small pots, requiring regular watering and perhaps occasional feeding to develop from seed into a garden-ready seedling. Though parsley takes about the same number of weeks indoors, before transplant (8 or 10), it doesn't go outdoors as early as leeks and onions do (4 weeks before final frost, compared to parsley's 1). The way the math works counting from my last frost date around mid-May means those two edible alliums lead off my lineup with mid-February sowings, and will make their way outdoors sometime in the second half of April. When to sow and transplant each crop relative to your frost date is presented in the charts in the Birth section of the book.

When they hear 10 weeks, gardeners think growing onions and leeks from seed is hard, and I did, too, for decades. Besides the investment of time, the seed is relatively small, and I was impatient and maybe clumsy in one early attempt at wrangling it into individual cells in a seedling tray. Forget this, I thought. As is commonplace, early each spring I bought seedlings by the bundle of about 50 at like $15 to $20—costly compared to a packet of a couple or several hundred organic seeds that can be had for under $5 (though still a great deal compared to buying organic onions at the grocer). As with any crop, buying plants also limits variety choice.

I haven't bought bundles of transplants since I got a tutorial from Don Tipping of Siskiyou Seeds in southern Oregon, a longtime organic onion grower and breeder, among other specialties. The time it takes hasn't changed—in Don's greenhouse it's about 8 weeks for onions and 10 weeks for leeks, and in my shed under lights about 10 and 12—but everything else did. He sows into open flats of potting soil—10-by-20-inch shallow wooden boxes built for the purpose, but I use plastic seedling trays minus the usual individual cells. Be sure the trays have drainage holes, or create some. His homemade seedling mix is 8 parts compost to 1 part sand, plus some eggshells and a little kelp powder; I use an organic brand of germination mix.

Using a finger or pencil, make little lengthwise rows in that tray. Sow in those tiny furrows, but not too thickly, aiming for 8 to 10 seeds per inch. In Don's flats he gets four or five rows, and the seedlings can reach about the size of a pencil.

At transplant time, Don employs another onion-growing trick, one he credits to Eliot Coleman of Maine, who has long provided inspiration for organic farmers and gardeners. If spaced in the typical manner—gridded out with about 8 inches between each plant in all directions—a well-grown onion can reach 1 pound or even 2, especially sweet onions. Who needs a 2-pound onion? Save transplant time and get recipe-size onions instead, by scooping up clusters of two or three seedlings at a time from the flat, planting them in the same hole, with holes a foot apart. Submerge the point where the seedlings change from white at the bottom, by the roots, to green, so that there is an inch of soil above where the root starts. As they're growing, they'll push each other apart. The wider spacing also leaves more room for weeding.

Onion seedlings are passing an early spring day outside in the bright sunshine, almost ready to be transplanted.

Saying No to Deer

During a garden workshop, a visitor commented as he looked around at the mature shrubs and big swaths of perennials: "You must have a fence, because otherwise this garden wouldn't be here," he said. Because it's mostly hidden in the surrounding woodland tree line, he hadn't spied the fence itself yet, but he just knew: It's a deer-free zone.

I'm a serious gardener, and my home is in serious deer country, adjacent to a 5,000-acre state park where groups of four or five animals browse my boundaries daily, and in winter I have seen forty at a time just across the road. I had no choice but to fence, but in some circumstances there are other tactics, from temporary or smaller barriers than my 2.3 acres of 8-foot-high wire mesh enclosure, to repellents, to limiting the choice of what you plant.

Be aware: These are very adaptive, voracious animals that are not picky when hungry, and will at least sample most anything. Their typical diet, referred to as browse, is leaves, buds and branches of mostly deciduous (but not always) trees.

In the growing season, they may focus on green vegetation, but it's often in the downtime when they can do the most lasting damage to woody plants. A hosta will typically grow back after being browsed; a prized specimen shrub that took 10 years to cultivate may not recover. The decision on how to manage against deer must take into account the local population and its patterns, the value of the landscape you wish to protect, how attractive your plant palette is to them, and also local fencing codes. In areas like mine of high pressure, it's unlikely you can gain 100 percent control except with a major fence.

Before I had mine, I tried other measures, including repellents. I didn't understand then that these products are best suited for low or moderate deer-pressure areas. Typically sprays, various brands either smell or taste bad to deer (or both). The most effective ingredients to check labels for are eggs (the sulfur scent of rotten eggs does the job) and capsaicin (the heat in hot peppers). Different brands require different reapplication intervals—as often as every two weeks—and are not appropriate for use on edibles, plus they can't be applied in the hottest times or coldest (below about 35°F). Besides all the effort, the products are not cheap if you have a large landscape to protect year-round.

But perhaps you have fewer deer, or a problem in one season only. Maybe certain plants, like arborvitae or yew, are being eaten in winter—repellents might work in that case—or young trees are being damaged by bucks in rut. When males are on the move leading up to breeding season and polishing their antlers by rubbing against trees in fall, it can be very destructive—and sometimes the behavior continues into January.

Even in an unfenced property, this kind of damage can be prevented by exclusion—employing the same keep-out tactic as my permanent fence, but in a temporary version. Individual trees or shrubs can be protected with 4- or 5-foot-high pens of reusable chicken wire and stakes or even snow fencing, so bucks can't rub them (nor can any deer browse them). Plastic netting could be used to wrap or drape over shrubbier plants.

I did this each fall years ago, but I preach a 365-day garden philosophy: to strive to look out the window every day of the year with pleasure. The last thing I want to create is an axial view half the year of imprisoned shrubs and trees. Similarly, I bristle at adhering to a narrow regional list of less-palatable-to-deer plants. Don't fence me in by my plant palette, please. Whole books are devoted to deer-resistant plants, but I didn't do the painful homework to qualify to write them; I got a 365-day fence. There are various kinds to consider.

A 5-foot mesh fence might keep a small area protected, such as an average-size vegetable garden, which might look to the deer like a tight spot it doesn't want to jump into. Speaking of tight spots: In a long-ago trip to the hillside Northern California garden of *Salvia* expert Betsy Clebsch, I learned that two parallel low fences will also work: specifically, two 4-foot fences spaced about 5 feet apart. The gap between is too wide for jumping over and too tight to look inviting, but it's big enough for your wheelbarrow and mower (or you can plant it, a garden ringing the garden).

This solution is great for small gardens or areas near the house where a tall fence would be unsightly. It creates a space like an old-fashioned dooryard garden, but with two rows of fence. Critical tip: No matter how tall your fence is, what you do at ground level to exclude the deer is just as important. Deer are happy to do the limbo anytime and wriggle on in, particularly fawns.

Following the same too-wide-to-jump idea, longtime willow collector and expert plantsman Michael Dodge suggested to me the unexpected possibility of a living fence. He recommends

Instead of extending 8-foot wire deer fencing along the front roadside, a hybrid of pickets, extra-tall fence posts, and heavy plastic netting can do the job.

creating dense "fedges" (fence meets hedge) of the most deer-resistant willows, *Salix purpurea* 'Nana' or 'Gracilis'.

Other effective fence designs that cost less are often electrified, though some local ordinances forbid them. Electric fences can be vertical or slanted, and recommended heights vary, including a seven-strand 8-footer for total control, or a 3-foot "peanut-butter fence" that uses foil packets of peanut butter every 3 feet along the upper of its two wires to entice deer to investigate—and get a buzz. Like the family dog with the invisible fence, they learn to obey it. The Internet Center for Wildlife Damage Management web page has designs for both of these and other fences, or search for "slanted electric deer fence" and "electric peanut butter deer fence."

A final trick: I didn't want the wire-mesh look along my front boundary, so I invented a hybrid. I have stretches of 4-foot-high pickets, punctuated by 8-foot fence posts spaced 8 feet apart. Between the posts and above the pickets, I strung 4 feet of heavy black plastic mesh, reinforced with wire, creating an 8-foot fence that looks like a mere white picket fence as you drive by—well, except apparently to the deer, who have never dared make the leap.

Suckers and water sprouts, in this case from an old magnolia, should be removed regularly. A telescoping long-handled pruner helps reach them.

Pruning, Pared Way Down

I admit I lack the artistic vision required to turn boxwood into crowing roosters, but I refuse to be held hostage by errant water sprouts or suckers and broken or badly placed branches. I am happy to pay a skilled arborist to do the really challenging work, but basic care and maintenance of shrubs, especially, mostly involves making a simple set of obvious cuts whenever I see a plant in need of them. By then also sharpening our powers of observation, we can even learn to answer the worrisome question of when, on which kind of plant, to go beyond those basic cuts, should some woody thing need more serious corrective measures.

If I can do this much, so can you. The top three tips apply to all woody plants, but with conifers, any more involved pruning is a little trickier, and requires extra research first because some (like yew) respond to harder pruning than others that are less forgiving. How my everyday, as-needed routine works:

Take out the three Ds anytime they occur The Ds are dead, damaged, and diseased wood. (Some people say there are five Ds, with dying and deformed being added to the list, but I lump those into my "damaged" category.)

Take out all suckers and water sprouts as often as required This means that mess at the base of a grafted plant that looks like a thicket of shoots, where the underground rootstock is trying to overtake the desired plant. It also means twigs that shoot straight up vertically off a branch at a 90-degree angle or thereabouts, very common on fruit trees, say, or old magnolias. Look at the architecture of these shoots (which sometimes emanate from the trunk of an aged tree, too): If you left them on, what would they turn into? Nothing very useful, or well-engineered. Remove them.

Similarly, off with the head of anything thinner than a pencil or turning inward Rubbing against another branch is no good, either. (Those are probably all in the D called deformed.)

Learn the "when" by studying new wood and old wood Some pruning tasks are not "do it anytime it occurs" like those three, but timed to coincide with a specific moment in the particular plant's growth cycle. Ill-timed pruning may eliminate the next flowering or fruiting, or in more extreme situations may stress the plant and even cause decline.

Each May and June I'm asked, "Why didn't my lilacs bloom?" only to find out in the next sentence that the questioner had literally nipped the plants in the (flower) bud with late summer, fall, winter or earliest springtime pruning—meaning sometime after the new year's blossoms had been set. Early bloomers flower on old wood. Go out and look at an apple or peach tree or a forsythia or lilac bush in winter or even early spring: Unless you pruned in summer or fall, you'll see flower buds already in place, dormant but there. If you prune them off, the plant won't flower that year. Make sense? It will not harm the plant to prune extra early, but in most cases, why not enjoy the blooms first?

My old apple trees are an exception. Though they may be laden with flower buds, I prune apples and pears and peaches and cherries in late winter, when they are leafless and dormant—and if I time it right, I can force some of those lopped branches into bloom indoors as a bonus.

Generally speaking, if you want flowers the next year, don't prune spring-blooming shrubs and trees more than a month or so after they finish blooming, because they will be starting the bud-setting process for next year. This means not pruning (except the three Ds) from late spring or earliest summer, nor anytime again until after the next bloom cycle. After they're finished flowering, prune immediately.

Woody plants that flower late in the season, such as *Hydrangea paniculata*, bloom on new wood. Again, go look; you won't see any flower buds that overwintered on the old twigs. Discovering where on the stems and when the plant creates its flower buds will help direct pruning efforts.

Sometimes a shrub is just too big, or got beat up in a storm or is otherwise a mess, and the only hope besides replacement is to attempt rejuvenation pruning—a more extreme version of ongoing removal of damaged parts. The process can be staggered over two or three springs, or performed all at once. I've used the staggered approach on old lilacs, at first removing the three Ds plus maybe one-third of the oldest stems down to the base. I may also lower the remaining ones down part way, to the junction of a well-placed side shoot. Meantime, I'm surveying the lower reaches to identify any strong, well-placed younger shoots that could figure into future architecture. The next year and perhaps a third year, too, I repeat the process.

The rip-off-the-bandage version is easier, but scarier—and best used on robust, fast-growing shrubs. Essentially, you cut the entire plant to the ground (usually 6 to 12 inches) and let it regrow. When such wholesale rejuvenation is required, I do it in spring, to allow the plant the entire season to recover. Sometimes, selfishly, I wait until after bloom; sometimes I sacrifice bloom in the name of getting the job done now. Some of my oldest shrubs, including several giant *Physocarpus opulifolius* (ninebark), have been cut to the ground more than once, rising back to major status. I have also employed the brutal approach on *Weigela*, twig willows and dogwoods, *Spiraea*, *Philadelphus* (mock orange) and *Cotinus* (smokebush)—and of course roses.

One time I never prune beyond the three Ds in my cold-winter zone is in fall. I don't want new growth to possibly sprout and then get hit by blasts of cold before the wood hardens off. Avoid undertaking rejuvenations late in the season, and even any reshaping. If I were in a frost-free zone, I might be more flexible.

Intermediate Witch Hazels

I lost a lot of shrubs in 2011, between deliberate culling required by the garden's age (at that time, about 25 years) and a freakish late-October snowstorm that took even more than I'd planned to surrender. One silver lining—or should I say gold and copper?—was that spots opened up for some witch hazels, or *Hamamelis*.

My choices were intermediate hybrids like orange 'Jelena' and yellow 'Pallida'. Intermediate hybrids, or *Hamamelis ×intermedia*, means that each is a child of two great parents: the Chinese witch hazel (*Hamamelis mollis*) and Japanese *H. japonica*. Their offspring (hardy in Zones 5–8) are mostly fragrant, and all bloom early, unfurling little streamer-like petals in a spidery arrangement, and boasting hot fall foliage besides.

I have said before that if garden centers were open in winter in cold-climate zones like mine, early blooming Asian witch hazels would knock the more vulgar (and admittedly later) *Forsythia* out of the ring. Mine bloom most years in February into March, but I have had them begin before New Year's.

'Jelena', with coppery, scented flowers, is more horizontal in stature than another I made a spot for, the vase-shaped 'Pallida'. I'm figuring on perhaps 10 or 12 feet in eventual height, and about as wide someday. Some varieties, like the best known of all, yellow 'Arnold Promise', are slightly bigger, perhaps 15 by 15 feet.

The intermediate witch hazels like a spot in full sun to part shade, with more light meaning more flowers, but spare them a hot, dry location. Like *Fothergilla* and *Corylopsis* (winter hazel), their cousins in family Hamamelidaceae, and two of my favorite shrubs of all, witch hazels have handsome foliage that seems to resist most insects and disease. Whether deer eat them or not depends where you live, as with many plants. Rutgers University, in its searchable online database of plants according to their palatability to deer, classifies intermediate witch hazels as "seldom severely damaged"; other such sources disagree.

My only caveat: Keep an eye on the base for the emergence of any suspicious, extra-vigorous shoots that may wish to overtake the desired cultivar. These are often sold as grafted shrubs, meaning the rootstock (our native American witch hazel, *Hamamelis virginiana*, which blooms in fall along my wooded property line) may try to out-compete the desired variety. Decades ago, my first hybrid witch hazel got engulfed before I understood what was happening. Remember who has the pruners and take no prisoners on suckers.

The harsh winter of 2011 made room for more witch hazels in my garden.

The intermediate hybrid witch hazel *Hamamelis ×intermedia* 'Jelena' can flower as early as New Year's, but will typically bloom in February into March.

Hamamelis ×intermedia 'Pallida' is likewise one of the earliest offerings to awakening insects.

Hellebores Galore

A strange-shaped box, much longer than wide or tall, arrived unannounced one day. Inside was a plastic plug tray—a seedling flat but with deeper individual cells than typical—packed with baby hellebores. The surprise gift was from a friend, Charles Price, who was trying his hand at breeding some of the so-called *orientalis* hybrids, or *Helleborus ×hybridus*.

I had never grown a hellebore except white-flowered *Helleborus niger*, the so-called Christmas rose, the first perennial to bloom every year since I acquired it at a local garden center. At the time the seedlings arrived, I didn't even know I could grow another hellebore species; now I also grow the stinking hellebore, *H. foetidus*, a short-lived and shallow-rooted perennial that likes to choose where it will colonize, somewhat like columbine, meaning where it damn well pleases (and in some pretty tough spots). For me chartreuse-flowered *foetidus* blooms at least as early as *niger*. The original plant will die off after a few years, but its seedlings carry on unless inadvertently disturbed.

What I have now besides my age-old same clump of *Helleborus niger* and the independent-thinking *H. foetidus*, are the hybrid Lenten roses, *H. orientalis*, in a delightful profusion where I put them in the first place plus two more spots where I have since repeated the good effect. Before the first of the extra-early perennials like *Pulmonaria*, it's as if the Lenten roses are in a race to beat the truly fearless early bulbs, *Eranthis hyemalis* (winter aconite) and *Galanthus* (snowdrops).

I enjoy weeks of their big flowers from darkest purple to reddish purple through uncanny slate shades and various pinks and amazing yellows on to white, plus some that combine more than one color in a single flower, marked with contrasting blotches, streaks, freckles or margins. Those aren't petals but sepals, and the sepals (in many shapes and sizes) will sometimes be slightly greenish, or more so, and even conduct photosynthesis. I just went out to measure, and from that long-ago gift now three large areas of about 700 square feet are dominated by *Helleborus ×hybridus*, plus many smaller groups.

That's not to say they are invasive, but some of those once-tiny seedlings I dotted a few feet apart around the original site under an old apple tree are now the diameter of bushel baskets, producing many dozens of flowers apiece. Prodigious self-sowers, the original plants have yielded enough offspring to send dozens of visitors away with their own gift of a trayful each, without making a dent in the supply. Experts say to move the self-sowns as soon as they appear, to limit root disturbance, though I also do so when they are a couple of inches tall, if a would-be adoptive parent happens to show up then. Before they bloom there is no way to tell what color seedlings will be, but no recipient so far has called to complain.

The hybrids seem as tough as any perennial; I don't feel as if I did much but plant them and keep them watered till they settled in. When transplanting from a nursery pot, loosen the roots first to help them get going. Flowering-size plants may skip a year of bloom after transplant, and so may young plants that haven't reached blooming age.

Avoid poor drainage and "wet feet," or spots in the baking summer sunshine (especially in more southern gardens). Hellebores are shade-tolerant, but not shade-dependent; mine get far more light than a hosta or hakonechloa would stand for long, and I think the brightest shade yields maximum flowers. (Speaking of other early "shade" perennials that can take more light than you'd expect and could complement your hellebores, *Epimedium* is one.)

As the garden comes alive, hybrid hellebores, trilliums, and the gold flowers of *Hylomecon japonicum* have their moment.

Many of the hellebore seedlings will bloom in rose tones.

Helleborus foetidus, the stinking or fetid hellebore, is a short-lived perennial that sows itself around at will in shady areas.

A slate-colored *orientalis* hybrid hellebore.

More virtues: Being naturally loaded with alkaloid toxins, like *Narcissus*, hellebores are essentially deerproof. The hybrids basically provide handsome evergreen ground cover, even in dry shade once established, though technically last year's foliage fades just as the bloom cycle begins (again, like *Epimedium*). I cut it off in late fall or during a winter thaw—or just before bloom if I got lazy, which makes for a harder job, working around the succulent emerging

Some of the progeny of my hellebores are bicolored, and their flowers are of different shapes.

The so-called black flowers of the *orientalis* hybrid hellebores are my favorite of all.

flowers. Don't cut off all the foliage of a *Helleborus niger*; just tidy the worst bits, which is what I do with *H. foetidus*, too. And remember: In the wild over the millennia, nobody ran around doing cutbacks; it's strictly optional.

The late Judith Knott Tyler, who co-authored an important book on hellebores and bred them in Virginia, told me many things that stuck, including this: Think of them as you would peonies, meaning they require nothing more than an annual cleanup and perhaps a bit of compost. Feed hellebores with a balanced, all-natural organic fertilizer in early spring—or don't bother. I never have. Tony Avent of Plant Delights Nursery confirms they seem to be fine even without that something extra. He also tells me they'll grow under black walnuts, but that I can neither confirm nor deny.

Plants with Structure

Looking good naked is a challenge to people and plants alike. Plants that manage to do so are especially appreciated at this difficult time. Taking at least one wintertime walk at an arboretum or public garden can help add names to your wish list of plants with good bare bones.

Garden books traditionally cited the same plant first up as being synonymous with "good structure" and "winter interest," and that is the contorted filbert, *Corylus avellana* 'Contorta'. Lately there is a version called *C. a.* 'Red Dragon', which I succumbed to because it boasts both purple leaves and good resistance to eastern filbert blight. Said to slowly reach maybe 8 feet high and 5 wide, it is a twisted, shrubby, wild thing, but by no means the only possibility, and not for every garden.

Likewise contorted, but bigger (15 to 25 feet by even wider) and faster growing is another often-mentioned structure plant, the Camperdown elm (*Ulmus glabra* 'Camperdownii'). Its branches arch to the ground and create a kind of secret world beneath when the tree is in leaf. Dutch elm disease would be my worry here, but what a magical creature an old example of this tree is.

This brings up the subject of weeping things, which can add intriguing off-season silhouettes to the garden—or sully it. I become agitated by obscene high-grafted cherries that look like a bad hair day (or the working end of a mop) glued to the top of a totem pole. Shop especially carefully for grafted weepers and choose one before they leaf out.

There is hardly any small tree more beautiful in any season than a naturally cascading Japanese maple (*Acer japonicum*), and even some more vase-shaped or otherwise upright Japanese maples have good structure and sometimes bark that is tinged with color, from greenish to coral-red depending on the selection.

I have a weeping kousa dogwood, *Cornus kousa* 'Lustgarten Weeping', bought as a truly tiny thing from the former mail-order nursery called Heronswood. I almost cut it down many times the first decade, when it was more gangly teenager than confident adult. Blessedly, I did not, and it is 8 feet high by 10 feet and offers flowers, fruit, and fall color besides its dome shape, with branches touching the ground.

There are good weeping forms of native eastern redbud, or *Cercis canadensis*, including a purple-leaf form that could fit a small yard at maybe 6 or 8 feet tall and slightly narrower. At Broken Arrow Nursery in Connecticut, a weeping form of Japanese snowbell, *Stryax japonica* 'Carillon', is a charmer, and in the nursery trade there are even smaller varieties than its 8 to 12 feet tall by similarly wide stature that I have not met in person.

Lately I find myself attracted to columnar plants, both evergreen conifers and deciduous ones like the purple beech *Fagus sylvatica* 'Dawyck Purple'. I have a feeling that my next adventures in adding structure will involve a number of exclamation points.

I do an annual late-winter cutback of a twiggy shrub with winter interest, the ghost bramble or *Rubus cockburnianus*. As its common name suggests, it has ghostly white canes that are arching and very thorny (and gold leaves in season). It does not flower or fruit here, so I have never had it seed about, just run a bit underground like other brambles.

Site these off-season highlights where they can be enjoyed from a cozy spot, or along the route you take from car to doorway no matter the weather. Underplant with the earliest blooming bulbs, perhaps, like snowdrops (*Galanthus*) and glory of the snow (*Chionodoxa*) and winter aconite (*Eranthis hyemalis*), to maximize the vista.

A broom stands at the ready at the top of the driveway for cleaning off the car, an endless task in winter.

Birth

MARCH & APRIL

GROUNDHOG DAY

TODAY IS THE DAY when thoughts officially turn to the potential coming of spring, but on Groundhog Day, my troubled mind can't let go of memories of the Fourth of July. Just the mention of anything groundhog, in fact, and those guilt-laden synapses of mine take me right to that Independence Day not long ago and an ill-advised display of underground fireworks.

I tried to off a groundhog with a smoke bomb.

There, I feel better now that I've shared it.

At that time, like many city people, I fought the way things are, or at least objected to it energetically. The first year in the country house, we—my ex and I—fought everything, I recall, not just the groundhog (or woodchuck, as we knew him to be called). On the morning after a harsh snowstorm, for example, we tried to travel back to the city, and in this self-important misadventure, learned a whole new meaning for the term respect.

We fought the deer, who for generations had been coming to eat beneath the apple trees we now insisted were ours; the mice, who asked only for a warm place—our bedroom wall—to raise their children. We fought the logic that says that moss, not flowers, grows on the north side of a house. And we even fought each other.

Neither skiers nor children eager to fashion Frosty on the front lawn, we moaned about snow simply because it was inconvenient, because it slowed us down. Now, many winters wiser, we pray for the stuff. It is nectar, sustenance. We have seen the devastation a winter windstorm can deal unto the naked garden, where no white blanket lies in place to soften the blow. When it melts around this time of year, we pray for more with all our might.

Beneath it, all manner of plant and animal life—even the groundhog—might sleep in safety until spring. Without it, they are like shivering homeless on the city streets.

This February morning, Punxsutawney Phil will raise his sleepy head toward the exit of his man-made bedroom burrow in Punxsutawney, Pennsylvania, aided by a human handler whose job it is to make him forecast the season ahead. The Blob, which is what a groundhog looks like, mostly, will either see or not see his shadow, depending on the strength of the late winter sun. If he does, it's back to bed for six more weeks; sorry, no early spring. The whole thing stems from an ancient Scotch couplet: "If the sun is bright and clear, there'll be two winters in the year."

I, for one, hope winter stays around a while longer. I hope the rest of the winter, which hasn't seemed like a winter to me at all yet, will bring enough water to the earth in whatever form, however inconvenient. I hope it snows and sleets and rains until there is enough, because recent droughts are too clear in my memory for me to hope otherwise.

I remember years when a third of the United States, or more, was parched deep into the subsoil, aching for those healing waters. Any gardener who has lost even one lettuce seedling to an unexpected April heat wave, or one potted plant when it baked on the radiator, should realize what that means: Without a proper sequence of the passing seasons, without the "inconvenient" weather like rain and sleet and even snow, there would be no farming nor gardening, no flowers and no food.

In April, *Berginia ciliata* emerges from the leaf litter.

I know, it's been bright and pretty a lot of recent mornings, and you haven't had to fight the chapping winds to get to work or school. Besides, you think, the trouble's worse in some other region, not mine, and so it's all right to feel safe and happy that it's spring two months too soon.

It's not right, and it's not safe.

My groundhog did not die, by the way, that unpleasantly memorable Fourth of July; he didn't even bat a droopy lid at the pair of fools who sealed off the doors of his burrow with big stones after dropping a smoke bomb down one end. He just sat up high on his haunches, as his breed is inclined to do, watching from the distant third opening to his subterranean home. If we had more experience, or if we had only asked one of the many local farmers, we'd have known the burrow might have more than two openings. We would have known that the groundhog had more sense than two flatlanders, as we of the city streets were sometimes not so fondly called in our unfamiliar rural home.

The rest of the summer—or was I being paranoid?—he seemed to devote to watching me garden, a kind of hairy conscience lingering over my shoulder. All would be well in the garden when, suddenly, a rustling in the brush on the nearby hillside would herald his arrival.

"He's planning his retaliation," I would say to myself, wondering what tasty morsel he planned to make his crudité. Day after sunny day, he watched me, until I finally lost it, and began to shout at him with conviction in my voice that he should listen, that he should understand, that he should even respond.

I was fighting again, a sorry sight, and though he never ate a thing from that year's summertime garden, the woodchuck had already won.

The cold-hardiest frog species, the wood frog, is also the earliest to engage in the mating embrace of amplexus.

A female wood frog, her sagging belly revealing a load of eggs, rests on a March afternoon.

The largest of the ancient apple trees in my garden, 125-plus years of age, is underplanted with hellebores and spring ephemerals.

Gardening for the Birds

I always say the birds taught me to garden. As I watched their interaction with what I planted, and the insects that showed up, too—some the birds ate, others pollinated plants whose seeds or fruits the birds then ate—birds became my first really intimate window into the web of life, or food chain.

Thirty-plus years ago, I didn't know much about plants, or much about birds. I knew I liked both of them, however, and with that very loosey-goosey mission at least subconsciously in mind—"I want to be surrounded by plants and birds"—I set about to make a garden. Simply wondering, "What plants will help me attract more birds?" ended up bringing about 65 species into the yard yearly, including many who nest in it or at its perimeter.

There is a more orderly way to go about attracting birds, and in hindsight I can recommend these steps:

Adjust your mindset Bird gardening and not-so-coincidentally what's now often called pollinator gardening or habitat gardening are all really *food-chain* gardening.

The bottom line: It's all about growing bugs Without beneficial insects, a lot of flowering plants don't get pollinated. Plus, most songbird species are at least in part insectivorous; even those that are vegetarians as adults generally feed their young some insects (especially caterpillars, the baby food of the songbird set). Many are so insect-dependent that they migrate southward in late summer or autumn, when insects wane up North.

No chemicals, please This organic commitment should be implicit in the mandate to grow more bugs, but just in case: no chemicals. Even the "safest" ones can indiscriminately kill beneficials, or taint soil and water.

Assess your habitat As the ornithologist Pete Dunne has written, "Birds are almost always where they are supposed to be." If you are adjacent to forest as I am, not a wetland, you won't get ducks. The only things quacking in my backyard are wood frogs in March and April, in mating season. No matter how many bluebird boxes or purple martin houses you erect, if the overall environment isn't right, they won't move in. Bobolinks, a grassland species, won't adapt to a half-acre of mown lawn.

Get informed, and target the right species with the right actions Sign up for a free account on eBird.org. When you go to create a checklist of birds you saw, eBird will offer up a list of birds known in your area (not all suited to your precise backyard, of course). Find the website of your nearest Audubon chapter or sanctuary or a local bird club, and ask for their species list, too, scanning it for birds that match your kind of site. This takes homework in books or on websites like Cornell Lab of Ornithology's All About Birds, but the sooner you learn the local birds and their life histories and preferences, the better. Shortcut: Go to a club meeting of keen local birders and ask questions.

Start imagining the garden as a giant, year-round living birdfeeder Plant so that it offers quality food at different times of year–for nesting times; in summer; big doses of fuel to support migration's energy demands; and persistent fruits and seeds to survive on in winter. A saner cleanup style, too, leaves standing whatever still has wildlife value, till it doesn't.

Strive for what scientists call functional redundancy of each moment in the food supply—not just one but several plantings representing different species that can support birds in each

A glade of devil's walking stick, or *Aralia spinosa*, occupies the garden, a large suckering shrub or small tree attractive to bees, and then birds.

Aronia melanocarpa, a native chokeberry, attracts pollinators when in flower and birds in late fall for its fruit.

month (in case one crop fails). Chart what you have to offer insects and in turn birds in each month, and deliberately order plants to fill in where there are not multiples. An informal, first goal to set is to have something blooming in every possible month your climate allows—information on what blooms when is readily available. Then work on achieving a similar succession of fruit and seeds, which will require more investigation.

Water is needed 12 months a year I am often asked what my most effective bird plant is, and I say, "water." Water is also a critical factor for many hard-working insects, like dragonflies. Keep a hole in the icy water-garden surface with a bubbler or floating de-icer; even a birdbath can be kept unfrozen with a special device.

Reduce mowed lawn, which lacks any biodiversity or potential to grow bugs.

'Winter Gold' winterberry and other pale orange and yellowish cultivars last a little longer than red-fruited cultivars that hungry birds devour first.

Spicebush, *Lindera benzoin*, an early blooming native that produces wildlife-friendly fruit (plus great fall color), is host to the spicebush swallowtail butterfly.

Staghorn sumac, a good nectar source for butterflies and bees, fruits up to delight birds and small mammals, too.

Create more "edge" habitat, called ecotone, the transition zone between two different systems, like where woods meet field in nature. This requires a layered style of planting, not disparate trees or shrubs stuck in the middle of dimensionless mown lawn. Edge habitat is where the action is for insects and therefore birds, too.

Native-heavy plantings in particular increase biodiversity, which should surprise nobody. An example: Audubon says that native trees, including oaks, willows, birches, and maples, and various native herbaceous plants, host numerous protein-rich caterpillar species vital to birds raising families.

Figure in elements of evergreen cover, particularly conifers, which provide shelter from wind and cold, nesting sites for some species, and seed-filled cones for others.

Install nest boxes—but only if you plan to maintain them for cleanliness, and if the proper design to match a target species' needs is used and properly sited, with predator deterrents installed. NestWatch.org's Right Bird, Right House search tool identifies cavity nesters in your area, and offers plans for the right houses for each; Sialis.org specializes in everything bluebird.

Better yet, cultivate a snag—turning a dying or dead tree into a wildlife tree, in which natural decay or the work of woodpeckers or a combination can create nest sites. More than 40 species of birds alone, not including the woodpeckers themselves (or many other animals), nest in woodpecker cavities in North America. Snags have many other functions.

Keep feeders clean, and well-stocked, even if supplemental-feeding can be offered only in the off-season as here, because of active black bears mid-March through Thanksgiving or so. Place feeders (and birdbaths) either closer than 2 feet from buildings, or 30-plus feet away, to reduce deadly high-speed window strikes when birds are en route.

Keep your cat indoors, and also safeguard birds from window glass Window strikes—when birds fly into glass after being confused by its mirror effect—and outdoor cats are two leading causes of songbird death. No outdoor cats, period, and consider special fiberglass exterior screens, streamers, or other preventive tactics if your windows are causing such deadly incidents.

Watch birds, count birds, know birds, love birds Join eBird, and Project FeederWatch online, and The Great Backyard Bird Count, and the local bird club, and . . .

Powerhouse Bird Plants

The following lists of mostly native woody and herbaceous plants are largely chosen for fruit or seed—meaning that they are key beneficial-insect plants, too, since they flower first. Appropriate species will differ by region; the Native Plant Finder launched in 2018 on the National Wildlife Federation website, searchable by ZIP code, can help you find yours.

Some personal notes: Though I never see them on recommended lists, I also rely on my native eastern *Aralia* (spikenard), the herbaceous *A. racemosa*, and a native from farther south, woody *A. spinosa*, called the devil's walking stick or Hercules' club. Both require ample space. Pollinators and then birds, especially thrush relatives and cedar waxwings, go mad. Though not listed in "bird-plant" references, either, my observation is that even the vegetable garden can contribute to diversity. Umbel flowers (parsley, chervil, carrot, fennel) and those in the brassica family (arugula, turnip, radish) are especially attractive to beneficial insects. I let a portion of each past-edible row "bolt" to attract them.

WOODY PLANTS

* *Amelanchier* (shadbush, serviceberry)
* *Aronia* (chokeberry)
* conifers, including *Picea* (spruce) and *Pinus* (pine) for shelter, nest sites, seeds
* *Cornus* (dogwood, shrubs or trees)
* *Ilex* (holly, including winterberry)
* *Juniperus virginiana* (eastern red cedar)
* *Lindera benzoin* (spicebush)
* *Malus* (crabapple; not native)
* *Myrica* (bayberry)
* *Parthenocissus* (Virginia and thicket creepers)
* *Prunus serotina* (wild black cherry)
* *Quercus* (oaks, for insects and caterpillars, plus acorn production)
* *Rhus* (sumac)
* *Sambucus* (elderberry)
* *Vaccinium* (blueberry, huckleberry)
* *Viburnum* (note: some Asian species are invasive in certain areas)
* *Vitis* (wild grape)

Daisy-like flowers such as *Rudbeckia triloba* 'Prairie Glow', a short-lived self-sowing perennial for me, have good insect appeal.

HERBACEOUS PLANTS

* daisy-like flowers (coneflowers, sunflower relatives, asters) for insect appeal and seeds
* wild grasses (*Schizachyrium*, *Andropogon*, *Bouteloua*, *Panicum*, *Sorghastrum*)
* hummingbird plants (*Monarda*, *Lobelia*, *Penstemon*, *Salvia*, *Lonicera*)
* mints like *Pychnanthemum* (and again, the *Monarda*) are very pollinator-friendly

When to Start Seeds

Need help remembering when it's safe and smart to start your first spring sowings of vegetable, flower, and herb seeds indoors and out? The following charts, based on an online calculator tool built for my website, are a good starting point. I find it helpful to jog my memory around now, and then organize my seed packets according to what needs sowing when.

Using any such calculator begins with knowing the final spring frost date in your hardiness zone; if you don't, a Google search can remedy that. Then it's simple math. Besides my last frost date (about May 15), I need to know the number of weeks indoors a particular crop requires from sowing to transplant time (say 6 weeks for a tomato). The last variable is, relative to that frost date, when a tomato seedling can safely go outdoors (1 to 2 weeks after the danger of frost is past). From mid-May, then, I count back 6 weeks, bringing me to April 1 or thereabouts, then I add 1 to 2 weeks to adjust for the post-frost transplant margin. Tomato sowing time here? About April 15 (for set-out in late May).

My chart dates suggest the earliest springtime sowings, but there is no hard-and-fast rule whether you prefer a 6- to 8-week tomato transplant (I like smaller), or whether lettuce needs 4 to 6 weeks indoors—or if you don't give salad a head start but direct-sow it. This is my best guidance, not doctrine.

Other factors: Using protective row covers can let you cheat on the earliest transplant dates by as much as 2 weeks, which is especially helpful for tender seedlings like melon (or insect-prone brassicas and cucurbits).

Choose the chart with the last frost date closest to the one in your zone, and adjust the results accordingly. Then scan the next-to-last column ("sow indoors, from-to") for crops where the seeding action overlaps—for example, tomatoes, peppers, and eggplant could be sown at the same time, or broccoli, chard, lettuce, and mustard could be lumped. Write such potential groupings down so you can mark your calendar for a few group sowing dates, simplifying indoor production (which began with onions and leeks). Finally, with starred items, look at the last column to identify what you could direct-sow into the garden on a common date (like beets, kale, lettuce, mustard) without a head start indoors.

Many crops that you want available over a long season (like salad, carrots, beets, bush beans, cilantro, etc.) are best sown in succession, a small amount every 2 weeks, starting at the chart date. In some climates, a later sowing timed for fall or winter harvest may do better than a spring-sown one, or you can get a second sowing in of, say, peas that you also sowed in spring, then pulled.

Seed-Starting Calculators

BASED ON A 15 MARCH FINAL FROST DATE

Crop Name	Weeks Indoors Before Transplant	Transplant (or Sow) Date, Relative to Final Frost	Sow Indoors From-To	Transplant (or Sow)
VEGETABLES				
arugula	direct-sow only	4 weeks before		15-Feb
beans (bush or pole)	direct-sow only	at frost date		15-Mar
beets*	5 to 6	2 weeks before	18-Jan to 25-Jan	1-Mar
broccoli	4 to 6	2 weeks before	18-Jan to 1-Feb	1-Mar
cabbage	4 to 6	2 to 4 weeks before	4-Jan to 1-Feb	15-Feb to 1-Mar
carrots	direct-sow only	2 to 3 weeks before		22-Feb to 1-Mar
cauliflower	4 to 6	2 weeks before	18-Jan to 1-Feb	1-Mar
chard*	4	2 weeks before	1-Feb	1-Mar
celery, celeriac	10 to 12	1 week after	28-Dec to 11-Jan	22-Mar
corn*	2 to 4	0 to 2 weeks after	15-Feb to 15-Mar	15-Mar to 29-Mar
cucumber*	3 to 4	1 to 2 weeks after	22-Feb to 8-Mar	22-Mar to 29-Mar
eggplant	6 to 8	2 weeks after	1-Feb to 15-Feb	29-Mar
kale,* collards*	4 to 6	2 to 4 weeks before	4-Jan to 1-Feb	15-Feb to 1-Mar
kohlrabi*	4 to 6	2 to 4 weeks before	4-Jan to 1-Feb	15-Feb to 1-Mar
leeks	8 to 10	2 weeks before	21-Dec to 4-Jan	1-Mar
lettuce*	4	2 to 4 weeks before	18-Jan to 1-Feb	15-Feb to 1-Mar
melon (muskmelon)*	3 to 4	1 to 2 weeks after	22-Feb to 8-Mar	22-Mar to 29-Mar
melon (watermelon)*	3 to 4	1 to 2 weeks after	22-Feb to 8-Mar	22-Mar to 29-Mar
mustard*	4	2 to 4 weeks before	18-Jan to 1-Feb	15-Feb to 1-Mar
onion	8 to 10	3 to 4 weeks before	7-Dec to 28-Dec	15-Feb to 22-Feb
pak choi*	4	2 weeks before	1-Feb	1-Mar
parsnips	direct-sow only	3 to 4 weeks before		15-Feb to 22-Feb
peas	direct-sow only	6 weeks before		1-Feb

15 March, Cont.

Crop Name	Weeks Indoors Before Transplant	Transplant (or Sow) Date, Relative to Final Frost	Sow Indoors From-To	Transplant (or Sow)
VEGETABLES (cont.)				
peppers	6 to 8	1 to 2 weeks after	25-Jan to 15-Feb	22-Mar to 29-Mar
radish	direct-sow only	3 to 4 weeks before		15-Feb to 22-Feb
spinach	direct-sow only	4 to 6 weeks before		1-Feb to 15-Feb
squash (summer)*	3 to 4	1 to 2 weeks after	22-Feb to 8-Mar	22-Mar to 29-Mar
squash (winter)*	3 to 4	1 to 2 weeks after	22-Feb to 8-Mar	22-Mar to 29-Mar
tomatoes	6 to 8	1 to 2 weeks after	25-Jan to 15-Feb	22-Mar to 29-Mar
turnip	direct-sow only	2 to 3 weeks before		22-Feb to 1-Mar
HERBS				
basil*	4 to 6	1 week after	8-Feb to 22-Feb	22-Mar
cilantro	direct-sow only	0 to 3 weeks before		22-Feb to 15-Mar
dill	direct-sow only	0 to 3 weeks before		22-Feb to 15-Mar
parsley	8 to 10	2 weeks before	21-Dec to 4-Jan	1-Mar
ANNUAL FLOWERS				
calendula*	6	1 week before	25-Jan	8-Mar
cosmos*	6	at frost date	1-Feb	15-Mar
hyacinth bean*	4 to 6	0 to 1 weeks after	1-Feb to 22-Feb	15-Mar to 22-Mar
impatiens	8 to 10	1 week after	11-Jan to 25-Jan	22-Mar
marigold*	6	1 week after	8-Feb	22-Mar
morning glory, moonflower	4	2 weeks after	1-Mar	29-Mar
sunflower*	3 to 4	at frost date	15-Feb to 22-Feb	15-Mar
sweet peas	4 to 6	1 to 2 weeks before	18-Jan to 8-Feb	1-Mar to 8-Mar
viola, pansy	8 to 10	2 weeks before	21-Dec to 4-Jan	1-Mar
zinnia*	4	1 week after	22-Feb	22-Mar

*Chard, collards, kale, kohlrabi, lettuce, mustard, plus many familiar herbs and annual flowers are probably easiest direct-sown. In short-season northern areas, starting heat-loving melons, cucumbers, and squash indoors may offer a head start, though they also do well when direct-sown.

BASED ON A 15 APRIL FINAL FROST DATE

Crop Name	Weeks Indoors Before Transplant	Transplant (or Sow) Date, Relative to Final Frost	Sow Indoors From-To	Transplant (or Sow)
VEGETABLES				
arugula	direct-sow only	4 weeks before		18-Mar
beans (bush or pole)	direct-sow only	at frost date		15-Apr
beets*	5 to 6	2 weeks before	18-Feb to 25-Feb	1-Apr
broccoli	4 to 6	2 weeks before	18-Feb to 4-Mar	1-Apr
cabbage	4 to 6	2 to 4 weeks before	4-Feb to 4-Mar	18-Mar to 1-Apr
carrots	direct-sow only	2 to 3 weeks before		25-Mar to 1-Apr
cauliflower	4 to 6	2 weeks before	18-Feb to 4-Mar	1-Apr
chard*	4	2 weeks before	4-Mar	1-Apr
celery, celeriac	10 to 12	1 week after	28-Jan to 11-Feb	22-Apr
corn*	2 to 4	0 to 2 weeks after	18-Mar to 15-Apr	15-Apr to 29-Apr
cucumber*	3 to 4	1 to 2 weeks after	25-Mar to 8-Apr	22-Apr to 29-Apr
eggplant	6 to 8	2 weeks after	4-Mar to 18-Mar	29-Apr
kale,* collards*	4 to 6	2 to 4 weeks before	4-Feb to 4-Mar	18-Mar to 1-Apr
kohlrabi*	4 to 6	2 to 4 weeks before	4-Feb to 4-Mar	18-Mar to 1-Apr
leeks	8 to 10	2 weeks before	21-Jan to 4-Feb	1-Apr
lettuce*	4	2 to 4 weeks before	18-Feb to 4-Mar	18-Mar to 1-Apr
melon (muskmelon)*	3 to 4	1 to 2 weeks after	25-Mar to 8-Apr	22-Apr to 29-Apr
melon (watermelon)*	3 to 4	1 to 2 weeks after	25-Mar to 8-Apr	22-Apr to 29-Apr
mustard*	4	2 to 4 weeks before	18-Feb to 4-Mar	18-Mar to 1-Apr
onions	8 to 10	3 to 4 weeks before	7-Jan to 28-Jan	18-Mar to 25-Mar
pak choi*	4	2 weeks before	4-Mar	1-Apr
parsnips	direct-sow only	3 to 4 weeks before		18-Mar to 25-Mar
peas	direct-sow only	6 weeks before		4-Mar
peppers	6 to 8	1 to 2 weeks after	25-Feb to 18-Mar	22-Apr to 29-Apr

15 April, Cont.

Crop Name	Weeks Indoors Before Transplant	Transplant (or Sow) Date, Relative to Final Frost	Sow Indoors From-To	Transplant (or Sow)
VEGETABLES (cont.)				
radish	direct-sow only	3 to 4 weeks before		18-Mar to 25-Mar
spinach	direct-sow only	4 to 6 weeks before		4-Mar to 18-Mar
squash (summer)*	3 to 4	1 to 2 weeks after	25-Mar to 8-Apr	22-Apr to 29-Apr
squash (winter)*	3 to 4	1 to 2 weeks after	25-Mar to 8-Apr	22-Apr to 29-Apr
tomatoes	6 to 8	1 to 2 weeks after	25-Feb to 18-Mar	22-Apr to 29-Apr
turnip	direct-sow only	2 to 3 weeks before		25-Mar to 1-Apr
HERBS				
basil*	4 to 6	1 week after	11-Mar to 25-Mar	22-Apr
cilantro	direct-sow only	0 to 3 weeks before		25-Mar to 15-Apr
dill	direct-sow only	0 to 3 weeks before		25-Mar to 15-Apr
parsley	8 to 10	2 weeks before	21-Jan to 4-Feb	1-Apr
ANNUAL FLOWERS				
calendula*	6	1 week before	25-Feb	8-Apr
cosmos*	6	at frost date	4-Mar	15-Apr
hyacinth bean*	4 to 6	0 to 1 weeks after	4-Mar to 25-Mar	15-Apr to 22-Apr
impatiens	8 to 10	1 week after	11-Feb to 25-Feb	22-Apr
marigold*	6	1 week after	11-Mar	22-Apr
morning glory, moonflower	4	2 weeks after	1-Apr	29-Apr
sunflower*	3 to 4	at frost date	18-Mar to 25-Mar	15-Apr
sweet peas	4 to 6	1 to 2 weeks before	18-Feb to 11-Mar	1-Apr to 8-Apr
viola, pansy	8 to 10	2 weeks before	21-Jan to 4-Feb	1-Apr
zinnia*	4	1 week after	25-Mar	22-Apr

*Chard, collards, kale, kohlrabi, lettuce, mustard, plus many familiar herbs and annual flowers, are probably easiest direct-sown. In short-season northern areas, starting heat-loving melons, cucumbers, and squash indoors may offer a head start, though they also do well when direct sown.

BASED ON A 15 MAY FINAL FROST DATE

Crop Name	Weeks Indoors Before Transplant	Transplant (or Sow) Date, Relative to Final Frost	Sow Indoors From-To	Transplant (or Sow)
VEGETABLES				
arugula	direct-sow only	4 weeks before		17-Apr
beans (bush or pole)	direct-sow only	at frost date		15-May
beets*	5 to 6	2 weeks before	20-Mar to 27-Mar	1-May
broccoli	4 to 6	2 weeks before	20-Mar to 3-Apr	1-May
cabbage	4 to 6	2 to 4 weeks before	6-Mar to 3-Apr	17-Apr to 1-May
carrots	direct-sow only	2 to 3 weeks before		24-Apr to 1-May
cauliflower	4 to 6	2 weeks before	20-Mar to 3-Apr	1-May
chard*	4	2 weeks before	3-Apr	1-May
celery, celeriac	10 to 12	1 week after	27-Feb to 13-Mar	22-May
corn*	2 to 4	0 to 2 weeks after	17-Apr to 15-May	15-May to 29-May
cucumber*	3 to 4	1 to 2 weeks after	24-Apr to 8-May	22-May to 29-May
eggplant	6 to 8	2 weeks after	3-Apr to 17-Apr	29-May
kale,* collards*	4 to 6	2 to 4 weeks before	6-Mar to 3-Apr	17-Apr to 1-May
kohlrabi*	4 to 6	2 to 4 weeks before	6-Mar to 3-Apr	17-Apr to 1-May
leeks	8 to 10	2 weeks before	20-Feb to 6-Mar	1-May
lettuce*	4	2 to 4 weeks before	20-Mar to 3-Apr	17-Apr to 1-May
melon (muskmelon)*	3 to 4	1 to 2 weeks after	24-Apr to 8-May	22-May to 29-May
melon (watermelon)*	3 to 4	1 to 2 weeks after	24-Apr to 8-May	22-May to 29-May
mustard*	4	2 to 4 weeks before	20-Mar to 3-Apr	17-Apr to 1-May
onion	8 to 10	3 to 4 weeks before	6-Feb to 27-Feb	17-Apr to 24-Apr
pak choi*	4	2 weeks before	3-Apr	1-May
parsnips	direct-sow only	3 to 4 weeks before		17-Apr to 24-Apr
peas	direct-sow only	6 weeks before		3-Apr
peppers	6 to 8	1 to 2 weeks after	27-Mar to 17-Apr	22-May to 29-May

Crop Name	Weeks Indoors Before Transplant	Transplant (or Sow) Date, Relative to Final Frost	Sow Indoors From-To	Transplant (or Sow)
VEGETABLES (cont.)				
radish	direct-sow only	3 to 4 weeks before		17-Apr to 24-Apr
spinach	direct-sow only	4 to 6 weeks before		3-Apr to 17-Apr
squash (summer)*	3 to 4	1 to 2 weeks after	24-Apr to 8-May	22-May to 29-May
squash (winter)*	3 to 4	1 to 2 weeks after	24-Apr to 8-May	22-May to 29-May
tomatoes	6 to 8	1 to 2 weeks after	27-Mar to 17-Apr	22-May to 29-May
turnip	direct-sow only	2 to 3 weeks before		24-Apr to 1-May
HERBS				
basil*	4 to 6	1 week after	10-Apr to 24-Apr	22-May
cilantro	direct-sow only	0 to 3 weeks before		24-Apr to 15-May
dill	direct-sow only	0 to 3 weeks before		24-Apr to 15-May
parsley	8 to 10	2 weeks before	20-Feb to 6-Mar	1-May
ANNUAL FLOWERS				
calendula*	6	1 week before	27-Mar	8-May
cosmos*	6	at frost date	3-Apr	15-May
hyacinth bean*	4 to 6	0 to 1 weeks after	3-Apr to 24-Apr	15-May to 22-May
impatiens	8 to 10	1 week after	13-Mar to 27-Mar	22-May
marigold*	6	1 week after	10-Apr	22-May
morning glory, moon-flower	4	2 weeks after	1-May	29-May
sunflower*	3 to 4	at frost date	17-Apr to 24-Apr	15-May
sweet peas	4 to 6	1 to 2 weeks before	20-Mar to 10-Apr	1-May to 8-May
viola, pansy	8 to 10	2 weeks before	20-Feb to 6-Mar	1-May
zinnia*	4	1 week after	24-Apr	22-May

*Chard, collards, kale, kohlrabi, lettuce, mustard, plus many familiar herbs and annual flowers, are probably easiest direct-sown. In short-season northern areas, starting heat-loving melons, cucumbers, and squash indoors may offer a head start, though they also do well when direct sown.

18 Seed-Starting Tips

Becoming a confident seed starter unlocks possibilities; you can try any catalog offering, no longer being limited to the local garden center's selection. Nervous? Remember, in nature seeds sow themselves successfully, usually emerging when the soil is moist and starting to warm.

Details of spacing and depth vary by crop. Your seed packet (or the catalog website) may offer specifics. Basic guidance: Except with large seeds like peas, beans, and squash, which I direct-sow outdoors and deeper, I make a shallow depression or furrow, press the seed gently in, spacing according to packet directions, and lightly cover with more planting medium.

If you're only going to do one thing on the following list to improve seed-starting results, *focus on the light*. Too little light is the most common reason for seed-sowing failure by home gardeners. The 18 seed-starting tips are:

Don't rush Get your timing right for each crop. Refer to the preceding charts to pinpoint dates.

Don't be cheap; buy fresh seed if there's any doubt Check on the average viability of a given type of leftover seed in the preceding charts, but also ask yourself how well you really cared for it. Seed is alive (but not if you left it in the hot, humid garage all summer).

Don't use just any potting soil; some may be too coarse Buy a fresh bag of sterile medium labeled "germination mix" or "seed-starting mix."

Cleanliness counts When re-using flats, trays, cells, and pots, wash with a dilute bleach solution (1:9 bleach:water) or at least hot, soapy water.

Do pre-moisten the mix before putting in flats or cells, so it's no longer powdery dust (but not sodden). Trick: Run water from the kitchen-sink sprayer or the outdoor nozzle into the plastic soil bag ahead of time; massage and turn the bag to distribute; then repeat a few times and let it sit a while.

Do use bottom heat, from a germinating mat, and a dome lid or plastic wrap to create a "germination chamber" of around 70°F.

But don't leave the heat mat plugged in, or the lid on, once the plants have emerged Seedlings don't like it as warm, or moist, as seeds trying to sprout do.

Don't let seeds dry out before they germinate (a recipe for death!).

But don't overwater seeds once they germinate Water requirements drop dramatically as soon as they're up and growing. Let the soil go slightly dry between doses.

Do invest in a watering device that's gentle enough for seeds and seedlings Bottom watering is great, and avoids washing seeds out of place or damaging transplants. I have a cheap mister that holds 2 liters; you pump to pressurize the contents, then spray. I also use a turkey baster and cream pitcher, among other improvised tools. If watering with a garden hose, use a breaker nozzle rated for seeds.

Don't skimp on light once seedlings emerge, or anytime thereafter Don't be surprised if they get spindly if you do. No windowsill growing.

Do take advantage of fair days to make up for the limitations of artificial light I carry my seedlings outside by day when possible. Even when closely spaced, efficient T5 fluorescent tubes might put out just one-fourth to one-fifth the light of a clear day in May outdoors, where occasional breezes also help toughen plants. Between indoor and outdoor light, I provide 12 hours daily.

Do direct-sow crops suited to it, but not unless you are committed to keeping the seedbed moist and free from competing weeds.

Don't rush to transplant, especially with warm-season crops like tomatoes, peppers, and eggplant. Nothing is gained, and much can be lost in wild weather.

Don't transplant seedlings into the garden that haven't been hardened off with a few hours a day outdoors for a week before, to allow for acclimation.

Do sow extra, and do cull the herd by discarding any weak or off-type seedlings at any stage of the process—like any that are extra-slow to germinate, for example. A seed-farmer friend starts her careful selection process before sowing, discarding the smallest seeds from each packet. Ruthlessness pays.

Do plan for succession sowings of many crops, sowing only a short row every couple of weeks and avoiding 40 servings of lettuce or 10 pounds of green beans in a single day's harvest.

Don't blame yourself for every failure Old seed or poorly stored seed or just crappy seed can outsmart your best efforts. Sometimes seed was viable (had the ability to germinate) but lacked sufficient vigor (the ability to thrive). And then you have the weather to invoke as the guilty party. This is gardening, remember? We can always blame the weather, and then try again.

Why Seedlings Stretch and Get Spindly

I haven't had a single spindly, stretched-out seedling since I started carrying my baby plants outside on each fair day during their young lives. But it took a conversation with a plant physiologist to get me to see the light—literally. Why do vegetable seedlings stretch and grow spindly, and can I prevent it? That was how I began a note to Thomas Nils Erik Bjorkman, Professor of Crop Physiology at Cornell, a botanist whose research focuses on the effects of environmental stimuli on plant growth and development, particularly in vegetables. Are leggy seedlings reaching for light, or is something else at work?

Scientific papers I'd read listed a range of causes: too little light (maybe also too much); light's intensity; temperature (even the day-to-night drop); improper use of fertilizers; leaving seedlings in "germination chamber" conditions (extra-warm and extra-humid) too long. The list went on—even factors like spacing, apparently, can affect the way seedlings grow. But all the cited research happened in light- and climate-controlled conditions of labs or commercial greenhouses, not in a home seed-starting environment. What could I do better?

The stretching that home seedlings experience is almost entirely from insufficient light, Bjorkman said. Those other factors play smaller roles, but we can safely concentrate on making the light brighter. That surprised me, since the improved T5 fluorescent tubes under my reflective seed-starter hood look so bright, and I keep them on, close to the seedlings, 12 hours a day.

"Our eyes have an incredible capacity to adjust to different light intensities," Bjorkman explained, "which makes it easy to underestimate how dim the light really is for seedlings. Putting them by a window is rarely enough. Fluorescent lights are rarely enough, unless they are almost touching the plants, but that can get hot."

And then to really make certain he made his point, the scientist offered data—truly startling numbers (measured in micromoles per square meter per second, or μmol/m2/s): Under regular fluorescent lights—the old-style ones—the light output in μmol/m2/s is typically 50 to 100. Even with Super High Output fluorescent lights spaced 2 inches apart—brighter than my current T5 tube setup—we can get to 400. But with a *cloudy* day outside in spring in my region, 500 to 800 is common, and on a *clear* day in late May (when volunteer seedlings would be up and growing on their own) the light will be 1,500 to 2,000.

The advances in new LED fixtures hold promise for putting out concentrated light with low heat, and I am watching as prices come down. Meantime, once the seedlings' true leaves appear, out go my seedling flats on each fair day, at first into a protected bright spot and then gradually into the open, where a bit of breeze makes them stronger, too. Part of each day (or all day on blustery or cold days), I use the lights to total about 12 hours of exposure.

My seedling physiology crash course with Bjorkman included a bonus element: Don't leave germinating heat mats under the flats or clear plastic domes over the flats once the seedlings poke through the soil surface. If the cotyledons (the seed leaves) even peek up above the soil surface in a hot, humid germination chamber, they'll quickly put up the dreaded thread-thin hypocotyls (the stem beneath those seed leaves). With brassicas, for example, Bjorkman needs to get them out of the lab's chamber within 36 hours. I shudder to think of the brassicas I have probably steamed before their time.

Another benefit to my outdoor regimen: By transplant time, my seedlings are already hardened off. To minimize shock, I transplant on an overcast day when it isn't too windy, or best of all, just before a gentle rain.

Native goldenseal, *Hydrastis canadensis*, is in the mix of Asian and American woodlanders in the April shade gardens.

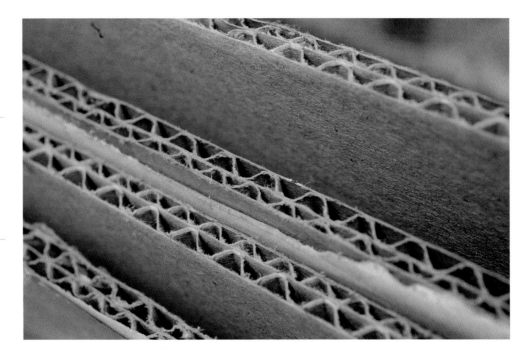

Making a Bed, with Cardboard

There are various more backbreaking ways to make a new garden bed, but in recent years I've often relied on the magic of recyclables: newspaper and cardboard. It's not all about being lazy, or getting older and less inclined toward the heroic double-digging of my first years here. Prepping a bed without turning or tilling may actually help reduce the number of weed seeds that sprout.

For all of us needing a shortcut, it's a good thing that cardboard is considered safe for garden use, whether a sunny patch of lawn is destined to house tomatoes or this fall's bulb garden, or an existing border needs some weed-smothering. Use the plain brown stuff, not versions that are printed with colored ink; likewise collect black-and-white newsprint, not glossy magazines or slick special color sections. Many modern inks are soy-based, but be extra-safe.

The explanation below assumes decent underlying soil, neither bog nor wasteland nor highly compacted, with mostly herbaceous vegetation (like lawn, not a blackberry thicket). If the residents are tougher than turfgrass or the equivalent, first use a spading fork, and dislodge then remove weedy or woody clumps after a good rain, or put a sprinkler on the area beforehand.

Over the weeded area, or right over turf mown short, layer on newspaper thickly, or spread out flattened corrugated cardboard as the underlayment. Moisten the paper and pin it down with earth staples if needed, then cover with mulch.

Depending on what I am planting, I may cut Xs in the cardboard and plant immediately, then mulch. This would work with substantial perennials or when making a shrub border, for instance, and I have even planted pumpkin seeds in Xs the same day if I pre-weeded. With delicate little transplants, or when I'm suspicious that the underlying weeds might need time to settle, I wait. With the worst weeds, I might fork them out, then solarize the area with plastic for a month or longer in a hot, sunny season, then remove the plastic and follow the steps of cardboard and mulch.

I also use the cardboard or newsprint system here and there in a spot approach, when an area of an existing bed has gotten weedy, such as the edge adjacent to lawn or good-size patches between plants.

Again, most important: The paper can be hydrophobic—repelling water. Don't just "set it and forget it," or plants will suffer. If the soil is dry and you layer cardboard on, rain won't penetrate until the paper softens, so don't maroon little plants in the island of cardboard without life support. Water the area before smothering, moisten the paper, and water individual plants regularly via the Xs.

I suppose I got my "lazy" gardener inspiration first from the late Ruth Stout, and her approach to "no-work gardening" (something like what people call lasagna gardening, a term I loathe). I think of it as passive composting in place, and advocate for rigorous mulching with the right materials.

If you have a spot that needs the more serious intervention of double digging to the 24 inches I once did, the longtime modern master is John Jeavons, of Ecology Action in California. He admired Stout, but quite correctly said that her "no-work" methods aren't suitable for all soils. His classic book *How to Grow More Vegetables* (one of my first garden books, many printings ago) includes the how-to of what he calls biointensive gardening, including soil prep, and there are YouTube videos as well.

How to Shop for Plants (and Not)

The first week garden centers reopen here can be perilous, particularly if the winter has been ugly. I suggest shopping with a strategy etched in mind—along the lines of the suggestion not to do the grocery marketing when hungry, especially not without a specific list.

To appeal to our appetite for color, the smart nursery staff will have assembled all the current showoff plants near the parking lot, so there is no avoiding their temptation. Lower your eyes and make a direct route to a helper at the counter, asking two questions: "Where are the plants that looked good in February?" And, "Where are the plants that will look good in November?"

I suspect that you, as I, already have plenty of spring bloomers, since we generally shop in person in spring. Do that long enough, and all those impulse buys will catch up, yielding a big show followed by hits and misses. We must shop to fill in, and extend, and work toward that 365-day garden goal. I go in search of plants to serve a mix of functions:

Ephemerals and other early birds: herbaceous woodlanders and so-called minor bulbs, the mostly miniature opportunists that start the season before it seems possible, extending it here back into March or even February (witch hazels, hellebores, and pussy willows come to mind).

Late-show stars: plants that stretch things at the other end of the season, whether late bloomers like perennial *Lespedeza thunbergii* (a big herbaceous mound of pea-like purple or

white blooms), or fruiting plants like winterberries, or some of the ornamental grasses that age well.

An army of soldiers: durable, unfussy plants with a long season of interest, often from colorful and texturally pleasing foliage such as painted ferns, or *Epimedium*, or low-growing *Sedum*, and so many more.

True powerhouse plants: the ones that fit into more than one of the previous categories, starring in multiple seasons, like *Viburnum*, crabapples, broadleaf evergreens, and colorful conifers.

Imperfect but irresistible types: plants with regrettably short peak moments, but even so, you cannot live without them. For me, this category includes lilacs, and martagon lilies—one-trick ponies you cannot build a garden of, unless the soldiers and powerhouse plants are there to support them.

I shop with these functional categories and my color palette firmly in mind, because in each month (and also at each design level or layer, from ground cover up to shrub or tree or climber), I can strengthen that theme. If I like red (which I do) I want red from late March with ground-covering *Pulmonaria rubra* into June with vining *Lonicera sempervirens* and the small tree called red buckeye (*Aesculus pavia*), on to summer and fall fruits of mid-size viburnums and hollies, to hot red fall foliage, too. See how it works?

Also, avoid bringing home just one of anything herbaceous for a change. Areas that suffer from too many disparate polka-dots of one-off plants could use some more sweeps and waves and other kinds of repeats to make it all hang together.

Ephemerals

Ephemerals are plants that come and go in a relatively short time, making their days with us all the more precious. Though the term can simply mean short-lived or short-lasting, we typically apply it to a number of coveted early springtime plants that complete their life cycle before the heat of summer comes on: emerging, reaching flowering size, then fruiting or setting seed and returning back underground for dormancy most of the year.

Many of the best-known ephemerals in my region are native eastern woodlanders, like various trilliums, Virginia bluebells (*Mertensia virginica*), and bloodroot (*Sanguinaria canadensis*). If you think about where their species originated—beneath deciduous trees—you get the answer to how they evolved to this catch-me-while-you-can lifestyle. Once the trees leaf out, light on the forest floor would be in short supply, so by necessity they learned to hurry.

How quickly they do the last bit—going dormant—can vary according to zone, and even the weather in a particular season, or whether you water, which can slow the disappearance. Heat will send them packing faster than a prolonged moist and cool spring. In my garden, many ephemerals don't go fully dormant at all, or do so quite late into summer, but I know that in friends' more southern yards, they do—sometimes in a mere 6 or 8 weeks, start to finish.

Bloodroot, even here, is fleeting, for example; so is Dutchman's breeches (*Dicentra cucullaria*), and squirrel corn (*D. canadensis*). But three other early favorites—merrybells (*Uvularia grandiflora*), blue cohosh (*Caulophyllum thalictroides*), and twinleaf (*Jeffersonia diphylla*)—remain standing, flowerless but present and accounted for.

Not all ephemerals are woodlanders. Other habitats have their temporary headliners, including the prairie, which features shooting star (*Dodecatheon meadia*) and prairie smoke

Eastern bluebells,
Mertensia virginica.

Blue cohosh,
*Caulophyllum
thalictroides.*

(*Geum trifolium*), among others, that then enjoy the protection afforded by the taller grasses and forbs of summer.

These plants and the natural plant communities they hail from—how they are constructed with a sequence of companions—have much to teach us about layering plants into our borders so they work visually over longer seasons of interest and also work functionally. Landscape architects and authors Thomas Rainer and Claudia West are inspiring many gardeners today, including myself, to pay attention to this issue and learn to plant smarter.

Using not just minor bulbs but also ephemerals can jumpstart your season—and also stretch the opportunities for local pollinators. Like the little bulbs, they kindly disappear and leave room for some main-season shade plant to show off next. Some gardeners view this disappearing act as a liability, but I say not so. Think of ephemerals as opportunity-makers instead, and plant something alongside that is glad to share the space.

Dividing Trilliums

Maybe it was while fixing something, or painting the house all those years ago. For some forgotten reason I was down at ground level, peering under the front porch, and there they were, in near darkness: two tiny trillium plants, specifically Northeast native *Trillium erectum*, the wake robin, with reddish flowers. I rescued them, and you know how it goes when a plant repays you for your help: Thanks to those first two, and to a tip handed down from a great gardener about dividing them when they're in flower, I have many.

The books, and many experts, often recommend waiting until late summer or fall to do so. But the "aha" that they are easier to locate at bloom time before they go dormant, and don't

Native *Trillium erectum*, or wake robin.

I divide trilliums at bloom time, when they are easier to locate in the garden.

mind being divided then, was imparted to me and Ken Druse by Evelyn Adams of Wellesley, Massachusetts, when we visited her garden awash in trilliums one spring, working on Ken's 1994 book *The Natural Habitat Garden*.

He and I have both been doing it this way—not waiting—ever since. The trillium rhizomes are barely below the soil surface, so you hardly have to dig. Each division must have at least an eye or growing point, but I don't cut them up; I just gently tease apart the clumps descended from those two rescued ones and replant each rhizome. They'll need to be watered well, especially the ones that have top-heavy flowers, then baby-sat till they resettle. My favorite day to do this: a rainy one.

Hopefully I needn't remind you, but wild plants must never be dug for this or any purpose. Commercially, trilliums are ethically propagated by seed, a four- to seven-year process—so next time you balk at the price, think about that.

Planting Peas, with Mendel in Mind

Since I first cultivated a vegetable garden, planting peas has been the task that marked its start. One recent March, I approached the welcome ritual with new reverence for the genetics built into a single *Pisum sativum* seed, and with a diversity of varieties to sow. It was 2013, and I had just audited an online class at MIT called "Introduction to Biology: The Secret of Life." The professor, Eric Lander—one of the principal leaders of the Human Genome Project—had been teaching it for 20 years, almost as long as I'd been planting peas. It was the first time he'd taught it simultaneously online, so besides the classroom full of MIT undergrads, there were thousands of us unseen virtual types learning about subjects that to my delight included Gregor Mendel and his early genetic experiments with peas.

It turns out that Mendel started his scrupulous research by simply going down to the market in Brno (in the Moravian region of today's Czech Republic) and buying 34 varieties of peas from several seedsmen. (Knowing this makes me less self-conscious that I order at least 10 kinds.) It was no accident that he chose peas as his subject. They didn't take up much space in the monastery garden confines, and the structure of a pea flower, with its enclosed fertilizing organs, makes random cross-pollination unlikely.

Mendel carefully set up his controls, then bred the 34 to see if they transmitted their traits faithfully. That took 2 years, and resulted in 22 making the cut for the actual experiments that followed—the ones about wrinkled and smooth seeds, and short and tall plants that most of us studied in secondary-school science.

Not long after the Mendel lecture, thanks to a few sunny days, it was time for pea planting in my nonvirtual life. I cultivated the soil along the edge of two raised beds, choosing the side that won't cast shade when the peas are trellised and render the rest of the space useless. In a generous furrow a couple of inches deep made with a hoe, I sprinkled legume inoculant very lightly. Sometimes I instead moisten the seeds slightly in a bowl and sprinkle the powder or granules onto them, mixing with a spoon.

Edible peas (whether they're seeds, pods, or flowers) come in many colors, such as 'Sugar Magnolia' from breeder Alan Kapuler.

Many edible peas have white flowers, but not all; some are pink or even purplish.

Peas form in the still-tender pods of 'Schweizer Riesen', called "puffer pods," which are like a cross between a snow pea and a sugar snap pea.

I sowed double-thick rows, a few inches across and an inch or so between seeds in all directions. I don't get all precise about it; years ago, I'd make a perfect grid of two staggered rows in the cultivated soil with my dibber, poking 1½-inch-deep holes every inch or two apart, dropping in one seed per hole. Although I was once more measured and controlled, I've lately become a scatterer. The peas cooperate either way.

I raked the dislodged soil back into place, tamped it down so the seeds are covered about 1½ inches deep, and then prayed the chipmunks don't notice what treasure I buried. I usually pin down Reemay or burlap on the soil surface until the peas are well up, when keeping wood-chucks or rabbits at bay later became my primary animal-control assignment.

I sat on the edge of that bed in the strengthening March sunshine, reading each packet while marking the labels needed to complete the job. Some promised tall vines; some short ones that require no staking (and will yield a little sooner). Some will have purple flowers, others white or even pink. I'd just sown seeds that were yellowish, or some green, and one cherished variety, 'Schweizer Riesen' ('Swiss Giant'), is a distinct rosy green. Mendel would have noted every detail, as had the modern-day breeders who created the ones I was growing.

A few of my choices are always for shelling, like 'Tall Telephone' (also called 'Alderman') or 'Green Arrow', which I freeze for off-season eating. Another couple are snow-pea types with flat edible pods, and a couple are snap peas with plump edible pods. Mendel—even with 34 kinds—would not have had those, a discovery that came about 100 years after his time. Calvin Lamborn of Gallatin Valley Seed, a sharp-eyed breeder not in Moravia, but in Idaho, crossed a tight-podded rogue pea with a snow pea, eventually leading to 'Sugar Snap', Lamborn's 1979 All-America Selection medal winner. Lamborn made *People* magazine that year.

I always grow his 'Sugar Snap' and his later, shorter stature 'Sugar Ann', plus the Swiss heir-loom 'Schweizer Riesen' with the purple flowers, which shapes up like snow pea meets snap pea. For this type, you let the extra-large pods puff up and fill with peas before eating. Dylana Kapuler of Peace Seedlings in Oregon, daughter of the longtime seed (and pea) breeder Alan Kapuler, calls peas like that "puffer pods," and indeed they are. Her father's star puffer pod is called 'Green Beauty', which was in my stash that day, too.

Inspired by Mendel to widen my genetic palette, I included various other Kapuler offerings, including a purple-podded snap pea called 'Sugar Magnolia' and a yellow-podded one called 'Opal Creek'. I'd chosen the pink- and purple-flowered peas—not just the usual white—because of Dylana's promise that hummingbirds would like them as much as I.

In 60-something days, the first of my peas flower and start to produce, and bring a few weeks of precious harvest if I dutifully pick daily to keep the vines productive. A girl cannot have enough peas in any year, so I get a good crop again in fall from a second sowing made in July, again with Mendel in mind.

Under an old Loebner magnolia called 'Ballerina', *Hylomecon japonicum*, *Trillium erectum*, and *Stylophorum diphyllum* begin the early spring show.

Hydrangea Pruning

Any garden writer's top question year after year is probably about hydrangeas, and when to prune them—particularly the bigleaf type, or *Hydrangea macrophylla*, an Asian species that produces mophead or lacecap blooms in blue (or sometimes pink, if your soil is more alkaline than acid). Gardeners commonly speak of frustration at a lack of flowers, and wonder what they're doing wrong.

Before the introduction in 2004 of so-called ever-blooming versions, starting with the variety 'Endless Summer', the answer was usually considered pretty straightforward. Conventional wisdom, at least in the North, said that because *Hydrangea macrophylla* generally bloomed on the previous year's growth, after carrying the coming year's flower buds over the winter on it, no flowers come summer usually meant someone had either pruned them off with untimely cuts in spring (or late fall), or nature had killed the buds with late frost or extra-deep winter freeze.

Once, I would have pretty confidently said to prune them just after flowering (in late summer) by removing some of the weaker older stems that have flowered right to the ground, and also any younger ones that are badly positioned, crossing inward, or weak. This makes room for the best-positioned, strongest new growth to develop, carrying with it the promise of future flowers. In early spring, you might have some cleanup, either from damage or if last year's flowers needed deadheading, or the removal of spent flowers.

But now, there are seemingly endless ones. To bloom repeatedly over a longer season, they must form flower buds on both old wood and new. With these I'd only prune if needed, cutting back each stem with spent flowers to a strong pair of buds, and cleaning out any damaged or badly positioned wood in early spring. If both old and newer wood had the potential to contribute flowers, I'd decide where to make my cuts based on creating a pleasing overall structure.

These most-beloved hydrangeas are technically hardy to Zone 6-ish, and though I am right on the cusp (and some varieties are labeled for Zone 5), I don't bother with them. My windswept site puts the flower buds at risk no matter how deftly I prune or preen, and besides, I'm not really a blue person except when it comes to sweet spring natives like Virginia bluebells (*Mertensia virginica*) or various amsonias. If I were desperate for one of the more delicate-flowered lacecap or variegated-foliage types, or better yet one of the choice hydrangeas such as *Hydrangea serrata*, I'd attempt to grow it in a big pot and carry it over in suspended animation in the unheated barn, simulating a winter of a slightly milder kind—not to prevent freezing, but to freeze without the combined evil forces of wind or ice, or alternating sun and temperature drops.

I don't lament the iffy nature of the *Hydrangea macrophylla* types, but grow the rest of the available hydrangeas for my zone as the backbone of summer through latest fall. The other common species, *H. paniculata*, another Asian, is just the opposite kind of creature: it flowers on new wood, so it can be pruned as hard as you like from earliest spring until it begins to push new growth. It can be trained to a single trunk, like a small tree, and in this form has long been a classic in the Northeast in front yards of older homes as *H. paniculata* 'Grandiflora', commonly called the Pee Gee. In high summer, giant cone-shaped white-tinged greenish flower heads begin to expand, and toward fall coloring up to a fleshy, old-fashioned pink like Grandma's powder-puff, and on to tan, if left to meet the frost.

Hydrangea paniculata blooms on new wood, and is pruned in early spring or late winter.

The straight species that Pee Gee was selected from, plain old *Hydrangea paniculata*, is large-flowered, too, but not quite so overblown. The way that the lacecap hydrangeas are daintier than mopheads, plain *H. paniculata* is more refined than 'Grandiflora'. These airier trusses actually combine two kinds of blooms: the larger, showy males, which are sterile bracts, and therefore of less value to pollinators and other hungry insects, and the tiny, tight female flowers that look like buds. I like these boy-girl ones best of all, and plain old beautiful *H. paniculata* has a place of prominence beside my front walk. Another similar selection, 'Tardiva', is in a few spots here.

I also am inclined toward ones like those of bigger stature that can grow into shrubs of 10 or even 15 feet and almost as wide. Sometimes I just go stand by one of the giant ones in my far borders at flowering time and listen and watch, since (though non-native) they are loaded with pollinators and other happy insects.

Lately, numerous little mounded forms of panicle hydrangea to just 3 or 5 feet high are more in vogue, such as 'Bobo' or 'Little Lime'. But I like mine big to suit the garden's scale, and I prune them only lightly—more like deadheading plus a little bit—to encourage maximum size. The recent explosion in breeding of the panicle hydrangeas seems a little crazy—who can keep track?—and I think there are close to 100 varieties, or at least the last time I checked there were already 80 or 90.

Even if you have multiples of the same variety, you may notice a difference in size of the flower heads depending how each plant was pruned. If the plant's a twiggy thicket, with less pruning, it will make many smaller blooms; to encourage fewer but larger panicles, reduce the number of primary shoots emanating from the trunk.

I also grow *Hydrangea quercifolia*, the southern native oakleaf hydrangea. Its large white flowers are produced on old wood, so its buds are potentially vulnerable to my winter. I have a couple that have shaped up well in protected spots, and I mostly don't prune the irregular, loose plants, with their peeling bark like a cinnamon stick and leaves that turn a great red-purple-bronze in fall. They bloom well in summer, even in shade.

As easy here as *Hydrangea paniculata* is *H. arborescens* 'Annabelle', a cultivar of an eastern U.S. native, with giant summertime white snowballs that fade to greenish and look good for months. It can be cut down as far as you like, to the ground like a herbaceous perennial, or just cleaned up of any wintertime damage and thinned of some oldest stems to be more than waist high. It will flower either way but take note: The mophead 'Annabelle', like the overblown paniculatas, is loaded with sterile male bracts, and of little pollinator value, offering very little nectar. The straight species, by comparison, is a great habitat-garden plant.

The other hydrangea I have grown is the climbing one from Asia, *Hydrangea anomala* subsp. *petiolaris*, which takes time to settle in and then becomes a large feature trained up a building or big old tree, or over a wall. It can reach 60 feet unchecked, with white summertime flowers that look like the lacecaps. Prune to keep it in bounds, just after flowering in summer.

My Gold Foliage Issue

When I try to defend why I use so much gold foliage—maybe an excess, admittedly, yet another impulse run amok—my head fills with soulful but divergent voices, from the Isley Brothers to Robert Frost, who would seem to have nothing to do with the matter (or each other).

"Nature's first green is gold," Frost wrote of the freshest, fleeting color of unfolding spring, in "Nothing Gold Can Stay," which is not just the poem's title but also its last line. Make it persist by adding other golds and chartreuses into your designs. Perhaps you don't wish to end up collecting gold-leaf plants, but here is what gleaming subjects used in key spots can do for a design:

They scream—a good thing if you want to draw your eye across the garden to an intended focal point, the punctuation to an axial view, and say "come here." A big gold shrub or group of them will do that, and I suggest using others here and there along the way, as well, to provide context.

They brighten—a good thing in semi-shade, where you want more "light" (something white variegation does even more). However, most gold-leaf plants sited in too much shade will be more yellow-green than gold. Given too much sun they may burn, so experimentation is required. Get out the shovel if you get it wrong at first.

They make things feel fresh, even after spring fades. Some gold plants, including the ninebark *Physocarpus opulifolius* 'Dart's Gold' and the spike winter hazel *Corylopsis spicata* 'Aurea', fade considerably to greenish-yellow after their spring peak, but are still plenty worthy.

From an extensive (some would say overboard) collection of gold-leaf plants, *Spiraea thunbergii* 'Ogon' is gold from May to December.

Spike winter hazel, *Corylopsis spicata* 'Aurea', is especially electric in spring.

They provide needed contrast to deeper colors Think of the role the gold parts play in the leaves of some favorite *Coleus* choices. Where would the other colors be without it to offset them?

Of my many gold-leaf plants, I cannot imagine being without certain ones, including long-time companion *Hakonechloa macra* 'All Gold', the yellow version of Japanese forest grass. *Aralia cordata* 'Sun King' is a big, lusty perennial that can reach 6 by 6 feet, and really makes a statement. The spreading yew *Taxus baccata* 'Repandens Aurea' is only gold in the growing

Japanese forest grass, *Hakonechloa macra* 'All Gold', still beams even in autumn.

Herbaceous *Aralia cordata* 'Sun King' will grow to its eventual 6-by-6-foot stature.

season, but wow. The gold Hinoki cypress, *Chamaecyparis obtusa* 'Crippsii', is gold all year, and though that one gets to 25 feet (don't believe listings that say 10 feet), there are dwarf forms like 'Golden Fern' and 'Nana Lutea'. And among Japanese maples, who could live without the ones referred to as Full Moon and Autumn Moon?

Truth be told, I make no apologies for this or any of my other design decisions, and that's where the Isley Brothers come in (circa 1969): "It's your thing, do what you wanna do. I can't tell you, who to sock it to."

Forsythia Alternatives

I say rude things sometimes, and admittedly have in various spaces and over many years done so about *Forsythia*, which I call the vomit of spring, owing to its overuse in the Northeast suburbs where I grew up. It is a genus I do not understand making room for except perhaps a gold-leaf form, though even there I could list many better options. Defenders always start with, "It's so early blooming," but so are these many worthier shrubs:

I have already praised the Asian witch hazels (*Hamamelis*), in a range of sunny to fiery colors. They bloom early and make forsythia look like a slacker.

Winter hazel (*Corylopsis*) is a witch hazel relative in the family Hamamelidaceae, with several species bearing dangling chains of yellow flowers in early spring, before the leaves unfold. In botanical terms, a plant that blooms when leafless is called precocious, and winter hazels are certainly that. (Precocious can also mean a plant that flowers and/or fruits at a young age, and magnolias—some of which bloom very early and could be recommended here on that basis—qualify in both meanings.)

There are a number of species to select from, including *Corylopsis glabrescens*, the hardiest of the lot, which can reach about 15 feet. Its pale yellow flowers are scented sweetly. *Corylopsis spicata* has about a 60/40 chance of flowering success here in Zone 5, since late frosts are common. It is smaller, more wide than tall, and I appreciate its spreading shape—perhaps 8 feet high and now astonishingly more than twice as wide after decades. Its choice leaves open tinged pinkish purple, then turn a beautiful blue-green for summer, retaining a touch of pink where they attach to the twigs.

Corylopsis platypetala is another 15-footer; *C. pauciflora* is the little guy of the bunch, 5 to 6 feet high and wide, and I added one lately. Its foliage is also about half the scale of its brethren, and unlike the others, which prefer sun here, it wants light shade. *Corylopsis* specimens may go a pleasing yellow in fall or just go brown and hang on a while. Underplanted with a mass of tiny blue bulbs like maybe *Chionodoxa sardensis*, chosen to coincide in bloom time, the effect is extra pleasing.

The native spicebush, *Lindera benzoin*, has tiny yellow flowers with a spicy fragrance in early spring, and astonishing yellow late-fall color. Its small fruits are appreciated by birds, and it is one host plant for larvae of the appropriately named spicebush swallowtail butterfly, whom I delight in making happy. The shrub can tolerate the shade of a deciduous woodland garden or woodland edge, where it fits right in.

There is no jasmine scent to yellow-flowered *Jasminum nudiflorum*, but that's the only drawback to it. A sprawling creature well-suited to arching over a wall, it puts out bursts of bloom anytime the sun shines and the days begin to warm in late winter and earliest spring, a welcome sight (but for slightly warmer zones than mine).

Shadbush, or serviceberry (*Amelanchier* spp.) are not yellow-flowered, but white, and also very early. The smallest among this genus of large shrubs or small trees, which includes many native American species as well as some from other areas in the Northern Hemisphere, is *A. canadensis*, which stays under 15 feet. Apparently even nurserymen and taxonomists are confused about which species is which and plants are often misnamed. All have clouds of delicate blossoms, fruit that's tasty (to birds and people) and evolves from green to red to blue-purple, and hot fall foliage and gray bark. Need I ask for a side-by-side assets comparison to forsythia?

I could go on: There are the Southeast native *Fothergilla* species (but hardy here) with white bottlebrush flowers, beautiful leaves not unlike those of its Hamamelidaceae relatives, and brilliant fall color. There is leatherwood, an eastern native (*Dirca palustris*, yellow flowers on a small shrub that can even take the wet). The various unusual pussy willows (*Salix* species) would be nice additions—ones with black catkins (*S. melanostachys*), or the giant pussy willow (*S. chaenomeloides*), including the pink catkin variety florists love called 'Mt. Aso'. If pink is more your taste, what about the deciduous native pinkshell azalea, *Rhododendron vaseyi*, which blooms in a woodland setting before its leaves unfurl (or those on the trees around)? Ready to excommunicate that forsythia yet?

Corylopsis spicata, the spike winter hazel, unfolds chains of gold flowers in early April, attracting a bumblebee.

Spanish bluebells, *Hyacinthoides hispanica*, are just one species of animal-resistant bulbs, and can take part shade.

Animal-Resistant Flower Bulbs

Inspired by photos of crocus lawns in England and who knows what other pipedream, I undertook a memorable planting some years back. I remember it because I added 2,000 crocus bulbs one fall and had four bloom the next spring, thanks to squirrels and chipmunks who teamed up to dig many bulbs and behead the rest at bloom time.

Now I focus only on animal-resistant varieties, because even with a deer fence I still have those demons, and occasional rabbits and woodchucks, too.

Before I fully reformed, I experimented with a big grouping of the "rodent-proof" *Crocus tommasinianus*, which managed to mostly stay in the ground but were felled before they opened, their botanical bodies lying everywhere. Most friends have succeeded with the Tommies, but it wasn't meant to be for me.

My thinking: Do not even think of growing crocus, or tulips, or lilies without protection.

Daffodils, or *Narcissus* spp., seem to have all-round resistance to nibbling or digging by animals. They are laced with poisonous concentrations of alkaloids, and apparently the fauna know that. The ornamental onions (genus *Allium*) have a built-in repellent as well, with that onion-y smell. Camassia and most fritillaria interest nobody most of the time, though I did find it funny to have some of the little fritillaria dug up by what appeared from the earth-moving handiwork to be a skunk—odd since the flowers smell like skunk. Heirloom bulb expert Scott Kunst, who founded the Old House Gardens bulb catalog, told me that hyacinths are pretty animal-resistant, too, but I have never grown them seriously—too formal-looking, but oh the perfume. Foxtail lilies (*Eremurus*) are also rated for deer-resistance, as are my beloved pineapple lilies (*Eucomis*).

Among the minor bulbs, better animal-resistant choices than crocus include snowdrops (*Galanthus*); snowflake (*Leucojum*); *Eranthis hyemalis*; glory of the snow (*Chionodoxa*); Spanish bluebells (*Hyacinthoides hispanica*); *Ornithogalum*, *Scilla*, and *Muscari* (grape hyacinth). The so-called autumn crocus (*Colchicum*), with its late flowers, is also apparently not tasty.

If bulbs or other plants in your garden are being dug by squirrels and chipmunks, many experts say to try sprinkling a little blood meal on the soil surface. Here on Animal Planet, that backfired, too, and simply served as an invitation to the raccoons or maybe skunks, who dug to investigate (the same happens when I use fish emulsion as fertilizer in outdoor containers). *Sigh*.

The Ever-Reliable Narcissus

The most accommodating of bulbs are narcissus, which not only make themselves naturally unattractive to animal pests by being poisonous, but also gladly multiply underground over time. Each of the first five years I was in my house, I planted many hundreds; today there is no regret about the mud-stained knees and wet, cold fingers I suffered. Onward they still go, and will, long past my tenure.

Last time I asked an expert, there were something like 28,000 named cultivars to choose from, which is the only tricky thing about growing narcissus (unless you live in the likes of Florida, which they don't like). I lean toward old standbys such as big white 'Mount Hood' with its classic trumpet shape, or double whites like 'Erlicheer' (with a ruffle of yellow, too, in its petticoat), but once upon a time I guess I got wild and planted bawdy double orange-and-yellow 'Tahiti', and so I am reminded each spring.

Each 6- to 8-inch-high stem of scaled-down *Narcissus* 'Hawera' produces multiple fragrant, pale yellow, nodding flowers with tiny cups. Its delicate stature is deceptive; this is one tough little bulb, and so is 'February Gold', the first to bloom among mine, at maybe 8 or 10 inches. A tiny and rare white species type I keep saying I will try, called *N. cantabricus*, would be even earlier, as would yellow 'Rijnveld's Early Sensation', among extra-brave souls.

To my eye (and nose) *Narcissus* 'Thalia' is a must-have, with highly fragrant white blooms carried in groups. It is called a Triandrus narcissus, and its clustered flowers are not as overblown as those of many daffodils, and therefore have a grace to go with their pristine color. I always scour catalogs for other fragrant offerings, since aroma is such a prize at this early moment. The pheasant's eye type or Poeticus narcissus called 'Actaea' is another particular beauty, and spicily fragrant, with flat white petals and a tiny, short golden cup rimmed in red.

And then there are 27,990-something others. Whichever cultivars your eye takes you to, select for very early, early, midseason, late, and very late bloomers, so you can enjoy drifts for at least two months.

Never plant in small groups—a dozen is a minimum cluster, and 25 or 50 is better, or 100. Daffodils can be a nuisance in flower borders, because inevitably you will pierce some with a fork or spade when digging something in or out, and once they've faded they leave a big blank spot in the bed. I like them in big islands in the lawn near my old apple trees, where their flowers and the apple blossoms overlap. I simply mow around the drifts until their foliage withers. Speaking of that, don't tie up or braid your bulb foliage. Leave it be; to do otherwise may sacrifice bloom

Narcissus poeticus, or the pheasant's eye types of narcissus, with flattened cups and fragrance, are a personal favorite.

Narcissus are long-lived, animal-resistant, and offer a diversity of bloom times, colors, and forms.

next year. At least six weeks of stems and foliage ripening after the flowers fade is the minimum requirement, and again: I wait until July Fourth weekend and rake it all up, scratching in some grass and clover seed and sprinkling with chopped straw to heal the messy spots.

Preventing the bulb from making full use of its foliage until it shuts down naturally is a leading cause of diminished flowering, but there are others, especially too much shade. I had some old clumps start to peter out, sending up just leaves but no flower stalks, and after some judicious pruning overhead and a topdressing with an all-natural organic bulb food, they returned to a strong show. I could have also transplanted them to a sunnier spot. Other things the bulbs dislike: Is the area very dry? Ample moisture is needed when in active growth. (On the other hand, a soggy area will rot them.) Is the area filled with tree roots, or with other competing plants that grab all the nutrients and moisture? Spaces under evergreens can be inhospitable, for instance. Dividing may be called for (or relocating).

Confession: I used to add organic "bulb food" or bone meal to the hole at planting time, but why bother? These stalwarts seem to thrive without the extra attention.

Pruning Clematis

If you know when each of your clematis vines blooms—or at least know its name so you can look that up—you are on your way to figuring out when to prune. Climbing clematis fall into three general categories, each having a favored pruning time, including some (called Type 3s) targeted now, during spring cleanup. A caveat: These directional guidelines are no substitute for pruning needed to foster a plant's health. Example: If a plant has just a couple of long, straggly shoots, I'd cut it back hard in late winter or early spring no matter what group it is in, hoping to encourage a fresh flush. The category system also doesn't take into account training the vines to do what you want them to do, such as follow a particular support. But generally, it's a great place to start, to get comfortable with managing these charming, versatile plants:

Type 1 are the earliest spring bloomers, including species *alpina*, *montana*, and *armandii*, with their flower buds carried on old wood. Clean up stray or damaged stems any time, but the ideal moment is just after flowering to limit loss of buds. Thinning every few years can be done then, too.

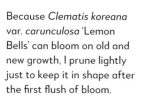

Because *Clematis koreana* var. *carunculosa* 'Lemon Bells' can bloom on old and new growth, I prune lightly just to keep it in shape after the first flush of bloom.

Type 2 are more versatile, and can bloom on old and new wood usually beginning in late spring. In late winter or early spring, when the buds swell, cut each stem back just above a healthy-looking bud at the desired height. Some gardeners prune again, after the first flush of flowers, by deadheading back to a lower bud or a strong side shoot, which may encourage rebloom. Most of the popular large-flowered hybrids are Type 2.

Type 3 bloom on new wood, beginning in summer or even later. Simply cut the vines nearly to the ground before spring growth begins, as you might a herbaceous perennial.

Nonvining clematis can be handled like Type 3.

A Particular Pulmonaria

Leave it to an asthmatic to fall in love with a plant named lungwort. And so I did, years ago, after the first bit of one was unceremoniously wrenched out of the ground by a nurseryman from his garden after I commented that I liked it.

"Have a piece," he said, and threw a plant, soil and all, into the back of my pick-up, along with the properly potted-up things I'd purchased. "Just cut off all the leaves when you get it home, and water it in well."

I still have a few plants of this unnamed, attractively spotted *Pulmonaria*, and have tried maybe eight other properly named cultivars whose foliage ranges from nearly all white ('British Sterling') to 'Margery Fish' (a ghostly silvery green) to plain green (my most beloved, *P. rubra*). Some are narrow-leaved, like 'Roy Davidson' and the even narrower 'Bertram Anderson', which are particularly appealing. They fall into different species and some are hybrids; look for them by their varietal names. They are among the easiest and earliest of perennials, and are fine informal flowering ground covers for shady spots where they will happily sow themselves around (though not always coming true to type in subsequent generations) so you can share your own pulmonaria crop, too.

Pulmonaria got its unfortunate common name from sixteenth- and seventeenth-century herbalists, who tried it for treating lung ailments. Their rationale, reportedly, was that the spotted leaves looked like a diseased lung. I beg to differ; they are simply beautiful. Most are blue or pink flowered (though 'Sissinghurst White', for one, isn't). But sign me up for the red one, *Pulmonaria rubra*, of which I have great masses since it comes true from seed. Spring, all pretty in pastels, doesn't have enough red for me, I suppose, which is why I like the wake robin (*Trillium erectum*), red tulips for cutting, and especially *P. rubra*. No fancy-pants, silver-splashed foliage like its more popular cousins, perhaps, and in hotter-summer zones I have read that it is less cooperative, but here it is the earliest and a gem. Just after or even as the hellebores begin and overlap them, *P. rubra* is the next perennial to open. The snow has barely melted, and there it is: starting to bloom, a foil to early bulbs. It has become a standby for massing in loose sheets in the shade under deciduous shrubs, where I want cover and a little early fun, but not a lot of extra work. It spreads and self-seeds happily but not aggressively, and is very easy to dig out. More diligent gardeners divide their lungworts every few years to keep the planting vigorous; I have never had to do that with this one.

Pulmonaria rubra, a lungwort with plain green leaves and very early red flowers, makes an easy ground cover in the big shrub borders.

The maintenance regimen includes a hard cutback after flowering. Lungwort will sulk and perhaps go temporarily dormant if dry, and doesn't want to be sodden, either. When lungworts are exposed to dry times and muggy weather, a bit of powdery mildew can form (more for me on the silvery and spotted ones than on *Pulmonaria rubra*), and if so I shear them again and water well. There are named cultivars of *P. rubra*, such as 'Redstart', that is most commonly seen, and even one with variegated, white-margined leaves called 'David Ward'. But to me all the white markings are overkill; the flowers are the point, an extra-optimistic flash of red that admittedly burns out after a good long show to pinkish red, the sign of warmer days to come. My only question about *P. rubra*: Why isn't it more widely grown?

Finding Room for More Natives

I know: The garden is full; there's no room at the inn. How do we layer in more native plants, then—thereby fostering diversity in all organisms, from pollinators and other beneficial insects to birds and more—when we have established, chock-full landscapes?

I began as someone who craved every new or rare plant, and my early acquisitions added up to more of a collector garden than a habitat. My interest in nature and science grew as I spent more time outdoors, though, and also as I have learned more about the intricate co-evolutionary relationships between native plants and other living things. Can a plant-collector's garden become a habitat garden, or do we have to start from scratch?

Thankfully, we do not. Even in a suburban-size yard I suspect there are hidden opportunities. Imagine a bird's-eye view of your property (or better, see an actual image on Google Earth, using the 3-D view). What would be sacrificed if at least one stretch somewhere along the boundary line moved in a bit, and a mass of low-care native shrubs like winterberry holly, viburnums, and highbush blueberries went there instead, underplanted with native ground covers like sedges, or *Pachysandra procumbens*? If there is already hedging at the property line, that's O.K.; extend the bed that is now just the hedge inward to make it deeper, even just an extra 6 or 8 feet, and let the hedging become the backdrop for the additions.

Walking around my property line I realized I had many such spots for even deeper low-maintenance beds at the woodland edge, just inside the fence, up to which I had always just mowed. In these spots large shrubs and small trees like shadbush (*Amelanchier*) and redbud (*Cercis canadensis*) could be underplanted with ferns and woodland asters.

Perhaps your opportunities are not at the boundaries, but somewhere in the middle of what is now lawn. I've been "unmowing" some areas into mini-meadows as one other native-adding tactic. Even a small island could become a native perennial planting—or even better, a mix of shrubs and perennials.

There is room.

What Is Native Where?

At a wildflower talk I attended, a lot of the audience questions after the expert finished her slides were ones like this: "Is such-and-such trillium native here?" or, "Have you ever seen [insert specific fern] in the wild locally?" We were all curious about the hyper-local version of native plants.

Yes, we know the nursery label on a coneflower, or lupine, or coreopsis, may say "native," but keen gardeners have figured out that that term is often used quite generically in marketing, perhaps implying U.S. native, or maybe regional at best.

As I consciously added more natives to my garden, I wanted to learn how to get a little more precise than that. Many states also have a searchable online "flora," or list of all their recorded plants, even down to county level; mine is the New York Flora Atlas, newyork.plantatlas.usf. edu, for example. Local wildflower or native-plant societies or preserves may have one for your location. A local wildflower field guide is another essential asset.

Some online databases use maps to indicate the distribution of a particular genus of plant, including ones from the Biota of North America Program, bonap.org, and though that site can be overwhelming, it was the BONAP maps that got me started wondering: What's really native right here? Other searchable sources I have since discovered about ranges of native plants are:

CalFlora
    A database of wild California plants. | calflora.org
GoBotany
    A database from New England Wild Flower Society. | gobotany.newenglandwild.org
National Wildlife Federation Native Plant Finder
    A database searchable by ZIP code, created with University of Delaware and National Forest Service. | nwf.org/nativeplantfinder
Native Plant Information Network
    A database of Lady Bird Johnson Wildflower Center. | wildflower.org/plants

Nature Serve Explorer

Data on 70,000 plants, animals and ecosystems of the U.S. and Canada. |
explorer.natureserve.org

USDA Plants Database

Plants of the U.S. and its territories. | plants.usda.gov/java

VASCAN

The database of vascular plants of Canada. | data.canadensys.net/vascan/search

Spring Water-Garden Regimen

Algae—especially tenacious filamentous string algae or blanket weed—can quickly turn a water garden into a battleground. I have been enjoying, and managing, two in-ground, rubber-lined garden pools for more than 25 years, and it's not that hard, despite the sometimes-relentless, gooey green stuff. And most important: There is no other garden feature that brings more joy or sustains more wildlife than a pool, even a small one. I host many more species of birds, salamanders, and frogs than my waterless neighbors, and have gotten to know a fascinating complement of insects including dragonflies, stoneflies, caddisflies, fishflies, and dobsonflies.

My essential spring maintenance tips are:

Reduce debris (organic matter such as leaves on the bottom), which adds nutrients to the water as it decays, and can feed algae growth. I leave a little, which overwintering frogs seem to like hiding in, but remove the bulk of it. Use a net just as the ice on the pool relents— typically in March here—then turn the plumbing back on. I make another pass with the net and my hands in April, once the perennial water plants start to sprout so I can see which parts are dead, and I remove them, but I'm careful not to disturb masses of frog and salamander eggs. I dump the smelly, mucky debris around shrubs; they seem to enjoy the treat, but you could compost it, too.

Excess nutrients can also enter ponds in the form of fertilizer runoff Are you feeding flowerpots beside a water garden, or is the lawn adjacent (and being fertilized)? Not good.

Think like the English, and add barley straw—whether actual straw stuffed into a floating sachet-like net bag, or one of the newer extract products (sold as pellets, powders, and even liquids). Barley straw helps make the water inhospitable for algae. The sachets last about six months, other products a shorter time.

Other nontoxic additives may help I have been experimenting with other nontoxic and/ or biological additives (liquids or powders, sometimes formulated in combination with bar-ley extract). They may help settle particles out of the water, and/or add enzymes and helpful bacteria, and I think I am favorably impressed. Add periodically, according to label directions.

Changing the water doesn't work, and can actually backfire Work to improve what you have, consistently keeping a vigilant eye out and adjusting things.

Aerating the water (with a small spillway or waterfall) can help fight some algae species, but not all, though it is much preferable to stagnant water for various other reasons. And who doesn't love the sound of moving water?

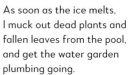

As soon as the ice melts, I muck out dead plants and fallen leaves from the pool, and get the water garden plumbing going.

Natural products, including ones containing barley extracts, may help in the effort to maintain clear water.

Filter, the biological way I have pumps and biological filters for both my pools, one in the water of the smaller pool, and a larger external unit the size of a wastebasket that's sunk in the ground at the larger one. Inside both are biological filters, hosting a community of helpful organisms including bacteria that build up on the filter "medium" made of foam or what looks like packing peanuts. The organisms help digest unwanted pond wastes. My units have lasted many years, though every few years the medium or the pumps that power the filters need replacing.

UV "clarifiers" can help, too Some pond filters incorporate the use of ultraviolet light bulbs. When the water passes by these clarifiers or sterilizers, as they are called, algae buildup is prevented. Independent clarifying devices—not housed within the filter—are also available.

Critical: Shade at least one-third of the water surface Experts cite that proportion; I shade more. Ponds in full sun will be most challenging, and algae will romp. Shading can be accomplished by siting your pond in part shade, or planting shrubs or grasses or other shade-casting objects nearby. Most important and easier:

Floating water plants will shade the pond surface (and some also help with overall water health besides blocking light). They are essential. I love the texture of fairy moss, or *Azolla*, for instance, and *Lemna* (duckweed), but you might prefer bold water lilies, or towering pots of large-leaved elephant ears. (Never discard water-garden plants into natural waterways, lakes, or ponds.)

One more shading tactic: nontoxic black water dye Sold as a powder or liquid, I like the dye because it helps hide the submersed plumbing. Various labels also claim it reduces light entering the water. The dye lasts a few weeks, and then needs to be reapplied.

If floating foamy-looking or stringy algae does occur, reduce it promptly Use a net, or a bamboo cane moved in a circular, swirling motion to entwine the long threads.

Net the surface in fall, or not? Experts advise netting to prevent debris from entering the pool, but my frogs, birds, and other pond visitors and residents would strongly object, and even potentially be injured navigating it.

Follow the fall pond-care tips in the final section of the book, which do not include water changes or scrubbing the liner. They do include keeping a hole open in the ice that might form, to prevent gas buildup that would suffocate inhabitants. The open water also welcomes wildlife who want to drink or bathe 365 days a year.

Name Game: Know Your Weeds

I know a lot of cultivated plants by their proper names, but when it comes to "weeds," my knowledge pales. A garden-benefiting task for days not conducive to actual outdoor chores is to study weed-identification websites and a regionally appropriate field guide, and learn to finally address *Alliaria petiolata* (garlic mustard) or *Galinsoga quadriradiata* (quickweed) with the proper (dis)respect.

I do not think we have a prayer of subduing or at least outsmarting an opponent we are barely acquainted with.

Before I started this rainy-day home study curriculum (wedged between sessions studying local birds, moths and butterflies, beetles and more), I didn't even remember the botanical Latin name for the ubiquitous dandelion, *Taraxacum officinale*. Learning names is the gateway to critical tactical knowledge, like figuring out which ones are native, and not, for example. Yes, we may call the native impatiens jewelweed, and *Impatiens capensis* will try to have its way

Galinsoga quadriradiata, or quickweed, is a common agricultural and nursery-industry weed.

Garlic mustard, *Alliaria petiolata*, is one of my worst weeds—and the first one whose proper name I learned.

sowing around a shady garden bed. I may weed it out of a formal spot, but as with clearweed (*Pilea pumila*), another native with -*weed* in its common name, I let it sow into a less conspicuous place so insects who use these as host plants (or even the ruby-throated hummingbirds, who so enjoy jewelweed flowers) can have a nibble, or a drink.

Mere common names—saying you have an issue with "bindweed"—won't do, either. Is it field bindweed, the wild morning glory (*Convolvulus arvensis*), or hedge false bindweed (*Calystegia sepium*)? The latter is native where I live, but still an impressive pest, with 10-foot vines and matching 10-foot root systems.

With a proper ID, we can also learn what a particular weed is related to—no small matter, since many weeds harbor various fungal pathogens or viral diseases, or attract insects. Queen Anne's lace or wild carrot (*Daucus carota*), for example, is closely related to the common garden carrot, and if you are growing both plants, transmission from the wild stand to your vegetables is possible. Common chickweed (*Stellaria media*) can harbor viral diseases that damage beets, cucumbers, peas, tomatoes, and turnips.

Proper weed identification may also inform how to time efforts for maximum effect, since some weeds are actually best tackled late in the season. Knowing whether they are an annual, biennial, or perennial gives us strategic insight, as do other factors of biology—such as if they form runners, or spread by seed, or both.

Besides using an overall North American plant encyclopedia and two indispensable region-specific weed field guides, I am a regular on such websites as the Rutgers New Jersey Agricultural Experiment Station's New Jersey Weed Gallery; the University of Illinois weed identification database, and the University of California weed ID site (part of their encyclopedic Integrated Pest Management database that I often turn to with all manner of plant troubles, though I live on the other coast). A web search for "weed identification guide" and the name of your state or region will turn up others, and then you, too, can start to really get to know your weeds.

Youth

MAY & JUNE

A SEASON FOR SISTERHOOD

WE HAVE FOUND neutral ground, my sister and I. After three and a half decades, there is at last a place for us to be at peace, a new mother tongue that does not have so many angry phrases. We talk not of what has been, or might have been had someone or the other done something differently. We speak the language of flowers instead.

"I have an urgent garden question" is how her phone calls begin these days, and with those words we start rewriting the story of big sister–little sister, a tale that did not go so well the first time around.

No matter that she doesn't always listen—she stored the dormant pot of calla lilies under the kitchen radiator, not exactly where I recommended, but they bloomed just as well the next year anyhow. Her "urgent" questions are the opening lines of our revised first chapter of growing up together, and for that reason, I am grateful, and not so picky about such details.

When we were little, and the grandma she is named for grew them, my little sister crinkled her freckled nose and objected loudly to the stink of marigolds. Their gaudy color shone— positively gleamed—as if Grandma had planted them exactly to match the child's orange hair. Young Marion was more inclined to horseplay than horticulture, however, her knees skinned and trousers shredded not from bending to the task of weeding but some far more hellish undertaking decidedly lacking in adult supervision. No time to stop and smell the flowers when you are playing cowboys.

Though not her namesake—perhaps they should have called me Lily, as hard as I tried to be demure—I never declined a chance to sit by Grandma Marion while she dried flowers from her garden in an old wooden press. From the lifeless bits she composed intricate arrange- ments that she later framed.

"Pressed-flower pictures," we called them, proudly, but I remember that it was my room, not Marion's, whose walls were covered in them. When she was not growing or pressing flow- ers, Grandma was painting pictures of them: a giant green ceramic vase of lilacs, a bowl of pansies, perhaps—and yes, of course, her precious marigolds.

Later, when Grandma was gone and growing pains were being felt full force at my end of the hallway, Marion was the sister who got bouquets from those who wished for her atten- tion. Even then, Marion loved a rose—preferably long-stemmed and by the dozen—but I never actually thought that she would grow one. Apparently, I had something to learn about my sister, and about humility.

"Are those roses you gave me ramblers?" she asked not long ago, because they had clambered up and over this and that as rambler roses do. "You know, the ones you said were dead?"

The plants in question had arrived in time for an unseasonably early bout of high heat. Because I was not home, they had sat in their package in the sun, right where the UPS man left them. They stayed that way for days. Attempting a rescue on my return, I soaked them awhile in a bucket of water, and cut the cooked parts back, but they were too far gone to my impatient eye to bother with.

"I'll take them," said Marion, seeing the "dead" creatures lying on the lawn one day when she visited, and so she did. Within what seemed like no time, the dead plants had undergone a resurrection, and then proceeded quickly to ascend, too. By summer's end, they were well up a trellis, where an enthusiastic tangle of vines—probably previous years' casualties from my own garden—already grew lustily, as if to get back at me for my rejection.

There is a certain hazard to passing on your outcasts, whether to family or to friend. You may very likely have to face the plants again; do not forget this fact. Some, sent away because they were so aggressive, will quickly overtake their new home as they did your place. This does little to enhance the sense that the spirit of generosity was behind your gift.

Other plants were banished because their color proved too jarring; no spot for them could be found, no matter how hard you tried, so out they went, too. Such was the case with a dozen peach- and melon-colored daylilies, and I was glad to see them go.

I was not quite so glad to see them as a focal point at Marion's, where somehow, magically, they fit right in as if custom-ordered for the spot.

It is not all having to grit teeth, of course, not all a test of one's semigood humor. I admit to an intense pleasure when she comes to pick my apples in fall, knowing I will hear about the pies and sauce for months to come. The image of them on her table is a good one, as if the act of sharing a harvest is deeply knit into the gardener's soul. The summer I planted three-dozen tomato seedlings, her own crop was lost to some animal invasion. No matter, between us there was plenty. Fruits heal all wounds, even those as old as childhood.

For now, the phone keeps ringing with the questions, although I suspect she doesn't really need the answers any more, and could even give a few herself. Admittedly, I will not try storing my callas inside the radiator cover, but there is a certain red poppy in her garden I'd like the name of, or better yet, some of its seeds.

We are actually beginning to look more alike as a consequence of this shared passion. They say that family traits are often revealed as the years go by, but that's not it. In our case it is the matching scratches on the insides of our forearms I refer to, the marks of rose thorns, or the ankle-encircling scars from wasp nests run over with the mower. It is the red half-circles behind each neck where the sun found its way in to sear our skin. Even our gardens have taken on a certain similarity: She, too, plants pumpkins in her flower beds, as if this idiosyncrasy were a familial trait.

There is more to this gardening stuff than planting, I guess, more than the books offer in step-by-step detail. No wonder, then, that the language of gardening and the language of life have so many words in common: words like tend and cultivate, words like grow.

An early adventure by a fledgling robin includes a pit stop on the backyard stepping-stone path.

'Golden Angel' peony, hybridized by Roy Klehm and Chris Laning, emerges in gold and even reddish tones before sending up single cream blooms.

Long, warm-colored shadows complete the garden picture at lilac and apple blossom time.

Nuisance Wildlife

Mole or vole, woodchuck, rabbit or deer? Who ate or uprooted my plants? By this point, I suspect every gardener has faced at least one fur-bearing opponent, all usually lumped in the general catchall of "nuisance wildlife." Identifying the specific culprit is the critical first step to future prevention, or to devising a safe, sane, and humane solution if the unwanted animal is already in residence.

With deer, I have already said I am a true believer in fences. With other animals, thanks to a long friendship with my local licensed nuisance-wildlife handler, Mike Todd, I have mostly learned to diagnose what animal is to blame, and how and when to intervene. Here's how I have been taught to think:

When was the plant damaged—during the night, or by day, and in what season? Dug-up containers at noon are probably the damn gray squirrels; at midnight, more likely it's raccoons (or perhaps a skunk) searching for grubs. Did it happen in the growing season, or winter? Rabbits (and deer) are active even in cold months, usually eating woody plants; woodchucks are hibernating then.

Where is the damage located on the plant? Within about 2 feet of the ground, it's probably a rabbit, or woodchuck, who can't damage branches higher up like a deer can. Sometimes added clues include tracks in the snow (or from dew-moistened feet, on decks or pavement), or the gift of scat, such as rabbit pellets.

What does the damage look like up close? Deer leave jagged edges because they don't have upper teeth but simply grab the plant between their lower incisors and their upper jaw then pull (and rip it). Rabbits are noted for their very tidy, clean cuts at a 45-degree angle, again a reflection of their dentition. Woodchucks, who like rabbits have upper and lower teeth, are a bit messier, and also (after deer) the most voracious, able to erase quite a swath of vegetable garden growth in pretty short order. Their favorite foods here are brassicas and legumes (and wild violets and asters). If half a row of peas is gone, I know it's no mere rabbit.

Any holes, or tunneling? Woodchuck holes are large and distinctive, and woodchucks normally forage in early morning and early evening quite near their burrows—making them relatively easy to trap. If I patiently scour the place (including along the roadside and driveway culverts), I usually find the holes.

Then there are much smaller moles and voles—often confused for each other, though their lifestyles are quite different. Moles are fossorial—they live underground—and also insectivorous, foraging for insects, grubs, and worms. They may dislodge plants while tunneling, but did not do so to eat them. You might see the occasional volcano-like mounds of soil—the proverbial molehill—but mostly the tipoff is that the lawn surface feels wobbly like a washboard, and if you step on it, the humps press back down.

Voles are rodents, and herbivorous—plant eaters, including bark of woody things, and bulbs and even seeds—and though they are semifossorial, with underground runways, what we notice is that their tunneling is at the surface, where they may also eat the turf they displace. A horrifying moment of vole awareness is when the snow melts, revealing mad squiggle patterns of missing grass, since they are active all year, and I discover surface runways at other times, too.

Was there damage to bark? Bark damage requires another when-and-where investigation. For example, male deer in what is called rut (mating season) polish their antlers against trees—especially young, flexible ones—from around September here, and sometimes into January. Over the winter, bark, especially near the base of young, vulnerable trees, may be gnawed by rabbits, voles, and mice. (Porcupines eat bark, too, but can climb, so their damage may even be found high up in trees, not merely at the base.)

Next, though, I have to take a hard look at myself, and how I figure into all this Conversations with my trapper friend, and with Marne Titchenell, a wildlife program specialist for Ohio State University, have helped keep me honest on this score. How can I expect wild animals to respect boundaries if I have put none in place—and in some cases have even issued an inadvertent invitation?

Titchenell teaches a five-element "toolbox" for dealing with nuisance wildlife, from lethal methods (from snap mousetraps to deer hunting), to exclusion (a fence, or individual plant protectors), to the use of repellents, or scare tactics—and maybe most important, habitat modification. The last one is where I need to ask myself what am I willing to give up, or to repair or modify, to make my place less attractive? If woodchucks have chosen beneath the back porch the last three years as a nursery, perhaps it's time to repair that loose board and bury hardware cloth as you do so. Gardeners being driven mad by squirrels or chipmunks cannot blithely hang birdfeeders and wonder why, and likewise feeding the cat on the back porch invites all manner of other dinner guests.

Planting young fruit trees without protective collars only to see most of them girdled the first winter by rabbits or voles should really be no surprise. I live in black bear country, and ask for trouble if I put out the trash the night before, or otherwise pique curiosity with appealing

smells of pet food, bird seed (or even the barbecue grill left uncleaned). Bottom line: To modify animals' behavior, we must start by modifying our own.

What level of pushback is really warranted? If the problem is merely occasional, and not on edible crops, perhaps spray repellents blending putrescent egg or egg solids (rotten eggs) and capsaicin (hot pepper) will work. These products are not cheap, and must be reapplied regularly. Fencing a vulnerable area like a vegetable garden, including burying wire mesh, may solve your problem.

Before you purchase a single trap, think very clearly What do you plan to do if and when you catch something? Not only can it be stressful for the animal and for you, but not knowing safe handling of live traps is foolish and even dangerous. Plus, many localities forbid relocation of wild animals—in some cases even by state-licensed trappers, let alone homeowners—meaning you would have to exterminate the animal on your own property to obey the law.

I cannot say enough how grateful I am to know an expert and considerate professional trapper, and I do trap in partnership with him when I have a woodchuck problem. I am able to trap them by the strictest humane guidelines he has taught me; he is licensed by the DEC to move the animals, and I hire him to do that. I always call before I set traps to ask if he will be in my area that day for a potential pickup, because I don't want an animal in a trap for an extended period. I check traps frequently throughout the day, and never leave full traps in the sun. Also: If you are trapping for woodchuck, say, who feed by day, close your traps at night or you may get a skunk or raccoon or even an opossum.

One thing I heartily endorse that everyone do year-round: Keep after mice, who are the primary vector in my region, along with chipmunks, for transmitting the bacterium causing diseases like Lyme to ticks, that ticks then transmit to us. At the same time, using the same tactics, I keep after the voles. I bait snap traps with peanut butter year-round for both rodents in all their respective hotspots, though with voles I use a larger number of traps per area. Outdoors, I place traps inside wooden boxes with removable covers and a small entry hole in one side that I made from plywood, to protect birds and other animals—a design modified from Eliot Coleman's vole boxes.

Whatever the havoc, mothballs are not the answer, and are highly toxic, and illegal for garden use. I hear from readers whenever I mention animal control who share the "tip" that they've discovered mothballs, and spread them in a vole-besieged bed, or along their deer-pressured property line, or even in a stone wall, perhaps, to deter snakes. No! Any use not specifically listed on the package violates federal law, and can harm you, pets, or outdoor animals, and contaminate soil and water. Mothballs (and flakes) contain either naphthalene or paradichlorobenzene, and do not belong in a garden (nor an attic, cellar, garage, car, or crawl space).

Tough-Love Transplanting

Though container plants—the standard of the nursery industry—are easier to work with than field-dug, balled-and-burlapped ones, and readily available, often they are rootbound and need a stern hand at transplant time to thrive.

The most common mistake with trees and shrubs in particular is failing to tease apart, examine, and even correctively prune the root-ball. Once unpotted, have a close look: Are the woody plant's roots wrapped around in the shape of the container, perhaps circling (which can lead to deadly girdling roots) or maybe hook-like or knotted? What you are seeking is not a congested lump to stuff in a hole, but more an architecture like the spokes of a wheel headed out in various directions to anchor the plant. I cut off the worst of the mess to try to guide it in that direction. (With pot-bound perennials, I pull apart the root mass or even score it with my pruners, to loosen things up.)

Another transplanting error that leads to poor performance or even plant death is planting at the incorrect depth. A tomato may be delighted to be buried up to its neck, because it has the ability to root all along its stem, but a tree or shrub buried too deep will not thrive. The old "wisdom" of digging a $10 hole for a $5 plant is now frowned upon, and can contribute to the too-low planting result, as amendments we all once used (like peat moss, formerly added to excavated soil before backfilling) are lightweight and eventually settle, as the plant sinks into a sump. I am careful not to put anything unstable, like clumps of sod or unfinished compost, into the bottom of the hole. Regarding amendments in general, it is illogical and unhelpful to give the root-ball, say, a foot of lightweight planting medium all the way around, then once the roots get through it have them confront the reality of the surrounding native soil. Better to let stimulation from the root pruning encourage them to be brave and explore their true home as soon as possible.

I use my hands, and also a stick, whether a half of a bamboo cane in a smallish hole or broom or shovel handle in larger holes, to prod around the edges and eliminate air pockets. I water slowly for a long period—usually with a donut-shaped sprinkler on low, or with a length of soaker hose (not a hose-end nozzle with a jet of water like when washing the car, please). One more piece of old-time advice I always still follow: I water plants of every kind well, a day ahead of transplant time, so they are fully hydrated before their move.

Editing Self-Sowns

Most people approach garden design like flower arranging, as a form of addition: You add more plants until you like what you see. But there is also a lot of subtraction, or at least moving things to other columns in the ledger, particularly with certain annuals, biennials, and short-lived perennials that tend to sow themselves about if allowed to go to seed. The best gardeners learn to identify their baby self-sowns each spring (which may not show until quite late), and capitalize—leaving some in place, perhaps, and relocating others.

This free shopping in your own garden can help minimize the polka-dot look of disparate onesies here and there by repeating some of your best plants, making them not accidents but your deliberate signatures. I arm myself with a tray, a sharp hori-hori knife, and an even sharper eye to scout for self-sowns to relocate into spots where they add up to more design impact. Simply pop them out, preferably on a morning after a rain, and poke them in their new homes, then puddle them in with a gentle shower from the adjustable sprayer nozzle or watering-can rose. Got it? Pop, poke, puddle. Then repeat.

Look for seedlings too close to bed edges for their own good, and scour the cracks in the pavement, or in gravel. Those places are where things like to sow—and where the Japanese weeding knife really comes in handy. I've learned to be careful when cleaning up near my most prolific self-sowers until they have yielded the latest crop; compulsively cleaning up in fall or too early in spring may squander a great resource.

I learned about self-sowns one spring when the shortest route across the lawn to the compost pile was suddenly turning purple. Apparently on the way there the fall prior, I had dropped something—*Perilla frutescens* seeds, to be specific (the herb called beefsteak plant). Like a Hansel and Gretel trail of bread crumbs, I could trace the paths I'd taken, when my wheelbarrow was apparently brimming with seed-filled plants.

What will self-sow is not consistent place to place, and a welcome volunteer in one region can be a pest in another. Here these worthwhile plants can be counted on to do it, among ones I've tried: various *Corydalis* spp., primulas, hellebores, dwarf goatsbeard (*Aruncus aethusifolius*), celandine poppy (*Stylophorum diphyllum*), *Verbena bonariensis*, clary sage (*Salvia sclarea*), annual poppies including opium poppy (*Papaver somniferum*), *Nicotiana* spp., *Angelica gigas*, common annuals including calendula and cosmos, plus copper fennel and dill. Tomatoes will, too, but you won't be happy about that from a design standpoint, and they can potentially carry over disease.

In spring I move volunteers from the biennial Korean angelica, *Angelica gigas*, into shady and semishady spots where I want them to bloom the following year.

Where they decide to place themselves is sometimes brilliant (other times not). Tall plants may march to the front of the border as if to say to the gardener, "Don't follow the rule of small at the front and large at the back so strictly!" I have come to cherish their resurrections, and their insurrections, too.

The celandine poppy, *Stylophorum diphyllum*, is an easy self-sower to transplant.

Various primulas, including *Primula sieboldii*, self-sow and can be moved around to semishady spots at will.

13 Things About Growing Tomatoes

From the first seed sown to the last fruit stashed in the freezer, homegrown tomatoes are a labor of love. Whether at tomato-sowing time (April 15 for me), or transplanting time (around Memorial Day), it's a good moment to review what goes into tomato-growing success.

Start with a homegrown seedling or a locally raised one—not a big-box-store plant that may have been shipped in from warmer zones, where more tomato diseases are endemic and overwinter. (That logic isn't tomato-specific; I buy local seedlings or grow my own everything—especially that basil I hope to have at tomato harvest time. Plants from far away can be vectors for disease.)

Getting great flavor out of a tomato is part nature, part nurture The genetics of the seed you start with—the breeding lines behind the variety, plus where that actual packet of seed you're using was produced—and the way you grow it both factor in. Choosing a Florida-bred variety and/or seed farmed in California's Central Valley for your New Hampshire garden will not let you hit the sweet(est) spot.

Grow a mix of both hybrids and open-pollinated tomatoes (including older heirlooms and newer nonhybrids) for the best overall insurance policy against failure. Whichever varieties you choose, read up on them first, and select not just by looks or extravagant flavor claims, but also for traits like regional adaptation and disease resistance.

Open-pollinated plants, including tomatoes, are not like uniform widgets, so a 'Brandywine' is not a 'Brandywine' is not a 'Brandywine'. Especially with such nonhybrids, there can be variability from seed-seller to seed-seller, based on where and how they raised the seed for generations, and what they had in mind as they selected each crop. Did they rogue out "off types" to keep it true to what a 'Brandywine' is meant to be, or did the genetics "drift" with neglect? Did they save their seed from the most robust or earliest to fruit or most productive plants, for example?

Good tomato hygiene counts With all the disease and "mechanical" issues a tomato can experience—biotic and abiotic challenges—it's a wonder we ever get a harvest. But blessedly we do, and we can even improve our odds. Most gardeners and farmers are fighting the presence of some soil-borne tomato pathogen, such as *Septoria* and early blight that reside in Northeast, mid-Atlantic, and upper Midwest soils. That means rotating tomatoes from one spot to another year to year doesn't cut it; we need to manage around disease presence. Start by choosing resistant varieties, and then following "good tomato hygiene," as founder Tom Stearns of High Mowing Organic Seeds taught me to think of it.

Growing tomatoes on black plastic increases soil heat that tomatoes love, provides weed suppression, and helps with soil-splash control–keeping some soil-borne spores from getting up onto the plant by creating a barrier. Even a layer of straw mulch can help. Stripping the lower leaves to eliminate the bottom rung of the "ladder" for spores to climb may help as well.

Water is best applied directly to the root zone, preferably with drip irrigation or soaker hoses, rather than by wetting the entire plant and possibly adding to favorable conditions for splashing and disease spread.

If you are worried about late blight specifically, the hygiene regimen also includes discarding any potato tubers missed at fall harvest. On advice of a Cornell pathologist, I also pull

Fluted, or pleated, tomatoes like 'Pink Accordion' may have been more common historically than they are today.

all volunteer tomato seedlings, which might carry other diseases like Septoria leaf spot. Some bacterial diseases can even get into seed left in the garden in rotting tomatoes, as can the early blight pathogen—but not late blight.

Whether you stake, cage, or trellis indeterminate varieties—ones that are more vine-like, producing new stem growth till frost—think about good air circulation to limit diseases. Never grow tomatoes trained together onto teepees or tripods; any tangle too closely spaced means a humid environment that invites more tomato troubles. Staked or trellised plants will generally ripen earlier crops of larger fruit.

Be realistic, though If you're not going to prune all season, don't stake or trellis; use a cage. Staking requires that each indeterminate plant be kept to one or two main stems of vine-like, not bush, habit. All small suckers that develop in the crotches between the leaves and the main stem must be removed, too. With such trained tomatoes, 18 inches between plants within a row is the minimum spacing, and 3 feet between rows (more is better).

Don't overfeed Yes, tomatoes are "heavy feeders," but a good soil that's high in organic matter (compost, compost, compost) is your best ally. Especially when nitrogen-rich fertilizers are used, plants that are overfertilized and too-fast-growing are a target for trouble, inviting pests and disease.

Sometimes, despite all the loving care, tomatoes fail to set fruit Assuming you did not overfeed, it may be weather-related. Nighttimes above 70°F or temperatures below 50°F interfere with pollination. Fruit-set can also be hampered (or the fruit damaged) by irregular watering. Hot, dry conditions at blossom time prevent proper pollination and can cause buds or tiny fruit to drop. If it's early enough, a next round of flowers may appear during favorable weather.

Don't forget: Plant enough of at least one plum (paste) type for last-minute freezing of whole fruits Forget purchasing whole canned tomatoes going forward; just pop homegrowns out of a freezer bag into that soup or stew or chili. Or go one step further, and lace "extras" of your favorite tomatoes with oil, garlic, and herbs on rimmed baking sheets to roast to a sweet gooey mess, then slide into freezer bags for the best "sauce" or soup ingredient ever. I also could not live without a stash of my easy, skins-on tomato sauce.

Skins-On Tomato Red Sauce to Freeze

Come September and October, it will be sugar-free skins-on pink sauce that I am processing by the vatful, when I turn the harvest of my ancient apple trees into applesauce. Right now, though, it's skins-on red sauce that preoccupies me—getting enough into the freezer, that is, to last the coming year.

Yes, in both cases, I leave the skins on, and with the tomatoes I leave in the seeds, too. I'm all for more fiber and vitamins, and besides, I love chunky sauce. If you really hate the skins, use a food mill to strain them out of either cooked mixture, or purée the cooked sauce right in the pot once it cools slightly, using an immersion blender.

I grow smallish, tender tomatoes for making red sauce—ones like the hybrid 'Juliet' or its close relative 'Verona', called a "cocktail plum" size. Both are borne in grape-like clusters, so you get loads of vivid-flavored, scaled-down fruits that don't need more done to them than to be quartered. Note that cherry tomatoes make their own distinctive, rich-tasting sauce, so if you have a late-season glut, why not halve them for the purpose?

Ingredients

2 tablespoons olive oil, for the pan

1 large head garlic, whole cloves peeled

3 quarts coarsely chopped fresh tomatoes (about a large mixing bowl's contents)

Handful torn or sliced fresh basil leaves, plus more if desired

Generous handful chopped fresh parsley leaflets

Salt and pepper, if desired

Directions

1. Warm the olive oil over medium-low heat in a large saucepan. Add the garlic cloves and slowly cook until soft and almost caramelized. While cooking, leave the cover on the pan so the garlic is almost sweating. Stir occasionally, so the garlic cloves don't get crispy (later, the cloves will sort of melt into the sauce).

2. To prep the tomatoes, I cut off any dings and occasionally the stem scar if it's tough-looking. Add the tomatoes to the garlic in the saucepan, and stir to combine.

Canning jars of skins-on tomato sauce cool before heading into the freezer.

3. Cover, stirring occasionally, until the tomato mixture starts to soften slightly, about 10 minutes. Add the chopped basil. Cover the pan again, stirring occasionally, until the ingredients get thoroughly soft, about 10 minutes. Remove the cover to let the steam escape and cook the sauce to thicken, stirring occasionally.

4. Remove the sauce from the heat. Add the parsley and stir so the leaves just wilt in the hot sauce but stay bright green.

5. This process will take about 30 minutes, longer for very wet tomatoes, prep to finish. Let the sauce sit, covered, in the pan in the refrigerator for a day so the flavors meld. Then ladle into straight-sided canning jars, leaving some headspace for expansion, and freeze. Store in a tightly sealed glass jar in the refrigerator up to 5 days, and in the freezer for up to 1 year.

TIPS Jars with "shoulders" and narrower necks can crack more easily when liquids push up during freezing. Vary the size of jars you fill. Sometimes you just need enough for one serving, like a half-pint jelly jar, or even half that, perhaps to use as the "liquid" in some sautéed vegetables or to enrich another sauce. Other times, company's coming: Make sure there are pints and quarts on hand.

Into one batch of red sauce I like to add homegrown green beans. I don't like them canned (all olive green and overcooked), and they can lose crunch or get ice-encrusted when blanched and frozen plain. Instead I cut them up and put them into my homemade tomato sauce

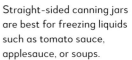

Straight-sided canning jars are best for freezing liquids such as tomato sauce, applesauce, or soups.

For variety, briefly blanch cut-up green beans in simmering homemade tomato sauce and freeze the combination.

for the last half-minute of cooking. Assuming the sauce is bubbling, they'll "blanch" in it immediately, turning bright green. This sauce-plus-beans recipe is delicious later on rice or pasta, with a heavy-handed drizzle of good olive oil and a generous sprinkle of freshly grated Parmesan cheese, of course.

Salad Days

If asked 20-plus years ago for lettuce suggestions, it would have seemed easy. Who wouldn't enjoy cooperative, tender 'Oakleaf' or 'Black-Seeded Simpson' and maybe a red one—the French heirloom Romaine 'Rouge d'Hiver', or the blushing version of my beloved oakleaf type? Add a little arugula, or spinach, and some leaflets from Italian-style flat-leaf parsley pinched on your way out of the vegetable garden, and you'd have a very nice salad.

Much has changed, both on the seed farm—where new varieties have proliferated through breeding and many old ones brought back—and in the kitchen. I (lovingly) blame people like Frank Morton out in Washington, an organic farmer who has been one of the influencers in the changed complexion of our salad bowls. "The plants showed me what they could do," Morton says of his 25-ish years of lettuce tinkering, "and what we could do together." From his start as a "salad guy" growing greens for restaurants, Morton watched as new traits surfaced, and evolved into a lettuce breeder, founding a company that grows everything it sells, Wild Garden Seed—and also supplies other seed companies.

There is just no comparison to those reds I grew decades ago when I look at Morton's breakthrough 'Merlot' leaf lettuce, positively loaded with blue-red anthocyanin pigments, or if I measure his current list against the choices I shopped from then.

Nowadays it will take longer to decide which varieties to grow than it will to learn to grow lettuce, which is easy if you follow simple guidelines.

Even in a cold climate, salad can be a nearly year-round accomplishment, if you have a cold frame or poly tunnel and purchase appropriate seed varieties for each season. Unfortunately, many gardeners enjoy only one harvest from a spring planting, which goes by in a bitter-tasting farewell, eventually stretching up its flower stalk and bolting. Most important: Don't plant 20 feet of row of one lettuce at a time. A short row or a block sown every two weeks is more the strategy for continuous supply.

Much of the time I direct-sow, but if you are not going to keep the seed bed moist, then transplanting is preferable. I do grow transplants to set out for a head-start crop around the time I make my first direct-sowing. Barely press seeds into a shallow furrow, or a divot in the cell-pack medium, and cover about ¼ inch deep, watering gently and regularly so the sowing stays moist. Those frustrated by germination failure in summer may wish to keep right on sowing in cell packs every two weeks, moving transplants to the garden as needed. Another trick: Sow in the garden, water the bed, then place a board or a piece of burlap over the row until germination. I give lettuce a bit of shade in midsummer by planting on the cooler side of tomatoes or pole beans.

One of my many dear friends waits for whatever delicious treat flies or crawls by.

Spacing depends not only on the variety, but also on the harvesting method. A full-size crisphead takes more room than each plant in a bed of baby mesclun; the newer mini-heads are a fraction of the size of their close cousins in full-size form, and so on. Generally, leaf lettuces like my old favorites mature quicker than heading types, like in about 45 days, and even sooner if grown as baby leaf (a month or less). Baby leaf lettuce can be planted in greater density than if you intended to harvest full-grown heads, even of the same variety, and cut a few times.

But which ones to grow? Take an hour (or three) and browse the listings and the photos of lettuces speckled and solid-color, flat, ruffled and frilled, best for harvest as baby greens if you like, or for multiple cuttings (cut and come again style), or as whole heads, whether the newer minis or big as an old-style iceberg. One of the latest developments are "one-cuts" that grow like a head, but when you cut it, all the leaves are uniform and baby-size.

Pick a few beauties and set up a seed trial, says Morton, to learn how well your choices actually do in your location and conditions. A basic "observation trial" can be as simple as 5 feet of row for each, sown at the same time, with each row then treated the same way. Their "contemporariness"—witnessing the varieties growing side-by-side—reveals what you like and dislike about each. You could repeat this with three heat-tolerant varieties in summer, and another handful of cold-tolerant types come fall.

And then there are the add-ons. Unless using a commercial mesclun mix of varieties tested for synchronized performance, I plant my extras separately, and use the packet days-to-harvest information to try to time sowings so everything coincides. Possibilities: mache, claytonia or spinach; herbs such as chervil and a foliage-focused dill, plus those flat-leaf parsley leaflets or ones of lovage (a perennial); baby 'Ragged Jack' or another kale harvested very young. For zest I like arugula, red mustard, or cress. And a farmer friend suggested this: mint. Try chopping up some mint leaves in your next salad (with a vinaigrette dressing) and see what you think.

Sow, Sow, Sow Again

Once is (almost) never enough. That's the basic idea of succession sowing, a practice aimed at a continuous harvest over as many weeks as your climate will allow, maximizing the output of every square garden foot.

It's one thing to sit indoors in winter and draw a layout of what you'll put where in spring, but it's not a static, one-time-deal, and instead is more a dynamic game of 3-D agricultural chess. As spinach goes by, then what—and what will go on the trellis when the peas succumb to summer heat? Some real estate gets three uses in a season here, like the spinach bed that then held various salads and bush beans before the garlic goes in around late October—actually various spots see that many, if you count a fall cover crop, or "green manure," as the third.

Organic grower Kate Spring of Good Heart Farmstead in Vermont charts each bed in its own multicolumn spreadsheet, with individual first crops down the left column, marked with sowing or transplanting dates—the latter indicated by TP, so "5/1" if direct-sown or "5/1 TP" if from seedlings. Possible replacements per crop are entered down each successive column to the right. Marking the desired transplants with a "TP" is a nudge to schedule sowing ahead in cells or flats so they're ready in time.

Not everything in a bed goes in on the same date. The trick is to start backward, from your desired major harvests—not stuff in everything at once, which may not prove strategic. Finding room for a row of beets or radishes or lettuce is easier than for your main crops. Want to can tomatoes or grow all your winter squash for storage—big things that demand a long span of substantial space? Block those out, then see what can happen there before or after. Example: spinach, mache, lettuce, and radishes, from a mid-April sowing, can precede those paste tomatoes, which might be followed with winter rye or field peas and oats as a cover crop to turn in next spring.

To maximize opportunities, it helps to have a fresh supply of not just seed but also seedlings on hand, though the latter aren't often available at garden centers after peak spring. The years I adhere to best practice and sow cell packs of second crops of edibles—more broccoli or cabbage, or lettuces, chard, kale, and even basil, to name a few—are when I make best use of my space. Sometimes a spot comes available for just a short window, like after early salad and then bush beans but before garlic time, and if I only had some seedlings that already had a couple of weeks' head start, I could squeeze out another harvest in that space. Transplants also help outsmart the hotter, drier soil of summer, when germination from seed can be tricky. Plugging in a plant you bring along in a kinder, gentler spot where you remember to care for it is key.

Exceptions to the transplant-on-hand strategy: Greens (whether kale or lettuce) that you want to harvest at the baby stage should be direct-sown, and more thickly spaced than for full-size plants. They can be cut more than once, so remember to plan for that extra time in the ground—like two months—for the double yield. Root crops that don't like transplanting, like carrots or radishes, are also direct-sown.

Musts for repeat sowings because they just don't hold, and are inclined to bolt or otherwise go past their prime fast: cilantro; salad greens including lettuces and arugula; spinach; Asian greens (including mustards); radishes. Sow carrots twice in spring (and later for a fall storage crop), and beets every couple of weeks. Chard, kale, and collards get a couple of sowings, and

Having a progression of fresh seedlings ready to plug in through the growing season helps maximize use of space.

stagger plantings of bush beans, too (and also grow pole beans for the longest possible bean season). With summer squash and cucumbers, I sow twice, a few weeks apart, meaning succulent fruits continuing into fall (plus often outsmarting an uprising of squash bugs or cucumber beetles or powdery mildew that can damage the earlier crop). The latest sowings, for fall supply and storage, are in July and August.

Investment Plants

I suppose each plant purchased is an investment, in that money is spent. But the return is not the same on the petunias you fill the hanging basket with as it would be on various other potential candidates for that job. I like to focus my plant budget on true investment plants whenever possible—ones that if well cared for may pay years of dividends.

What goes in pots for outdoor display spring through fall? Anything from a perennial, to tender bulbs like eucomis, to a columnar conifer like *Thuja occidentalis* 'Degroot's Spire'. Of course all my houseplants do temporary outdoor duty in shadier spots (especially fancy-leaf begonias, clivias, and bromeliads). True annuals or other tender bedding plants sold in flats or small pots in the "annual" section of the garden center are what I actually use the least of for creating spots of seasonal color.

Hosta pot? Why not. I always keep a few big clumps of hostas ready to do container duty, overwintering them in the empty vegetable garden, then lifting them out to pop back into pots to display in shady areas spring through fall. Bits of golden moneywort, *Lysimachia nummularia* 'Aurea', or of *Sedum rupestre* 'Angelina' stolen out of the ground here and there could

Looking across the vegetable garden back to the house in peak spring, past Siberian iris toward the old rhododendron in bloom.

become the trailing element at their feet, no extra charge. It's easy, showy, and the hostas don't seem to mind being shuttled back and forth.

Maybe 10 years ago I bought several young Japanese maples in 3-gallon nursery pots. Yes, each one cost more than a flat of marigolds, but they are still with me, having moved up to ever-larger pots every couple of years till they were in the largest ones a helper and I can wheel on my hand cart to the barn, where I overwinter the dormant trees out of wind and ice. Each one serves as a major focal element, surrounded by other containers to form vignettes, and has long since paid back its initial cost many times over.

Sometimes at late-summer garden center sales I splurge on an irresistible tropical or sub-tropical plant that I'm not sure will overwinter successfully but I just cannot resist trying. Cannas, of course, are easy, and about the highest dividend-payers of all, with their inclination to reproduce enthusiastically underground. Not long ago I lugged home something labeled variegated shell ginger, *Alpinia zerumbet*, knowing nothing about it except how beautiful its gold-and-green-striped leaves were. I took a lucky guess at where to stash it (a spot with a temperature in the mid-40s, with some light, and watered periodically) and now, several years later, it's a massive showpiece and giving no sign of regret that we ended up together.

Ornamental Onions

I first grew ornamental onions in self-defense against animals, and began with the usual suspects: the June-blooming kinds with large purple globes atop long stems, like *Allium giganteum* and *A. aflatunense*. There are others of this classic allium appearance: *A. rosenbachianum* (a bit earlier and shorter than *A. giganteum*, and it also comes in white); and 'Globemaster', with giant heads.

But *Allium* is much more than purple spheres. For the look of fireworks exploding, there is the startling *A. schubertii*, about 2 feet high with a foot-wide lilac-pink loose sphere on top. There is tiny *A. moly*, with bright yellow flowers on 8-inch stems, which I have come to love for here and there in between things. And *A. christophii* is a real winner, with nearly foot-wide heads of a silvery lavender that are airy, not dense. It is exceptionally long lasting, looking good for many weeks while blooming and then for many weeks more while turning a straw color. I like the faded look right in the garden, but eventually carry off some of the dried flowers for years of indoor use.

There is rose-pink *Allium unifolium*; a number of species, including *A. rosenbachianum*, come in white forms; and true blue in *A. caeruleum* (or *azureum*). Don't forget the most famil-iar of all, common chives (*A. schoenoprasum*, with lilac springtime blooms) and garlic chives (*A. tuberosum*, bearing white flowers in summer). The latter is a prodigious self-sower, but oh how the pollinators go mad for it in late summer, so I have afforded it two big patches in full sun for us all to enjoy. There is even one to grow for its foliage alone, *A. karataviense*, with large, low blue foliage topped with pale mauve puffs.

Maybe your taste runs to the bizarre? *Allium* 'Hair' is at your service, a mutation of the common drumstick allium, *A. sphaerocephalon*, and somewhere between undersea and outer space in appearance. Maybe it should be called 'The Hairy Eyeball'?

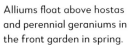

Alliums float above hostas and perennial geraniums in the front garden in spring.

For those who prefer blue to purple, there is *Allium caeruleum*.

Even garlic chives have their place, and are a popular destination for a wide range of insects in summer.

Winner of the prize for oddest ornamental onion, *Allium* 'Hair' is a mutation of the common drumstick allium and a June bloomer in my garden.

Fumitories and Aroids, Oh My

I am no systematic botanist, but I am intrigued by the relationships between plants, a curiosity that is sometimes a theme for purchases. I find one thing I like and then want to know what it's related to, and I try that. It started with what are called fumitories—the bleeding heart (*Dicentra*, now *Lamprocapnos*) and its cousins in the genera *Corydalis* and *Adlumia*. Taxonomically, they are part of the poppy family.

The name fumitory derives from the words for "smoke of the earth," and their foliage does have a grayish blue or yellowish bronze cast, like smoke, in some cases. It also looks like they might melt in your hand, like a puff of smoke, but they stay around—though sometimes as seedlings emerging at a distance from where you sited the parent.

My garden came with few assets: three ancient common lilacs, a somewhat dubiously valuable evergreen rhododendron about 15 feet high and wide, and several giant clumps of common bleeding heart (*Lamprocapnos spectabilis*, formerly *Dicentra*), with its bright pink flowers (or a white one, 'Alba'). I like to cut its arching flower stalks for springtime arrangements, and every year find myself in renewed disbelief that such an intricate, cunning flower form could possibly have evolved. My favorite is the gold-leaf form 'Gold Heart'. Though not native, bleeding heart is the first thing the male ruby-throated hummingbirds sample when they arrive back from their long journey south. The only drawback, particularly in hotter zones or dry seasons, is that bleeding heart is ephemeral.

A smaller cousin, the Appalachian native fringed bleeding heart, or *Dicentra eximia*, keeps at it at least intermittently all season, blooming from May through frost. It is inclined to sow itself around a flower garden in an inoffensive manner. The native Dutchman's breeches, *D. cucullaria*, is a true ephemeral for me, going through its whole life cycle in short order and disappearing underground about summer, until next year.

The first *Corydalis* I grew was *C. lutea*, with yellow flowers mid-spring through fall and beautiful, ferny foliage. It sows itself even into rock-wall crevices but is easy to pull. I did badly with the electric-blue flowered *C. flexuosa*, but lavender-colored *C. solida* is here and there around the place still. A climbing bleeding heart (*Dactylicapnos scandens*, formerly *Dicentra scandens*), is another possibility for our list of fumitories but not unless you are Zone 7 or warmer, with delicate foliage and yellow flowers. I go instead with old-fashioned *Adlumia fungosa*, a climbing cousin and a Northeast native with pinkish white flowers that climbs over shrubs and all the way up some old lilacs.

My collections of oddball relatives doesn't end with the fumitories. Apparently I have a thing for aroids, too—plants whose exotic-looking inflorescences combine a spathe and spadix. I stash pots of two voodoo lilies in the cellar in winter, though at Zone 6A-hardy they might just make it here outdoors in this changing world. They are *Typhonium venosum* (also *Sauromatum venosum*), originally from Southern India, and *Amorphophallus konjac* (East Asian). The latter have not reached flowering age, but like the former they will be otherworldly (and smell like rotting meat—the better to attract pollinator flies, thank you).

Doing a fast mental lap around the garden, I realize there are more aroids: the native Jack-in-the-pulpit (*Arisaema triphyllum*); various tender elephant ears I stash for winter (*Colocasia* and *Alocasia*); and (I learned with some research) a tiny water plant floating in my garden

Why grow a plain old green-leaf bleeding heart when you can have the gold-leaf one called 'Gold Heart'?

Corydalis lutea, a cousin to bleeding heart, sows itself around in the nicest way.

Chloranthus japonicus is a choice Asian woodlander.

pools, duckweed, or *Lemna*. Beyond the garden, there is native skunk cabbage (*Symplocarpos*) blooming in the moist places nearby in earliest spring.

You might have an aroid collection: tender bulblike caladiums and calla lilies (*Zantedeschia*), or houseplants like *Monstera* and *Philodendron* and pothos (*Epipremnum*).

No surprise if many of us are connoisseurs of the Berberidaceae or barberry family. *Epimedium*, from Asia, is related to the shrub *Berberis thunbergii* that has been cast out of most places for its invasive tendency, and so are *Caulophyllum thalictroides* (blue cohosh) and *Podophyllum peltatum* (the mayapple), two graceful eastern native woodland plants.

One could march about connecting the dots among all the many daisy or aster relatives in the garden, from lettuce to goldenrod and sunflowers, but this slightly esoteric version is more fun. Start an adventure at www.theplantlist.org/browse, and find the way to a hot-linked list of families and go from there. You may learn that you are already a sophisticated collector after all—or that some of your prized accessions are like only children, as I learned about the Asian shade plant *Chloranthus japonicus*, with no close relatives in the garden at all.

Euphorbias

Probably the most familiar *Euphorbia* of all is the poinsettia, *E. pulcherrima*, but it is many zones too tender (and also many shades too loud). In dismissing it, however, I do not wish to imply that I am not a fan of the sun-loving, animal-resistant perennials called *Euphorbia*, also known as spurges, because if there is one genus I wish had more Zone 5–hardy members, this is it. I rely on the toughest of the lot.

One of the most reliably cheery plants of early spring is the familiar, widely available *Euphorbia polychroma*, with its startling gold bracts brighter than a male goldfinch in mating season. I cut the plants back in late winter or earliest spring so they develop into even mounds of color, and again when they start to look past their prime a few weeks after flowering. An even showier form, *E. p.* 'Bonfire', has foliage of a dramatic, contrasting reddish and purple.

My *Euphorbia*-growing career started with *Euphorbia myrsinites*, the donkeytail spurge, a succulentlike blue-green perennial I've let seed into the cracks and crevices for decades. *Euphorbia myrsinites* doesn't look anything like *E. polychroma*, or the rest of the lot that I can grow, but rather it is sculptural with sprawling, snaky, spiked stems more like a sedum or cactus.

I still have random seedlings here and there—which come true to form—of another beautiful purple-leaved euphorbia, *Euphorbia dulcis* 'Chameleon', that I used to grow but apparently let get lost in the tangle of the bed it used to star in.

Perhaps my most cherished euphorbia has red-tinged leaves and startling orange bracts, and is one they said I couldn't grow for reasons of hardiness. I tried anyhow with *Euphorbia griffithii* 'Dixter', a foot and a half tall, and for well more than a decade, it has been perfectly happy showing off despite my winter temperatures. With more familiar chartreuse-yellow coloration is *E. palustris*, a shrubby 2-footer and a close competitor for favorite honors. Were I in Zone 7 (or even 6), I'd crave tall, handsome *E. characias* subsp. *wulfenii*, but no.

The euphorbia I like the best displays orange and reddish tones, called *Euphorbia griffithii* 'Dixter' after the famed English garden.

One important caution about euphorbias: They all contain a latex sap that can cause severe skin irritation for some individuals. Wear gloves when working around these plants and most of all, keep your hands out of your eyes.

Ferns

Thoreau wrote that, "God made ferns to show what he could do with leaves," and I think we should make gardens of them to show the same. These ancient plants, dating back several hundred million years, evolved into a moist world where there were not yet flowers or seeds. Instead of blooming, perhaps relying on animal pollinators and then setting a crop of seed, they reproduce from spores, dustlike material that contains their living germplasm. The spores gather into what are called sori, which may resemble brown dot candy orderly arranged on the undersides of fronds or broad brushstrokes of cinnamon-colored velvet, the way the nonhardy

Ferns such as *Dryopteris erythrosora* (top, the autumn fern) and *Athyrium niponicum* 'Pictum' (Japanese painted fern) seem to make flowers superfluous.

staghorn fern has, or even entire separate fertile fronds like the ostrich fern (whose emerging croziers, or fiddleheads, are edible).

In our worthy commitment to add "pollinator plants" to our landscapes to sustain insects under pressure, we shouldn't overlook the roles ferns play in providing cover for birds, mammals, and other creatures. Besides the habitat they create, ferns support unexpected interactions, such as when hummingbirds collect the fuzz of cinnamon fern to line their nests. Ferns often come in as early colonizers to heal a tough spot—even in the extreme example of the lava fields of Hawaii after a volcanic eruption. No condition in your garden could be that challenging, but ferns are resilient.

As garden plants, they are also naturally deer-resistant, in most cases adapted to shady gardens, basically pest- and disease-free, and require neither staking nor deadheading. What more can you ask?

It is hard to choose from the astonishing assortment, each with its own character. The native ostrich fern (*Matteuccia struthiopteris*) is a lusty spreader of about 3 feet that must be given its own area, but is unequaled in creating a sense of romance (and of the primeval).

The Japanese painted fern, *Athyrium niponicum* 'Pictum', is a flashy standout—who needs flowers when you look like this? When I shopped for them at the nursery years ago I grabbed all the pots of plants with maximum purple in their foliage, since when grown from spores this is a variable variety. Now there are named ones like 'Ursula's Red' if your taste runs like mine, to more purple than gray or green.

The autumn fern (*Dryopteris erythrosora*), another Asian species, has striking pink-bronze new growth in spring, and some autumn color, too (to 2 feet or just a bit taller). An eastern North American cousin, the Goldie's wood fern (*Dryopteris goldiana*), is a real standout, a specimen plant that can reach at least 4 feet high and several feet wide.

And there are even evergreens, such as native Christmas fern (*Polystichum acrostichoides*). Lately I have adopted a relative from Asia, *P. polyblepharum*, a so-called holly fern whose species name—or specific epithet—means "many eyelashes" because of the bristles on its stipe and rachis (the stalk from above the roots to below where the foliage begins, and the main stalk that bears the foliage, respectively). I did not buy it because it batted its eyelashes, but because its foliage (pinnae) were so lustrous. Next I am off to find *P. makinoi*, with likewise lustrous foliage and vase-shaped habit, to about 2 feet wide and high.

Peonies

When all seems hopeless, I think of the peonies that grew in the narrow space between the flagstone walk and the stucco-and-brick wall at the home of my youth. No matter that there was hardly room for anything, or that they'd been there probably 30 years. Every year at my birthday they bloomed like mad. "Onward," they seemed to say. "Keep at it." If they could thrive between a rock and a hard place, I figure I, too, can go on.

HERBACEOUS PEONIES

The typical herbaceous peonies, *Paeonia lactiflora*, are best planted or moved in fall, when nurseries sell clumps by mail. If you don't yet have a coral-colored one like 'Coral Charm', I recommend an investment. Though these are really durable creatures, the gardener must do a few things right to insure bloom. Here's a diagnostic checklist in case your plants are not blooming well:

Light Has a nearby tree or shrub grown and reduced the light, prompting a gradual decline? Nearby trees can also pose another challenge: Extensive root systems can outcompete peonies and reduce bloom. Peonies ideally want six hours of full sun a day (you can skimp in the Southern part of their range, Zone 8).

Nutrients Overfeeding of nitrogen can result in bountiful foliage and no blooms. It's best to apply a side dressing of compost yearly, and perhaps a balanced, all-natural organic fertilizer like a rose formula.

Foliage The untimely removal of foliage (too soon, before it can nourish the roots below by "ripening" intact) will reduce or eliminate bloom. Cultivate healthy foliage all season long, and then cut back after frost.

Planting depth With the big herbaceous peonies there is also the "too deep" thing–they really do know if the growing points, or eyes, are buried more than about 2 inches. Though the roots will work to right themselves gradually, too-deep planting can delay bloom (or prevent it if you go deep to the extreme).

Excess soil moisture Damp, poorly drained spots will be havoc for peonies. Why waste such a wonderful plant there?

Recent upheaval Recently acquired or transplanted peonies can sulk for a year or more, especially when moved in fall. Though that's an ideal time, it can also distract from their otherwise primary bud-production task then.

I grow herbaceous peonies in a big bed for cutting, though not in the borders. I like the coral ones best.

Diseases and weather Cold, wet spring weather can trouble buds, and some may be lost to fungal outbreaks, or frost. Other reasons buds will "blast" (fail to fully develop, often blackening first and drying up) can include the stress of dry conditions. Always clean up well around peonies if there are fungal issues, and destroy (do not compost) affected plant parts.

UNASSUMING WOODLAND PEONIES

I love the blowsy, fragrant herbaceous peonies, but they don't really match my garden, which is more woodsy shrubberies with mixed ground covers beneath than formal flower borders. I grow most of my extravagant-looking types in an out-of-the-way row specifically for cutting use. What I love in the garden (but not the vase) are smaller, more unassuming species (non-hybrid) peonies.

I have the white-flowered form of Japanese woodland peony, *Paeonia obovata*, tucked in a semishady spot or two (there is also a pink version to be had). But my favorite is *Paeonia mlokosewitschii*, more easily referred to as Molly the Witch. It gets to maybe 2 feet tall, and what I love most—yes, even more than the flowers—is how from its first hint upon emerging, its foliage is tinged with a little (or a lot) of purple-red. Molly's blooms are a beautiful pale yellow, and like those of *obovata* are single and cuplike. As if their unassuming grace were not enough, each of these produces insane red-to-blue seeds in star-shaped seedpods, another treat for giving them a spot among the ferns and hostas, and the time to grow up to reproductive age.

The woodland peony called Molly the Witch, *Paeonia mlokosewitschii*, is a little treasure in the semishade.

TREE PEONIES

Apparently I am the kind of person people give tree peonies to, because over the years I have been gifted four by different people. Call me the accidental tree-peony gardener. And then (on expert advice) I bought myself my favorite so far, *Paeonia ostii*, a fast-to-shape-up Chinese native whose profuse big white flowers have pink centers. This selection seems to ask for nothing but a spot in the sun, and every part of the plant is beautiful, from the fine-textured leaves to the flower buds (all with delicate hints of red).

Tree peonies—more shrubs than trees—are deer-resistant, extremely cold-tolerant, long-lived, and really don't require complicated pruning. Simply trim the stem tips down to an expanding bud in earliest spring. If a shrub grows leggy, I might remove some stems at the base to gradually rejuvenate it to fuller form as with another woody shrub.

Most tree peonies are propagated by grafting onto the roots of a herbaceous peony, so sometimes those shoots might grow up, too. Break them off by gently pulling the herbaceous shoot just below the soil level to separate it from the root system.

One of my gifted plants, with yellow flowers, is actually a cross between herbaceous and tree peonies, a so-called intersectional or Itoh hybrid (after the Japanese man who did the first such cross). Displaying aspects of each parent, it gets shrubby but then dies to the ground in winter, the oddball of my gifted plants.

If you treated actual tree peonies like you would the herbaceous ones (or the Itoh), cutting them to the ground during cleanup, you would never get flowers, because they flower on old wood. Another difference: Tree-peony blossoms are more delicate, so if your spring warms up fast, site them where they get morning and late-afternoon sun, but shade in the hottest hours.

Paeonia ostii is an outstanding Chinese species tree peony whose brilliant white flowers have flashy pink centers.

A lush yellow flower from one of the Itoh intersectional peonies, which combine traits of herbaceous and woody tree types.

(top) A toad has chosen a discarded broken flowerpot set down inside a window well as a temporary home.

(bottom) A detail of *Lonicera sempervirens* vine in bloom, a hummingbird favorite.

(opposite) I have added 10 crabapple trees to the garden to keep the five-century-plus-old apples company.

A Moment for Lilacs

Being Northern-raised, it is hard not to have a soft spot for lilacs, with those voluptuous flowers and that scent. At the start I made room for many, but as they have in some cases outgrown their spaces I find that I have likewise outgrown lilacs a bit. Now I treasure the special moment of a select few of 2,000-plus named lilac cultivars, but generally do not give them prime positions, since I have no delusions that these are multiseason plants or of much wildlife value—the two traits I have come to collect plants for more than in my earliest shopping adventures. In muggy summers they will often get powdery mildew, which is not damaging but not pretty, either.

Fussy as I have become, I am very glad each year to have allowed 'Mt. Baker' a permanent spot. It is a *Syringa hyacinthiflora* cultivar, blooming a week or more ahead of the common lilacs (*Syringa vulgaris*), and this one is like a low-hanging cloud of white, shrubby and wider than tall (maybe 8 by 10 feet). I spared a few others, including my favorite deep violet, the *S. vulgaris* called 'Agincourt Beauty', and a pink one called 'Marie Frances', both of which get to 15 by 10 feet.

These lilacs, like other spring-blooming shrubs and trees, produce flowers on last year's wood; dormant flower buds are produced late summer through fall and carried over winter. Pruning after about July 4 here (or in winter or early spring) reduces next year's bloom.

Once established, regular pruning amounts mostly to nothing more than cutting off bundles of flowers every year. How nice when a chore yields a side benefit like bouquets. Before putting the stems in water, I strip off most of the leaves and also split the stem ends vertically with a pruner or knife, or hammer them on a stone or other hard surface outdoors to split them. Whatever you do they won't last long as cuts, but what a happy couple of days.

With a telescoping long-reach pole pruner, I deadhead any faded ones left behind. Sometimes certain branches are extra vigorous and make for a lopsided plant, and these can be tipped back to rebalance things. Regular removal of suckers jutting up from the base is an ongoing task, unless they figure into future architecture.

An aged, out-of-shape lilac is usually rejuvenated over a few years with a portion of its oldest or worst positioned stems cut to the ground each summer. That task will bring the flowers down to nose height, and make for a bushy plant, which all the experts talk about, but sometimes I think that's missing the point. Apparently they have never lain upstairs in bed while their century-old common lilac bloomed right at mattress height by the window. An ancient lilac, with gnarled, twisted trunks, can be a real treasure, but will need to be cleaned out regularly in the center and deadheaded religiously.

A violet-purple common lilac, 'Agincourt Beauty', is underplanted with gold cutleaf staghorn sumac Tiger Eyes, which is just unfurling.

Making Mosaics (Underplanting)

It is easier to bring home several flats of some extra-sturdy ground-covering perennial, plug it in under trees and shrubs, and check that bed off the list. *Done!* In fact, in the outermost beds, to serve as living mulch and reduce weeding chores under big groups of woody plants, that's what I did with *Geranium macrorrhizum* and some other strong but not invasive souls.

Near the house, where I come and go—as do visitors—that would be boring, no fun at all for a *she's-gotta-have-it* gardener. In high-profile areas, I make mosaics, not masses—layered, intermingling compositions aimed at visual interest over the longest possible season. They are a bit more work to tend than sheets of the stalwart geranium, but worth it. Here's how to do it:

No ring-around-the-rosie, thanks anyway Rather than circling the dripline of trees or shrubs (or a group of trees and shrubs) with ground covers and bulbs and such, you have to get all the way in there, even nearly right up against the trunk, to make it look unman-made, as if it just happened.

No polka dots (except at first) It's all about learning to "think mosaic," which doesn't mean polka dots of onesies, but sweeps and drifts and deliberate repetition of said sweeps and drifts. At first, though, no matter how many plants you buy or what you feed them, the new underplanting will look like polka dots. Which leads to the next lesson:

Patience is required This gardening nonsense is all about patience—frankly I think it's a patience-building practice more than anything else. Your bed will look better next year, and almost great three years after planting. After the fourth, you can start harvesting divisions to repeat your success elsewhere.

Notice I say "divisions," as in small pieces of plants When working in the root zone of trees and even established shrubs, I work with a small trowel or a hori-hori, and plant very small things. I use divisions made from older plants, or order "liners" from my local nursery (the baby plants they get wholesale in late winter, then normally pot up and grow on to sell). I ask them to order me a tray of liners and mark it up accordingly—but to skip the repotting and growing on. No digging with a shovel (or tiller, heaven forbid) in root zones. Again, patience is required, and a gentle hand, too.

Select a palette that relies on several key plants, with another (or a couple) as punctuation—little gems to pop up from the carpet. Buy or divide so you have lots of each mainstay to get started. The late-spring-to-fall palette under my oldest magnolia is glossy European ginger (*Asarum europaeum*), *Hakonechloa macra* 'All Gold', a very choice Japanese painted fern, and turquoise and gold *Hosta* 'June'. An all-native idea: At the must-visit native plant research facility and garden in Delaware called Mt. Cuba Center, creeping phlox (*Phlox stolonifera*), maidenhair fern (*Adiantum* spp.) foamflower (*Tiarella cordifolia*), and Pennsylvania sedge (*Carex pensylvanica*) intermingle as a long-lasting and winning combination.

Include ephemerals, whether early spring bulbs or perennials, that rise and take advantage of the sunshine before the canopy leafs out, then vanish underground or at least don't take up much space. Winter aconites, trilliums, Dutchman's breeches, bloodroot, twinleaf, Virginia bluebells—the list goes on. I get about six extra-early weeks of color from my underplantings, before my mainstay plants fill in, by using ephemerals lavishly.

Don't just ring a shrub or tree with herbaceous plants around its dripline; get all the way in, as with this old *Corylopsis spicata* underplanted with hellebores, *Corydalis lutea*, and ephemerals.

Even without flowers, mosaics of a few choice foliage plants like *Hosta* 'June', European ginger, *Hakonechloa*, and Japanese painted fern offer many months of enjoyment.

Epimedium spp. are indispensable for making mosaics, providing multiple seasons of beauty but requiring just one shearing in late winter.

In April, *Primula kisoana* and *Hylomecon japonicum* do their thing as the ferns, grass, and hostas are still emerging.

Real gems like *Lilium martagon* 'Claude Shride' can add an extra moment to a mixed ground cover planting.

A detail of *Primula kisoana*.

Include some "ground cover" types, meaning plants that form thick mats (but not English ivy or pachysandra or vinca). For this part of the plan, I am partial to epimediums, European ginger, *Hakonechloa*, and hellebores.

Make space for some real gems These might include species peonies, choice hostas (I love gold ones for this purpose), or even bulbs—like an effusion of martagon lilies such as red-flowered 'Claude Shride'. What about an unexpected outburst from the bawdiest of primroses, *Primula kisoana*, with orchid-pink flowers and lovely scalloped, fuzzy foliage?

Spring is not all pastels if you add deciduous azaleas in fiery flower colors.

Even the border of the vegetable garden is a mosaic of sorts: various fine-textured ground cover sedums consort with bold rhubarb and horseradish foliage.

When choosing plants, remember that leaves are your best friend Plan on a mix of textures and colors, coming mostly from foliage (as the leaves will be there all season or even all year, the flowers just briefly). Think of the color range of heucheras alone you could employ, or hostas—foliage is hardly boring. Which relates to this lesson:

Texture is also a great ally. Work it I cannot imagine "mosaics" working without some linear things (grasses, or sedges), contrasted against some ferny things (like, well, ferns, or *Aruncus aethusifolius*), and against some larger-textured things (like bigger hostas, *Astilboides tabularis*, or the Northwest native *Darmera peltata*—which also offers extra-early pink flowers on naked stems). Speaking of large *and* textured: the *Astilboides* cousins in the genus *Rodgersia* are among my most prized shade ground covers.

Once you've selected a palette, repeat, repeat, repeat Not just in the first area you underplant, but (if it works) in another area, where it may be all mulch right now, or a sea of a single ground cover. Soon your first mosaic will fill in and afford you divisions, and you will move on to making the next beautiful carpet.

Confidence Builders, Rethought

Every gardener deserves a boost in confidence when new to horticulture. Inspired by this, many years ago I recommended a list of Certified Confidence Builders as starter plants. They were the ones that had given me early encouragement, a mismatched lot with vigor their only common trait. They delivered the positive reinforcement required to stick at a "hobby" as demanding as this. Things would have likely taken a different turn had I begun with delphiniums and alpines.

There pretty quickly proved a caveat: You will spend the advanced-beginner phase of your gardening lifetime digging these plants out. With some, that means they are invasive thugs and need to be struck from not just the bed you put them in, but also from the list of things for sale anywhere ever (though most remain in catalogs and on nursery racks). With others, they are just lusty enough to provide a good lesson in the vigilant management of mixed plantings—or why some otherwise worthy choices (like mint) are best grown alone, or in containers.

Impressively, bee balm (*Monarda*), a mint family member, still tops my Certified Confidence Builder list, adapting to sun or half-shade and growing about a mile—sideways—a year. It does what its name implies and draws the bees, and also hummingbirds. It had a prominent place, blooming for weeks in July, until it just crept into everything else and also got powdery mildew, not great in a conspicuous spot. Now I recommend those needing confidence (or one of the best pollinator plants) first do homework on which bee balms have a little more restraint and a little less mildew, and site them carefully. Chicago Botanic Garden in Illinois and Mt. Cuba Center in Delaware have each published research on mildew-resistant *Monarda* that can be found online, for example.

Some of the ground cover sedums (like *Sedum spurium*, or *S. kamschaticum*, and sunny *S. rupestre* 'Angelina') make me feel like I have a green thumb, but are easy to dispatch when the time comes. In contrast, a couple of *Lysimachia* spp. that cheered me onward at the start will be with me till I die and beyond: the gooseneck loosestrife (*L. clethroides*) and the widespread U.S. native fringed loosestrife (*L. ciliata*; I have the purple-leaved form called 'Purpurea' or 'Firecracker'). Neither is related to the dreaded pest of wetlands called purple loosestrife (genus *Lythrum*).

Today I think it safer to get your boost from a literal Jack-in-the-beanstalk plant like pole beans, including 'Scarlet Runner', another hummingbird favorite and edible both as tender pods and later as dried beans. As I look out the window, I am reminded of many more shot-in-the-arm types: innocent-looking little nursery pots of *Ajuga*, or bugleweed, that I brought home, and bigger ones of the giant of ground covers, *Petasites hybridus*. I am still digging bugleweed out of the lawn decades later, but I do like its defiant blue flower wands. Fuki, as *Petasites* is called in Japan, has umbrella-size, tropical-looking leaves and spreads like crazy, particularly in moist and partly shaded areas. When I was a beginning gardener, I was proud of its performance, and even now I'd be sorry to live without it (and will never have to). Like any aggressive plant, it must be managed by the gardener—not allowed to wander from the space assigned. Remember who carries the shovel in the family (a hint: not the plant), and trench around your spreaders every year to keep them in their places, tossing the uprooted bits in the trash, not the compost. Better yet with the lustiest, like fuki: Don't get started. It is one plant I will never share with anyone, knowing now its formidable energy.

A confidence booster from the early days that I never share now because of its thugishness is *Petasites hybridus*, seen barely halfway emerged in spring.

Rosa glauca, formerly *R. rubrifolia*, is a must-have rose for its red-tinged blue leaves.

A Must-Have Rose

Roses are notably scarce here, but there is one I actually have in multiple. It's *Rosa glauca*, the blue-leaved rose, and that's why I grow it: for its beautiful foliage.

I first came to know *Rosa glauca* by its former name, *Rosa rubrifolia*, meaning red-leaved, because they're tinged with red, as are the stems. Whatever the name, it has arching canes that may get to about 6 or 8 feet tall, forming a roughly vase-shaped shrub, and is hardy to a brutal Zone 2 (where I never wish to test it). The foliage color will be best in light shade, emphasis on light, but don't ask this (or any rose) to live in the dark or fungal problems will prevail. In early June here, a bonus of small, single, vivid pink flowers appear, followed by good-size orangey rose hips.

My oldest *Rosa glauca* is underplanted with bigroot geranium, *Geranium macrorrhizum*, whose hot-pink flowers coordinate nicely with the rose's, and with lots of *Nectaroscordum siculum*, an *Allium* cousin, whose mauve-blue-green blooms complete the picture, poking up from that. The rose's blue leaves make a distinctive addition to a mixed shrub border, especially vivid in contrast to purple-leaved plants.

Because *Rosa glauca* is a species (nonhybrid) rose, it will self-sow around after setting hips, and the babies are true to form. Not a bad thing, if you happen to want more and have patience. When my old one got out of shape, I cut back the rose to near the ground and started afresh.

I confess, occasionally I pass a planting of some nonstop-blooming modern rose series and have a pang of longing. For now, though, it's still just me and my *Rosa glauca* and an old suckering *R. rugosa* (I love its attractive orange hips), plus one super-hardy pink climber, 'William Baffin' from the Canadian Explorer series, who's been cut to the ground a time or two himself in our decades together.

Two big terra-cotta troughs become seasonal water gardens, the water shaded by duckweed and fairy moss. Fancy-leaf begonias summer in pots beside them.

Water Garden in a Pot

Mosquitoes? That's the most common question I'm asked when people see my seasonal water gardens in two ceramic troughs. "What about mosquitoes?" After that: "How often do you change the water?"

Making an "instant" seasonal water garden—one with no plumbing required—merely requires a watertight vessel, water, and some floating plants to shade the surface. I top up the water as needed during the season, but do not change it completely (nor do I in the in-ground water gardens).

For containers you can use galvanized cattle tanks or tubs; earthenware pots with glazing at least on their interior surface (like my big troughs) and no drainage hole; or some other found object. Level the pot with a carpenter's level while still empty, inserting shims beneath as needed to adjust and stabilize.

I prefer to place these temporary water gardens in a part-sun spot, rather than full sun, to reduce algae growth. The shade provided by floating plants like *Azolla* (fairy moss) or *Lemna* (duckweed) helps, too.

You can add fish, but I don't, since fish in a barrel are easy prey for cats or raccoons. The frogs add themselves at my place. Frogs (or fish) eat mosquito larvae and mosquitoes, as do dragonflies and birds, who also crave the water, so I have no mosquito issue.

One funny note: If the pot is topped up to near the rim, heavy rains will cause overflow—not just of water but also of floating plants. So don't overfill, or when downpours are forecast, cover the pot most of the way (I leave an opening in case any frogs are in residence).

In my cold-winter zone, the seasonal water gardens must be emptied and the vessels stored in a shed for winter. I happily check for tadpoles before I do the emptying, lest any inhabitants have used them as a nursery.

Organic Lawn Care

"Your lawn looks so great," visitors say, and I think, "What lawn?" They don't realize that I am actually mowing a mix of turfgrass and weeds, to which I have added loads of white clover (*Trifolium repens*) that bees love and stays green in the heat. No herbicides involved, ever, and as for fertilizer, perhaps an organic formula once every five years in the heaviest traffic areas, if that. Here's a quick review of my overall approach to managing a lawn organically:

Always use a sharp mower blade; tearing grass invites trouble. Dull blades can cause raggedy edges that invite discoloration or even provide entry for disease, and can also pull at the grass plants rather than cleanly clip them. I bet most of us rarely check, sharpen, or replace blades. Do so now, while we're talking about it.

Don't cut too low Though I lower the deck to about 3 inches for the season's final mowing, my normal height is 3.5 inches. I could probably cut at 3 inches if we have even summer moisture and it's not scorching hot, then 2.5 inches at the season's finish. The most expert organic lawn care person I know cuts his mid-Atlantic lawn at 4 inches, until the weather cools in October.

Never let grass get so long that you cut off more than one-third of the height in one cutting. If weather forces you to skip mowings, rake up and compost excess clippings rather than let them mat down. Otherwise, always let clippings lie to return nutrients to the lawn.

With fall leaves, a reasonable amount can be ground up right in place, too, especially if your mower's a mulcher, but not so it deposits shredded leaves in mats. Rake and compost heavy accumulations.

Don't feed if the "grass" is thick and green A green, vigorous lawn doesn't need fertilizer, and all you're doing is causing yourself more mowing.

If you think you need to feed next year, first do a soil test Some high-traffic or weak areas may need it, or at least a layer of compost, but probably not the entire lawn. Stop fertilizing as a reflex, no matter what marketers of lawn products say. Use only all-natural organic products when you do feed.

Never feed in winter or early spring In New York State, where I garden, it has been unlawful since 2010 to fertilize in winter, to protect fish and avoid conditions that favor algae bloom. The danger of runoff when the ground is frozen is just too great. Research guidelines for your area through your county cooperative extension. Ideally, when needed, fertilize in early fall.

Take time to look at your lawn's diversity, and "read" its weeds, then research what they are trying to tell you. For instance, certain weeds such as plantain spell "compaction"—and what's needed isn't an herbicide application, but rather soil aeration, a top-dressing of compost, and over-seeding. Moss suggests too-acid conditions, so liming is in order. Crabgrass seeds may germinate if you scalp some spots in summer, or there are otherwise bare spots where dormant seed is exposed to light. (Some weeds, such as dandelions or crabgrass, may not be showing off in every season, so don't forget those.) Know your weeds.

Make a commitment to stop using weed-and-feed products if you still are In spring, I make it a practice to dig at least a dozen dandelions a day, which I have been doing for years and years, so they have never taken over my home turf.

Clematis climbs a 'Helmond Pillar' columnar barberry and the vegetable garden fencepost.

(opposite) The garden makes its own combinations as foliage and flowers from *Chionanthus* drip onto hostas, with a self-sown *Nectaroscordum* for good measure.

Mulch Wisdom

"Plants are the mulch," landscape architect Claudia West reminds us lately, her message both aesthetic and environmental—and I discuss such ground covers elsewhere in the book.

The kind you shovel on, or dump from a wheelbarrow then spread, isn't meant as décor, and that's the unsaid part of what Claudia implies: We aren't going about the hard work of gardening to show off big swaths of mulch, but rather well-grown plants.

However, the right mulch material used well serves several purposes, and is critical in new beds where the living mulch—the plants—hasn't knitted together yet. In established beds, the kind of mulch I use also serves as a sort of passive soil-amending regimen (more on that below). I credit another great woman of gardening, from another era, for instilling my faith in mulch.

"God invented mulching," wrote Ruth Stout, who followed her 1955 book *How to Have a Green Thumb Without an Aching Back: A New Method of Mulch Gardening* with the equally offbeat early-'60s classic *Gardening Without Work*. She promised freedom from weeds and optimum soil health to gardeners who piled on 8 inches of hay mulch, and not a blade less. (Stout's ideas were re-packaged in 1971 as *Ruth Stout's No-Work Garden Book*, and some version has been variously repackaged since.) Long before phrases like "lasagna garden" were making the rounds of the as-yet uninvented internet, Stout (sometimes gardening in the buff) was layering all her organic materials on top of the soil—sheet composting, as it might be traditionally called, more the stuff of homesteaders than backyard types. Her tactic served to suppress weeds, reduce fertilizer use, conserve moisture, and spare her the work of composting in a conventional heap with all the toting and turning.

Her foundational principle was applying mulch, mulch, and more mulch, and then simply moving it back a smidge each year to make room for each row of seeds. No till, no weeds. She said the "aha" moment came one spring when the plowman hadn't come yet to till, and she was eager to get planting. She saw that the asparagus (a long-lived perennial) was already up, poking through the fallen leaves, so she walked over to the plant and asked it why she had to plow for the other vegetables if not it. Apparently the asparagus answered that she didn't.

Mulch also keeps root zones cool; it fosters abundant soil life from microbes to earthworms, and it improves soil texture as the mulch breaks down. Raindrops, not just footsteps, can compact soil, which mulch can buffer, and it can help prevent the crusting over of bare soil that causes moisture to run off.

Using the wrong kind of mulch, or the right one at the wrong time, can defeat the purpose. If I mulched too early, I might smother would-be volunteers, or self-sowns. Mulching too thickly, especially around tree trunks and shrubs (often called "volcano mulching") is bad for trees; bark wasn't evolved to live in the dark and damp. Never put mulch right up against the trunks of woody plants.

What makes good mulch? This can be confusing, since what's sold as "mulch" in many cases isn't suitable for the full range of duties. I seek a material that is:

* **an organic substance** (meaning deriving from some living or formerly living matter)
* **fine- to medium-textured** so it will break down into the underlying soil
* **but substantial enough to stay put**

A pair of red Wave Hill chairs gets moved around as needed to brighten spots in the garden.

* **preferably aged** before I use it
* **dark in color**, like soil is (if for the ornamental beds)
* **available locally at a good price**, preferably in bulk delivery unbagged
* **not a source of contaminants, pests, or diseases**

In ornamental beds I use fine- to medium-textured, dark-colored mulch, never anything that's going to sit there without breaking down, like big bark hunks (which I call "baked potato mulch" because they are as big as spuds), or anything orange or black or otherwise dyed. Also avoid very fine-textured materials like sawdust that cake, blow around, and fail to decompose.

Using a product that has been aged or composted means the mulch is ready to do its job as a soil-improver. I can dig with my hands in all my beds where I have let this passive composting, in effect, happen by topping up the mulch over the years. So could Stout.

Years ago I used bagged mulches, but switched to local materials delivered in bulk, sans plastic bags (and minus the fuel used to truck it to my local garden center). My preferred mulch is a composted stable bedding—a local agricultural by-product from horse or dairy farms. It's wood shavings (not too fine, not too coarse) that farmers spread on the floors of animal stalls to absorb manure and urine, and then muck out, age at a high enough temperature to destroy pathogens, and recycle into mulch.

Leaf mold (partially rotted, shredded leaves) would also be great, if your local landfill offers it, or start a leaves-only compost heap, pre-chopping with a shredder or mulching mower. I use all my homemade leaf compost on vegetables. In rough areas along the roadside or the paths between the raised beds, I use wood chips the power company or local arborist may share from a fallen tree, or the occasional bag of nugget-size bark chips.

Sometimes when prepping a new area, or rehabbing one that's weedy, an organic mulch alone may not suffice to keep troubles at bay until the desired plants fill in. An underlayment of thick layers of black and white newsprint or a sheet of brown corrugated cardboard may add the extra oomph.

Growing Potatoes

An organic potato farmer moved to my little town not long ago, and I count him and his family as friends—meaning I can just buy a few bagsful to eat, though I'm not a restaurant or other wholesale customer. What I miss out on is the annual treasure hunt of wriggling my hand in from the side of the straw-and-soil hills I'd gradually formed on each of my own homegrown rows, looking for those first new potatoes—a prize equal to the first ripe tomato.

Potato planting preparations really start in the fall, since with any early sown crop I want the soil ready. During October cleanup, I top up my raised beds with compost, enriching the loose, deep soil that is ideal for potatoes. They will adapt to other soil types, but the more organic matter the better. If you use manure, make sure it's very well-rotted and aged or you invite the bacterial disease called scab—that pitting or raised corky surface patches on the potatoes that don't render the harvest inedible but aren't very inviting.

What often arrives in the bag of organic "seed potatoes" is a range of sizes. Many gardeners cut up the large ones into pieces that each have at least two "eyes," letting the pieces sit overnight in a *humid* place to callous before planting. I never bother to cut up my potatoes, which probably lowers the yield a bit but may afford some protection from soil pests including wire worms, which like the open flesh.

No earlier than 2 to 3 weeks before my average last frost date, once the soil has begun to warm and drain, I dig a shallow trench about 6 to 8 inches deep with a hoe, and space the seed potatoes 10 to 12 inches apart in the trench—a little farther with the large starts I didn't cut up, a little closer for fingerlings. I make one trench down the middle of my raised bed, but if you are doing multiple parallel rows in the ground, leave at least 3 feet between them, or more for easy access during hilling and harvest.

I cover the tubers with about 3 to 4 inches of soil, so they are still in a shallow trench, then once the plants are up about 8 to 10 inches high, it's time to do the first hilling. Carefully bring the soil up around the vines from both sides with a rake or hoe until just the top leaves are above soil level. A couple of weeks later, I hill again, bringing another several inches of soil up around the vines. Though the second hilling could be a straw mulch instead, I think I get the best results with two soil hillings, followed by straw or rotted leaf mulch.

Assuming you chose a variety that is good immature, like one of the waxier-fleshed varieties, new potatoes should be formed several weeks after the plants flower. The signal that the main harvest is near is later, when the vines start to fade. Don't worry if they are in the ground through a couple of light frosts, but not hard freezes.

A few years ago I actually figured out the "right" storage spot at my house, and finally had my own potatoes right into spring. A closet in my mudroom was as close as I could come to their desired high humidity combined with dark and cold (ideally 40°F, but ranging from 38 to 45°F). First I cured them in a just slightly warmer place, in baskets or trays—unwashed, just as they come from the ground with heavy soil clods brushed gently off—in a dark spot that was counterintuitively humid (like 90 percent) and between 50 and 60°F. I got resourceful here, and turned off the dehumidifer in my very primitive Victorian-era basement. This treatment lasts for 2 weeks, and then they go colder for storage.

Room has opened up when the peas came out alongside a row of potatoes that are already hilled up with soil and then with straw.

Adulthood

JULY & AUGUST

THROWING IN THE TROWEL

I GIVE UP. Enough is enough. I've had it.

These are the kinds of phrases, tired but true, on my mind by sundown each of these days, when latest spring has slipped into the reality of summer, after eight or ten hours spent trying to solve the puzzle I started in the dirt some years ago.

Where do all the plants go to make a pretty garden? I wonder, close to tears, surrounded by pots and pots of this and that. At the nursery, I had been certain I had to have all of them, but now, in their company, I am feeling kind of lost.

What goes next to what? How many of these with how many of those will make the picture perfect? And why did I put that there—what was I thinking? Oh, why didn't I draw a plan, the way I tell others to do, and then stick to it?

If only it were a jigsaw puzzle of cut-up cardboard pieces, and there was in each plant a clue—an interlocking edge or some other clever device that fit it into place and let you know you'd got it right. But that is not how it is, as anyone who has tried this business of designing even a single flower bed will certainly confirm. The purple asters look good with the purple-leaved heuchera, and the allium is good spiking up through the artemisia, but those were merely good guesses—there are plenty of bad guesses around the place, too. No wonder so much of gardening is accomplished on one's knees.

My love-hate of garden-making has been running perilously close to the dark side lately as I desperately dug and dug some more, determined to find the answer. But then came early June, and not-so-early June, and I was still out there, searching for the "right" arrangement. If I moved the smokebush one more time, or that poor, peripatetic pulmonaria, I would surely self-destruct. A weekend or two ago, I felt certain I could dig no more.

"If only I could plant everything in alphabetical rows, instead of trying to make it look good, I'd be off the hook," I whined to a friend.

"There is no hook," the wiser gardener replied, performing horticultural phone therapy. "You *created* the hook."

That sounded very clever, and quite important, so I filed the remark carefully in my head. I wish he had told me where to put the damn Dutchman's breeches, or the buckeye tree still sitting in a pot, but he did not. His garden is a showplace; he must know what he's talking about, I figured.

But I did not really understand his words until the following weekend, back in the dirt. I found myself feeling stressed and panicky, starting 10 tasks and finishing none, fixating on all the holes in the puzzle all over again. Then I was overcome by a wild, freeing thought: how liberating it would be to borrow the neighbor's tractor and mow the whole place to stubble. If there had been a helpline for suicidal gardeners, I would have called it. Oh, if only for a 12-Step meeting of Gardeners Anonymous.

Yes, the hook is my doing, and I had hung myself on it, by my nasty habit of only seeing the problems, the weak spots, the areas in need of more tinkering. Perfectionism and the task of starting a garden do not mix, I learned just at that moment. My half-empty mentality gave

A frog is flocked with duckweed and surrounded by perennial parrot feather.

no gold stars for what had been accomplished, only demerits for what had not. Something would have to change.

If I created the hook, then it is my prerogative to unhook myself, yes? I am therefore declaring this Throw In the Trowel Week, a horticultural holiday I heartily recommend that any other gardened-out souls adopt in their localities, too.

Admit it: spring is not just aging; it is past. So I say enough, and quickly set about to fill in any really embarrassing bare spots with annuals, or even pumpkin vines (where my puzzle's weaknesses were on a grander scale). An even layer of mulch can work miracles in uniting plants that have far from knit together, too, and a cleanly cut edge around the bed makes things look almost bearable. After these last touches, only maintenance will be allowed till fall, when planting (hopefully without the panic) may be permitted once again.

Conveniently, it is especially good timing for such a declaration. The first official day of summer and the onset of consistently hot weather (hard on transplants and transplanters) have been marked. Time to plug in the last babies and crawl into the hammock with a glass of tea. Time to give it—the seedlings, the soil, the soul—a rest.

From this freshly liberated perspective, I think back upon my panic as if it were years in the past.

"All I seem to be doing is moving the same things around," I recall saying to the same wise friend.

"Well, then you are learning the secrets," he said, ever inscrutable.

And so I'll swing awhile and think of what I'll be able to move to where when the time comes, when the weather cools again and I am feeling refreshed, too.

Gardening is a process. Even great gardens don't start out great; they take time, and lots of reshuffling, the kind of thing we're all out there doing from early spring through right about now. *Gardening is a process.* I repeat this new mantra now as I find myself with time to take a walk or watch the birds. Or—dare I say it?—with time to simply look at what I have accomplished.

Bits and pieces of leftover garden succulents spend the summer stuffed into a strawberry jar.

The old apple trees I inherited make a 365-day statement with their massive presence.

An overgrown tangle of *Sedum*, *Agastache*, and *Nicotiana* make the front garden a spot of high appeal for pollinators and hummingbirds in August.

The back hillside, including an unmown bluestem meadow, glows in the late-summer sun.

Fall Vegetable Garden

In July and even August, after the longest day has passed, I make sowings in my northern garden of crops that will come to harvest in fall. Though summer is coming on strong, I am thinking about fall, too. Here's where the math of days-to-maturity listed on the seed packets needs a bit of adjusting, though, since those estimates are based on spring sowings, when temperatures and hours and intensity of light are strengthening, not declining.

What to do to adjust for what is often referred to as "the fall factor," counting back from the first expected frost date of fall and adding two weeks (some say closer to three) to the time that crop will be expected to reach maturity. Remember that with some crops the days to maturity are calculated from the moment seed is sown, while with others, it's from transplant time, so you have to figure in the time it takes to produce a seedling, too. It's hard to get it exact, so I err on the side of starting earlier (but not so early that I subject these generally cool-season plants to too much summer heat).

For best results, select varieties bred for or useful at the target time of year—you'll want a storage carrot, for instance, for winter use, plus a carrot for fresh fall eating. Sow a cold-tolerant lettuce latest of all (versus one whose outstanding trait is standing up to heat without bolting), or in general, shorter-day varieties of everything. Remember to plan not just for the fall table, but also for putting up—like a row of shelling peas to shuck and freeze in portion-size bags, or plenty of the ingredients in your favorite soup recipe.

Add fall-factor weeks to times noted in the following latest-sown crops, which include direct-sown seeds and also some I started earlier in cell packs:

arugula, 21 to 40 days (baby or mature leaf size)

bush beans, about 60 days (have insulating fabric ready if early cold threatens)

beets, for roots and beet greens, about 50 days

braising greens mix (mustard, kale, collards, Asian greens, etc.)

broccoli rabe, about 40 days

broccoli, 60 days from transplants started about 15 weeks before first frost

cabbage, 60 days from transplants started about 15 weeks before first frost, or napa cabbage (about 10 days faster)

carrots, a storage kind, plus some smaller types for fall eating

cauliflower, 60 days from transplants started about 14 weeks before frost

chard, about 55 days

chicory, leafy endive, radicchio, 45 to 60-plus days, depending on variety

cilantro, about 50 days

collards, about 60 days, but nice in half that time as a baby green

dill, 50 to 60 days

kale, about 60 days, but nice in half that time as a baby green

lettuce, leaf and head type and mesclun mix, about 21 to 30 days to first cutting

mustard greens, about 45 days, or faster as baby greens to spice a salad

peas, shelling, sugar snap, and snow pea types; plus a row or block of thickly sown peas for harvest as shoots for salad, at 3 or 4 inches tall

radish, smaller fast ones, plus larger Asian daikon (60 days)
scallions and other hardy bunching onions, for fall use and to overwinter
spinach, 25 to 30 days
squash, summer variety, fast bush type (I sow a 48-day variety July 1)
turnips, 40 to 50 days, faster for greens; also **rutabagas**

When loading up beds with fall-harvest crops, leave room for the all-important garlic, which goes in several weeks before frost is in the ground and stays till the following summer.

A Few Good Living Mulches

Cautionary tale: A Manifest Destiny approach to making beds and borders around the place can quickly lead to a spotty set of outdoor features. A grouping of shrubs here, a bed of perennials there, a tree across the way: I'd planted and planted and planted, but, frankly, what did it all add up to? It didn't flow, until ground covers helped unite elements that otherwise look like so many disconnected islands.

From a prostrate conifer like Siberian cypress (*Microbiota decussata*) or the Japanese plum yew (*Cephalotaxus harringtonia* 'Prostrata'), to ornamental grasses or sedges, a vine left to scramble, or the tiniest, ground-hugging moss: They can all be used as a ground cover, if massed, or combined into a large area with other plants of a similar scale. Generally speaking, the most successful ground cover is a low-growing plant that fills in quickly to create a continuous cover—the underplanting, or ground-level parts of a design that has various other layers above it, up to trees. I even underplant larger shrubs and small trees with lower-growing shrubs—such as prostrate golden yew (*Taxus baccata* 'Repandens Aurea'), like a colorful, textural ruff.

Ground covers act as living mulch, reducing weeding and shading soil, which offers the shrubs or trees above them a cooler, moister root run. By doing this, ground covers reduce watering requirements, compared to bare soil, and can camouflage ripening foliage of spring-time bulbs interplanted among them, prevent erosion, and camouflage harsh edges, like the corner of a porch or deck.

I prefer planting ground covers in combination, as what I refer to as mosaics, rather than monochromes, as I have mentioned. But sometimes you need the simplicity of wall-to-wall carpet—like in the various large shrub borders at the farther reaches of the landscape here, each mosaic segment maybe 750 to 1,000 square feet and containing multiple shrubs. The trick is selecting ground covers that do the "living mulch" assignment well—good cover, not a lot of maintenance—without being invasive thugs like some of the first plants I tried back in the day, when nobody warned you (or knew better).

The one I settled on as my workhorse is the bigroot geranium, *Geranium macrorrhizum*, so named because instead of a clumping habit, it grows from a ropelike rhizome that seems to barely need to touch the ground to thrive. It spreads but is easy to just pull up, and does not seed here. Its attractive weed-suppressing foliage has an aromatic, spicy scent, and is nearly evergreen even in Zone 5B. It seems to tolerate sun or shade, and even dry shade (but

Geranium macrorrhizum, low maintenance and easy to remove as needed, is a go-to workhorse ground cover under big shrub borders.

A gold-leaf prostrate English yew makes a great "skirt" for larger woody things like a kousa dogwood.

not a wet spot), requiring just an annual haircut. Shear with hedge clippers or a pruner (the former is faster for big masses), timed right after bloom. Deadheading would be another option, but shearing keeps each the expanse of plants tighter and denser. The straight species is pink-flowered but not pastel; if Pepto Bismol makes you queasy, there is the more prim, pale pink 'Ingwersen's Variety' and even white 'Album'.

Bulk-delivered mulch is not the focal point of beds, but is rather nearly obscured even in early spring by a herbaceous layer of living mulch.

In the shade under a grouping of native *Aronia melanocarpa*, *Heuchera villosa* puts on its fall show.

Epimedium is expensive to get started with, but then offers loads of divisions once established. The same can be said for *Helleborus orientalis* or *H. ×hybridus*, which make many seedlings once they get going that are good for relocating to extend the planting. Both are semievergreen, the old foliage fading before the new arrives. I use a lot of *Hakonechloa*—a graceful shade grass—too. On a semishady steep bank above the backyard, shrubs, like

Microbiota and *Cephalotaxus* and also the Northeast native low-bush blueberry (*Vaccinium angustifolium*) do the job.

In recent years, the native woodlander *Asarum canadense*, a herbaceous ginger, is one perennial I am moving into wider areas of coverage, as is sturdy *Heuchera villosa*—a southeastern native, but perfectly hardy in my zone (and offering easily transplanted seedlings). 'Autumn Bride' is a popular form, and since it blooms similarly late, I like it combined with white wood aster, *Eurybia divaricata*. They both live under *Aronia melanocarpa*, a chokeberry that's native to the East, in semishade.

Or plant ferns—loads of ferns. One of the most striking ground cover plantings I ever saw was ferns, in the woodland at ancient Powis Castle in Wales. As I came upon the glade it looked as if the ferns were in flower (which of course ferns do not do, since they predate the evolution of flowering plants, the angiosperms). It was a colony of species lilies interplanted in the mass of ferns, a memorable sight indeed.

Meadow Plants, Mowing Strategies

I'd been mowing a couple of acres regularly for years when I suddenly had one of those "aha" moments, realizing how many hours and gallons of fuel I had wasted. Allowing the grass to grow up to field height right around the house wasn't practical, but in the outer areas a change might be fun.

The hilly acre above the backyard was the first target. I had visited Madison, Wisconsin, where some forward-thinking gardeners called The Wild Ones have long timed their mowings to encourage prairie-like meadows instead of close-cropped lawns. I had also traveled to England, where selective mowing is an art form that complements the more formal beds and borders of noted gardens. The sensual texture of unmown grass against the cropped green paths cut through it invites movement through the landscape.

But what would sprout on my hillside if I stopped subduing it? The first step in deciding not to mow, or rather when to selectively mow, is an evaluation of the resident plants. At the start of claiming this place, I had fought my way through a tangle on the hillside—the remnants of former forage crops meant for a cow long gone, and every manner of thorny invasives like brambles and multiflora rose, plus Oriental bittersweet and an alien honeysuckle. In the mess, there existed a sign of hope in the form of the native bunchgrass called little bluestem (*Schizachryium scoparium*). Though there were other mostly welcome herbaceous things, from goldenrod to yarrow and sedges, the bluestem became my target species: the one I'd coddle and favor above the others, the one I'd design my mowing strategy around.

This plant would teach me many lessons, and continues to, including one about the benefits of creative mowing—or unmowing, as I think of it. The cheapest, simplest, and most effective thing we can do to increase diversity is to stop—or at least reduce—mowing. Turfgrass is dimensionless, supporting no beneficial insect life (that in turn supports birds and other wildlife, and pollinates plants). In 2015, a NASA study estimated the nation's total expanse of turf at 163,812 square kilometers—about the size of Texas, and about three times the amount

Little bluestem and native goldenrod planted themselves in the upper field, which is mowed once annually in early May.

of space allotted to any irrigated crop (corn being the most common). Can't we each find 500 or 5,000 square feet of grass to give back?

To give back that first third-acre, I began by researching how to favor my target species, which turns out to awaken later than the species I don't care for. I therefore time my mowing around the start of the second week of May, when the undesirable cool-season plants are already well up, but just before the bluestem reaches tractor-blade height, giving the bluestem (and other late plants) the edge. In a few years of once-a-season mowing, I went from having a few stray clumps of bluestem to about 30 percent coverage, and steadily to more than 60 percent. I mow one other time, as early as I can in spring before anything emerges—perhaps the first of April—to chop up the debris left behind by winter, which I compost. Then I'll mow at the moment already described. I dig out and discard periodic eruptions of *Rubus,* and edit the lustiest of the goldenrod occasionally, too, but that's it.

In return—and without planting anything—I got a meadow that probably delights me more than any bed or border I have toiled over, and what has proven the second-best attraction (after the apparently irresistible water gardens) to the widest diversity of insect, avian, and animal life. Even gray fox and bobcat wait at the edges of the longer grass to pounce on whatever vole or mouse might dare move within. In late summer through winter, the bluestem truly glows, from an initial reddish or coppery hue to a warm golden-tan. I will never be lawn-free, because unlike any other plant, mown grass is great to walk on, allowing us to move through the landscape. More outer areas here are getting unmowed each year, though.

Cutbacks

If it featured spring-blooming perennials and bulbs, the garden may have a bad case of what a friend calls "the shaggies"—unwanted frowsiness that make it look a fright. Add to that the inevitable first few blasts of 90-degree weather and you probably wonder: Is there life after spring (or heatstroke)?

Here is where a shorter haircut, a deep drink, and an adherence to the strategy of the long game help garden and gardener. Being a bit savage with deadheading, shearing, and other cutbacks and aftercare beginning in mid-June (and in smaller bursts throughout the summer) means that my garden can be open for tours in August, and in fact looks quite presentable until it is felled by late fall freezes. As I tidy up frowsy plants, I top up mulch where needed, and also give any fuzzy stretches of bed edge a crisper cut.

I've already tossed the stretched-up violas that filled the big bowl-shaped pots in April and May, and I've begun deadheading any plant whose blooms just look ratty. But starting around mid-June and into early July I need to take to some perennials not with pruning shears but hedge clippers (the way I used them to make short work of tidying big patches of *Epimedium* in early spring) or at least shop shears—bigger, sturdier versions of craft scissors, with comfortable molded plastic handles.

The plants and I will feel much better, once we get past 2 or 3 weeks of stubble growing out. I shear pulmonaria and the earliest euphorbia like *polychroma,* and various perennial geraniums hard just after bloom (including not just *Geranium macrorrhizum* but also G. *phaeum,* a good choice for shadier spots). Catmint (*Nepeta*) and any *Artemisia* that flowered or is trying to get the treatment, and if I grew perennial salvias, I'd whack them after bloom, too. A sentimental old patch of lady's mantle by the vegetable garden gate (*Alchemilla mollis*) will before long need to be shorn, plus my most rambunctious groundcover sedum.

The wood poppy, or celandine poppy (*Stylophorum diphyllum*), whose gold flowers shone in the April-May garden, will soon look peaked as its foliage fades. I simply cut each rosette at the base, and a new crop flushes—and even some occasional rebloom is coaxed from this native plant that doesn't naturally range as far east as my garden. These are just examples, by no means the only ones needing a stern hand. If a plant ends up looking wretched, cut it back (unless you plan to save seed). One thing I might deadhead but I never shear until their foliage has completely faded to tan are the spring-blooming flower bulbs. Cutting bulb foliage back too soon doesn't allow the bulb to build up enough nutrients and may sacrifice next year's blooms.

Are there other perennials not gone by yet in terms of bloom, but that in previous years got so big they flopped? A preemptive version of cutbacks, maybe best referred to as pinching by about one-half, may help Joe Pye weed, for instance, or even some of the taller asters and sedums and garden phlox (*Phlox paniculata*) or bee balm, to bloom slightly later than if left to its own, though at a stature that is slightly shorter, sturdier, and bushier. For proof that this is possible—that the plant will still grow up and come into flower—think of garden mums that have been pinched (but employ a gentler hand than is inflicted on those poor things).

Once you have performed your barber's tasks, the drink follows. Water slowly and deeply; hotter, drier weather is coming on.

Geranium phaeum 'Samobor', the mourning widow, produces a froth of tiny May flowers on tall stems, and will soon be cut back hard and re-flush.

Fetid but Fantastic Eucomis

Give me a plant that looks otherworldly for many weeks but is happy to sit in its pot, dry and sleeping, in my cellar all winter here in Zone 5B, asking nothing. Give me *Eucomis,* the pineapple lily—and the bigger and odder, the better.

The only bad thing I have to say about some of these hyacinth relatives, whose genus name means "well-haired" or "lovely haired" because of the crown-like tuft of bracts topping the flower head: Some smell bad; like something died. (Or like they're related to voodoo lilies, but they're not.) Blame the sulphur compounds in the scent of the most common one, *Eucomis bicolor,* chemicals aimed at attracting carrion flies. If you're a flower needing to reproduce and survive, you had better appeal to the right insect somehow: color maybe, or flower shape, or scent. Smelling like a dead body is the secret in *E. bicolor*'s case.

Thankfully, some others (like *Eucomis comosa*) are sweet smelling, or scentless. The fetid ones didn't stop me, and I grew medium-size *E. bicolor* for years before declaring it the start of a collection, and adding others. You know where that led—no more room on the basement floor for any more pots.

Choices included descendants of 10-inch-tall *Eucomis vandermerwei* (the dwarf pineapple lily, with offspring like 'Octopus' barely 6 inches high, and the Tiny Piny types) to others with *E. pallidiflora* genetics, the well-named giant pineapple lily, which I learned from the Pacific Bulb Society includes subspecies with flowers to 6 feet at maturity. I adopted a big pot simply labeled "giant pineapple lily" and it topped 3 feet the first year, with white blooms and lusty green foliage. 'John Treasure', with purplish flowers and tinged foliage, got to 30 inches.

Next I prowled for more little guys, and others with dramatic, darker foliage, such as 'Sparkling Burgundy', which Tony Avent selected in 1983, and more recently 'Rhode Island Red' from Ed Bowen of Rhode Island, close to 3 feet with pink flowers and maroon-green leaves, or petite, very purple 'Dark Star'.

Larger *Eucomis* 'John Treasure' has purplish stems, purple freckling at the base of its leaves, and reached 2½ feet tall in its first year with me.

The bulb's age and growing conditions will affect the height of the flower, or whether you get flowers at all. Many *Eucomis* species come from areas in South Africa that offer summer rain, so I offer sun and don't deprive them moisture once up and growing, but I am careful to avoid waterlogging, as if a saucer were beneath them.

I like everything about pineapple lilies—well, except maybe that occasional smell. I like the lush leaves; the stems (which can be dark-colored or freckled, too), and even the showy seed heads, after the long-lasting flowers are gone.

Unless you adopt *Eucomis* from a nursery that sells them potted and growing, you'll wait until spring to order more, since loose bulbs are not sold in fall. Many eucomis are hardy to about Zone 7 (with *E. bicolor*, catalogs often say Zone 6, if deeply planted and well mulched in winter). I'll stick with my pots, and every couple of years, give them fresh potting soil in very early spring, but otherwise there is not much to do—except wait for their welcome, though often late, reawakening.

In peak summer, the backyard is leaves of all scales, from tiny sedum in the pavement cracks to canna and even giant petasites.

Southeast Native, Northeast Garden

It felt like such a big score the day decades ago when I found bottlebrush buckeye, *Aesculus parviflora*, in a nursery in New Bedford, Massachusetts, even though the plant was just a small thing in a plastic pot. Now it's my biggest shrub, and also a treasure, for its hummock shape, handsome leaves that turn impressively gold in fall, and easy, basically disease-free disposition. Pollinators agree it's a winner when it covers itself in creamy bottlebrush flowers in July.

I had only seen a bottlebrush buckeye once, at the public garden called Wave Hill in New York City, a giant suckering mound of a thing probably 20 feet across and 10 feet high. It grew in the semishade of tall trees, as it does in its natural habitat of the southeastern United States, specifically the rich woodlands in Alabama, Georgia, and northern Florida. I loved its big mountain of a presence right away—and then on that shopping trip to Allen Haskell's former nursery, there it was.

But why is this southeastern native hardy up here—and come to think of it, why are several of my other most-prized woody plants likewise labeled as southeastern natives but so well-adapted, including *Fothergilla gardenii* and *F. major*; *Chionanthus virginicus* (the super-fragrant fringe tree); *Oxydendrum arboreum* (the small tree called sourwood); and *Hydrangea quercifolia* (the oakleaf hydrangea)? Apparently regional boundaries of the pre-Pleistocene era weren't quite as we perceive them now. As transformative glaciers expanded over more of a cooling continent, paleontologists say that forest plants from the Northeast took refuge farther south, and in the ca. 12,000 years since, some haven't regained their former ranges. The details are not fully understood, but it's not just here, either. One of the most extreme examples, I was told by Peter Crane, former director of the Royal Botanic Gardens Kew, was about the ginkgo, and went back a couple of hundred million years. Today we think of *Ginkgo* as having just one species, the Chinese *G. biloba*—but fossil records of pollen indicate that ginkgo was once native in places as diverse as Afghanistan, northern England, and North Dakota!

Though from a distance *Aesculus* flowers appear to be cream-colored, each tiny one on the long wands (technically panicles) is delicately splashed with drops of orange-red paint— actually the red anthers and pinkish filaments inside the little trumpets. Butterflies and many insect pollinators love to visit them, including silver-spotted skippers, and the occasional group of Baltimore orioles, who explore them enthusiastically, as they do earlier apple and wild cherry blossoms.

After many years, my *Aesculus* started producing an occasional crop of nuts that delighted local chipmunks and squirrels but are reported poisonous to humans or livestock. I now have multiple bottlebrush buckeye plants, too, including the later blooming 'Rogers' (a selection from *A. parviflora* var. *serotina*). It's slightly larger with very large flower stems (about 30 inches long) and blooms a couple of weeks after the species, so there is a longer season of *Aesculus* for us all to enjoy, and more of the giant mounds of fall gold.

In warmer zones like its native range, planting bottlebrush buckeye in shade to part shade is recommended, and it does well in shady spots here, too, or in sun, where the plants get bigger and flower more heavily. The only disclaimer I have to offer is: Give it serious room.

(top) Female fringe trees will set blue olive-shaped fruit in late summer if a male tree was nearby at flowering time.

(middle) Two species of *Fothergilla*, *F. major* (shown) and *F. gardenii*, are native to the southeastern United States but hardy to Zones 4 and 5, respectively.

(bottom) The bottlebrush buckeye, *Aesculus parviflora*, another Southeast native, is a giant hummock of a thing with early July bloom.

Southeastern native *Chionanthus virginicus*, the fringe tree, is intensely scented and extravagant at bloom time.

Clematis recta 'Lime Close' is a nonvining clematis with rich purple foliage in spring preceding frothy white flowers.

Weavers and See-Throughs

A professional gardener visited a renowned public garden known for its effusive plantings and unexpected combinations. Upon returning home, her boss asked her how she had enjoyed the place. "I didn't really like the way that all the plants touched," she said, apparently having missed the point.

In a good, established garden, no plant is an island (and the mulch isn't meant to be the focal point). Many gardeners would offer money to make the plants touch faster, rather than waiting two to five years (longer with woody things) for that mature, filled-in look a garden gets if you stick with it. I am one of them.

One functional class of plant that helps make this happen a little faster—and a lot more romantically—is sometimes referred to as weavers. Weavers' natural habit is not some tidy, perfect mound, but rather to reach out and touch their neighbors, or even wrap their arms around them. When I think of weavers, I immediately think of what baby's breath (*Gypsophila paniculata*) does in a traditional bouquet. White-flowered *Asteromea mongolica*, the Japanese aster, would be an especially effective way to accomplish that in a border, and is a more cooperative grower with longer bloom.

In my late-season garden this effect is created by some of the cloudlike, low- to medium-height native asters with small flowers, such as the calico aster I know as *Aster lateriflorus*, especially the cultivar 'Lady in Black' (now *Symphyotrichum lateriflorum*), and the heart-leaved aster (*S. cordifolium*). Such asters are among my favorite weavers, because by the time they flower, in fall, you really need something to tie the tired garden together, some of which you may have had to cut back. In shadier spots, the white wood aster, *Eurybia divaricata* (formerly *A. divaricatus*), does the job.

Knautia macedonica is another weaver, not because it has tiny, cloudlike flowers (they are bigger and vivid crimson) but because it is inclined to flop here and there and combine with other plants in an appealing way. You get the idea. Some of the looser perennial geraniums like 'Ann Folkard' or 'Rozanne' scramble around nicely, knitting while they go—and I use *Geranium phaeum* (such as the variety 'Samobor' with a distinctive dark purple blotch on the foliage) as effective filler, even in semishade.

Often overlooked are the shorter stature nonvining clematis, like *Clematis recta* (seek the purple-leaved ones, like 'Lime Close', lately marketed as Serious Black), which will scramble happily through the other inhabitants of a perennial bed or shrubbery instead of up a trellis, making a froth of ivory flowers at maybe 5 or 6 feet maximum height. Cutting 'Lime Close' to the ground after bloom will yield a fresh flush of that gorgeous purple foliage. *Clematis durandii*, with purple flowers, and other members of the Integrifolia Group, are especially good for scrambling duty, with the potential for longer bloom season, too.

Another class of plants named for their useful habit in designing are sometimes called see-throughs, taking up little room on ground level, but instead giving an airy appearance up above. Tall verbena (*Verbena bonariensis*) is the classic see-through, a self-sowing annual in my climate. Its tall, wiry stems seem to come up out of nowhere, supporting flattened clusters of tiny purple flowers that make ideal landing pads for colorful butterflies. It blooms from midsummer till hard frost for me, from hefty seedlings set out in May, or once established and allowed to do its thing, the many self-sowns start their bloom a little later. Some tall alliums are like that in springtime: virtually no mass at ground level, with spectacular blooms on high that seem to float.

Insect Love (or at Least Respect)

I propose a moratorium on killing insects that the gardener is not on a first-name basis with—ones we have not at least taken the time to key out and identify using BugGuide.net or a field guide, to be sure they are actually a foe. Resist the wish to squish, please. Do your homework, and in the process get to know "the little things that run the world," as Harvard biologist E. O. Wilson referred to invertebrates, including insects.

Extend the moratorium to all spiders, who occupy an order within the second-largest class of arthropods after insects, the arachnids. No matter how visceral the case of arachnophobia might be, never harm a spider, the leading insect predator without whom the world might be uninhabitable.

Why do we rush to crush everything on six, or eight, legs—or revile those on many more, like the giant millipede (*Narceus americanus*), a detritivore whose essential job is to recycle debris at ground level? All too often gardeners are revolted by the sight of a caterpillar, for example, and move to exterminate these seemingly voracious eaters. But how many besides the tomato hornworm or gypsy moth or Colorado potato beetle or eastern tent caterpillar, perhaps, do you really know by name or can identify? Do you know their favored diet—and who eats them? Without caterpillars during nesting season, songbird parents would lack the highest quality baby food their clutches rely on to fledge and thrive.

Spiders are critically important arthropods in the ecosystem and should be appreciated, not feared.

Handpicking Japanese beetles and destroying these alien pests, seen here on *Astilbe*, is fair game.

It's smart to learn to identify destructive vegetable garden pests like the Colorado potato beetle.

In adopting an attitude of curiosity about insects, I have come to marvel at how many have evolved to take on aposematic coloration—a warning color pattern—and perhaps even a suite of behaviors that potential predators understand on an innate or learned level are dangerous, and look for something else to eat. The monarch caterpillar and its adult butterfly is the famous example, but have you noticed how many other insects (locust borers, syrphid flies or hover flies, or the snowberry clearwing sphinx moth, to name several) mimic bees' yellow and black coloration? Birds, who presumably would happily eat them, might not innately know that bees are dangerous, but after sampling one bee, studies have shown that birds such as blue jays will never eat something furry and yellow and black again.

Don't misunderstand: After careful identification, I am all for hand-picking alien insects that are confirmed true pests, like squash bugs and Japanese beetles, or imported or cross-striped cabbage worms, or brown marmorated stink bugs. Better yet, I am all for examining the undersides of the leaves of some pests' favorite crops each morning with my three middle fingers wrapped in duct tape, sticky side out—a kind of insect-egg "lint" brush at the ready for easy removal duty. Get them before they hatch, and with a nontoxic mechanical intervention.

One August years ago, a lot of little fuzzy black-and-white creatures were eating the canna leaves, which is what got me started wondering who's who. It was the larval form of a hickory tussock moth, whose usual diet is ash, elm, oak, hickory, maple, willow, and other trees. I learned so much from this visitor, whom I have greeted every August since. Though he is furry, look but don't touch: The long "lashes" are hollow tubes connected to poison glands, and touching the bristles (called setae) can give susceptible people a stinging nettle-like rash. The tussock moths are cousin to the familiar woolly bear, and in the taxonomic subfamily Arctiinae (the tiger moths). Since they're not deforesting the entire region or anything, I just let them be–and eat—and I even clean up less obsessively in fall with such Lepidopteran well-being in mind. Many beneficial species at various life stages overwinter in places like leaf litter. We just don't understand enough about nature's tiniest creatures to go blindly rampaging against them, do we?

(top) The pot-filled landing is at the top of the front path, the main thoroughfare to the kitchen door.

(left) The duckweed-covered, parrot feather–filled back water garden is edged with a ground cover sedum blooming in the paving cracks.

(opposite) *Hydrangea paniculata* and *Nicotiana mutabilis* tower over gone-by geraniums and sedum in the front garden in late September.

One of the shade garden's boldest foliage plants is *Astilboides tabularis*.

Foliage, the Garden's Wardrobe

I frankly shop for leaves most of all, not flowers, so I bristle when I see charts of perennials or shrubs where they list just name, height, bloom time, and flower color. Why isn't there a column about the leaves? Flowers alone do not a garden make, since they represent the reproductive portion of the plant's life cycle, a mere moment in its year.

Even in the commonest leaf color, green, the range of shades is infinite, from nearly chartreuse to olive, gray, and blue, with countless mid-green tones in between. Add to that the diversity of leaf size, shape, and texture, and you start to get the picture. Then take it one step further, to plants with variegated leaves (whether splashed or striped or edged in white, silver, or gold, pink, or red), and on to purple-leaved plants and gold ones, too.

Many gardeners, especially beginners, are afraid of showy leaves, particularly unusually colored ones, because they aren't sure what goes with what. Green is the garden's neutral, and seems safe, but too much plain old leaf green is pure monotony. One place I find inspiration for combining foliage colors is in plants themselves—particularly ones like *Coleus* and *Acalypha* (the copperleaf plant, one of my favorite nonhardy choices for summer pots). Select a favorite one of either that combines two or more colors in its leaf, and make that your scheme. (On a smaller scale, at container-design time in spring, you will find me walking around the garden center holding one of these plants, looking for good companions—both flowers and other foliage—that pick up on its palette.)

Designers Glenn Withey and Charles Price of Seattle, friends who rely heavily on colorful-leaved plants, explain their strategy this way: To make colorful-leaved plants work in a design, you have to have several "incidents" of their usage around the yard. Don't just go buy a purple-leaved or golden shrub and stick it alone somewhere—the recipe for an eyesore. Tie it into the larger

Rhubarb gets a front-and-center position owing to its extra-large leaves that feel almost tropical, despite its origins in places like Siberia.

A single leaf of copperleaf plant (*Acalypha*) or of a showy coleus can suggest a sophisticated color scheme for a container planting or bed.

Ostrich ferns, bottlebrush buckeye, and rhododendron make a textural green-on-green combination, attractive even when the rhodie is out of bloom.

picture by repeating the motif with an underplanting of coordinating purple-leaved perennials (*Heuchera,* for instance, and the dark-leaved *Cimicifuga simplex* 'Brunette', now often labeled *Actaea simplex*), or gold ones, like golden hostas, *Acorus gramineus* (sweet flag), or grasses. Then in the not-too-distant background, repeat the idea once more, with a small tree in the same general color. When viewing the garden, the eye will be drawn across the scene from one incident to the next, instead of just focusing on the single out-of-place oddball.

Colorful-leaved plants can play important tricks with perspective and light, too. Golden-leaved plants and white-variegated ones advance, making dark corners or distant views pop; dark-leaved shrubs tend to recede, giving a sense of distance even in a tight space. They also make an exciting foil for flowers (try purple clematis draped over a golden-leaved shrub, or a bright-colored annual vine like canary creeper, *Tropaeoleum peregrinum*, over a purple smokebush).

Whatever color the foliage, a plant's leaves should also be evaluated for the ornamentality of their texture and shape. If you put ferns, *Astilbe,* and dwarf goatsbeard (*Aruncus aethusifolius*) next to one another, it would just read as a blur of ferny texture. But one of those near an *Astilboides tabularis*, with its large, bold leaves, and something linear or even spikey alongside that—*Hakonechloa macra,* for instance—would be a lot more interesting.

Very large-leaved plants are underutilized, probably because people are timid with anything so out of the ordinary scale-wise, just as they are of variegation or colored foliage. I cannot get enough of either. Plain old rhubarb has a prominent spot here—beautiful (and delicious). Remember if such subjects make you nervous, there are no mistakes in gardening, just experiments with a variety of outcomes—some more pleasing than others, but every one a critical bit of the gardener's education.

Squash Madness

I do not know where my special affinity for pumpkins and squash began, for I am no great fan of trick-or-treat. But I admit being reduced each year to child age when I tap their giant seeds out of the packet, or later on move among their giant leaves to giddily count the big fruits forming on the vine. At harvest time, I cannot wait to finally hug the offspring, to cradle a well-grown 'Blue Hubbard' in the crook of my arm as if it were my own flesh (if somewhat thicker, sweeter, and more vividly colored).

I never met a pumpkin I didn't like.

The best have another endearing quality: They'll stick around on the kitchen counter until you're ready for them, rather than melt into a sloppy mess of spoiled fruit the way a tomato does. The so-called "good keepers"—thick-fleshed cheese pumpkins or 'Butternut' squash—will last all winter in storage, versatile ingredients as a base for soup, a mashed vegetable, the stuff of pies or cakes, or even puréed and folded into biscuit batter. Good cooking is not the specialty of thin-walled, stringy jack-o'-lanterns, whose flesh is watery and doesn't last.

Though the genus *Cucurbita* is a bit of a tangle, not unlike a field of pumpkin vines, the ones we grow most commonly fit into four species, all natives of Central to South America.

Insect-resistant and prolific, 'Butternut' is my main-crop winter squash. The selection from Turtle Tree Seed has been bred for long storage.

For beauty alone, though both make good eating, try 'Pink Banana' and blue-skinned 'Triamble'.

The summer squash, usually eaten immature before their skins harden, all fit into the popular species *C. pepo*—and if you want company for a day or week, grow a zucchini. Also in *C. pepo* are some popular winter squash like 'Delicata', 'Acorn', and 'Sweet Dumpling', tiny pumpkins like 'Jack Be Little', and white-skinned 'Little Boo', plus sugar pumpkins and the carving kind.

The best keepers are generally in the species *C. moschata*, which also have the sweetest flesh, usually dark orange. This is where we find 'Butternut', 'Canada Crookneck', and the cheese pumpkins (their shape is flattened, like a wheel of cheese). Because of its resistance to squash bugs, and because I have found a very long-keeping variety selected over many years for that trait by Turtle Tree Seed, 'Butternut' is my main crop of winter squash. A gradually decreasing supply is stashed in my cool, dry, dark pantry closet, lasting at least until the following spring and even summer.

Cucurbita maxima includes the plant kingdom's largest fruits—the contest winners approaching half a ton—as well as many other outstanding eating varieties, like 'Rouge Vif d'Etampes' and the Hokkaido pumpkin, kabocha and Hubbard types. For beauty alone (though both are delicious) I love blue-skinned 'Triamble' and the dirigible called 'Pink Banana'. The least grown species is *C. argyrosperma*, which tends to want a hotter summer than I can offer, but I have succeeded occasionally with one of its outstanding members, 'Green Striped Cushaw'.

For best results, start with seeds of a regionally appropriate, disease- and pest-resistant variety whose days-to-harvest are within a reasonable span to match your season. Like with all cucurbits, pumpkins and squash require heat, a steady supply of nutrients, and good garden sanitation to limit pests. In the spirit of prevention, I am very particular about thorough fall cleanup to eliminate overwintering invitations for squash bugs in particular, removing all vine debris to a distance, hopefully giving me a good start the coming spring.

Pre-warm the soil with black plastic sheeting for a week or more before the set-out date (which is just after final frost). An extra benefit to soil-warming, weed-suppressing plastic: it limits nutrient leaching from rain.

Many gardeners transplant cucurbits into slits cut in the sheeting after a head start of 3 to 4 weeks indoors. I direct-sow, staggering each half of my seedings about 2 weeks apart as extra insurance against insect pests (who seem to go for one age or the other of plants when they have a choice, leaving me the other). Cover transplants with lightweight row-cover fabric for extra warmth, removing the wraps at flowering time to allow pollination. The covers may prevent squash bugs and vine borers from finding vulnerable young plants and laying their eggs. Rotating where cucurbits are planted may help outsmart pests, though rotation works better in a large-scale setting than small gardens.

To create a high-organic-matter soil, I top-dress before laying down plastic with compost and/or organic fertilizer such as seaweed meal, and then I add a little into each planting hole. Provide regular, thorough watering throughout the root zone during the growing season, without waterlogging. If you've looked at the root system of a spent cucurbit plant while pulling them at cleanup, they don't have a deep root system—meaning the moisture and nutrients in that top layer below the plastic are most critical.

Viburnums feature spring flowers, fall fruit, and often hot autumn leaf color, too, and the fruit will bring in the birds.

Viburnums

It was the stately doublefile viburnum (*Viburnum plicatum* var. *tomentosum*), with its outstretched arms covered in double rows of flat-topped white blooms and the promise of red fruit and maroon fall foliage to follow, that got me started with this outstanding genus of flowering and fruiting shrubs. The doublefile's growth habit is so distinctive I could not help but notice it. I cannot imagine a garden—especially a garden with a focus on attracting birds or on creating a long season of visual interest—without a complement of *Viburnum*, but lately growing them has posed some ethical and practical challenges.

Sadly, in various eastern U.S. areas this long-popular Asian species has proven to be an ambitious self-sower, and some states have put it and some other non-native viburnums on the list of plants to be careful about, which may invade wild spaces. The European cranberrybush, *V. opulus*, is advised against in spots across the Northern tier, and in the mid-Atlantic region, I see *V. dilatatum* with that warning attached.

I have *Viburnum dilatatum* 'Michael Dodge', with gold fall fruit, and its pollinator Cardinal Candy (red), and they don't seem to seed in—at least not yet. Nor do some other Asian types, like the highly fragrant *V. carlesii*, the Koreanspice viburnum, with daphne-like fragrance from barely pink-flushed white flowers in late April. You can smell it across the yard even when it is young, and by the time this rounded plant reaches maturity, you will smell it down the road. *Viburnum ×juddii*, Judd's viburnum, is also highly perfumed (*V. carlesii* is one parent), as is *V. burkwoodii*.

I have grown many other non-natives, but these days to avoid the possible non-native conflict, I focus on adding native ones only, and the choices here include *Viburnum dentatum* (arrowwood viburnum); *V. lentago* (nannyberry); *V. prunifolium* (blackhaw viburnum);

V. nudum (witherod), and *V. acerifolium* (maple-leaf viburnum, but sometimes hard to find in the nursery trade).

The European cranberrybush's native counterpart and native near-lookalike is *Viburnum trilobum* (sometimes lately referred to as V. *opulus* var. *americana*), the American cranberrybush viburnum, another informal shrub with bright red fruit. Its presence led to my first encounter not so many years ago with the viburnum leaf beetle, itself an invasive pest from Europe that apparently particularly adores that species (and also *V. opulus* and certain others). Cornell keeps a helpful online list of species ranked by their susceptibility to VLB (from highly susceptible to most resistant).

One spring day I noticed a gray catbird intent on what looked like a dead shrub, but was a defoliated (but alive) American cranberrybush. The catbird was gorging on larvae (which turned out, once I did my homework, to be of the viburnum leaf beetle). They in turn had just finished eating the shrub's foliage. The food chain at work—until I interrupted it, squashed hundreds, and cut off the worst branches to bag tightly as trash. Now I use these most susceptible species in out-of-the-way spots as a kind of beetle "trap crop," to hopefully entice them away from the other shrubs, and between October and the start of April, I check young twigs for little bumps that are overwintering egg cases, and prune and dispose of them.

Viburnum nudum, whose fruit goes from pink through blue to almost black against waxy or even shiny leaves, gets devoured by the beetle, which doesn't seem to have an appetite for the *V. dilatatum* types, and leaves 'Michael Dodge' alone. I am therefore weighing various factors. Whichever you choose, know this: viburnums are not in general self-fertile, and for the heaviest fruit set they like the company of another close but not genetically identical relative—a plant in the same species, whose bloom coincides with its own, but is not the same cultivar. Do your research and mix up the plantings—not just all 'Winterthur' if you are growing *V. nudum*, for instance.

With pruning, less is more. Usually viburnums need relatively little, assuming you planted the right species and cultivar in the right-size space. Even the lightest pruning, like deadheading, isn't needed, since what you want is fruit after the flowers (unlike deadheading lilacs to prevent messiness). If a little fine-tuning or gentle reshaping is required, I time my cuts right after bloom. Cut stems back judiciously to just above a node so the plant makes new shoots in a somewhat natural-looking style. Do not disfigure viburnums by topping or shearing branches halfway.

Not Your Average Morning Glories

Hummingbirds, butterflies, and even the Royal Horticultural Society (by bestowing its Award of Garden Merit) agree: The annual vine called *Ipomoea lobata*, formerly *Mina lobata*, a.k.a. Spanish flag or exotic love vine, is the bee's knees (and those pollinators agree, come to think of it).

Fusing flags with the exotic erotic, what about calling this July-through-frost morning glory relative the fan-dance vine instead? That's what the flowers, which are borne in clusters called racemes, look like: a string of little fans, or pennants, dancing in the breeze. The tubular

The Spanish flag vine, *Ipomoea lobata*, is an annual morning glory relative.

A little red morning glory called the cardinal climber, *Ipomoea ×multifida*, is a magnet for hummingbirds.

blooms start out red, but fade gradually so that each raceme includes some red, yellow and white individuals.

I'm happy to accommodate the Northeast's only breeding hummingbird species, the ruby-throated, so I also always make room for plants it likes to visit, including the hybrid cardinal climber or one of its parents, the cypress vine. The cardinal climber, *Ipomoea ×multifida*, is a cross between *Ipomoea quamoclit* (the cypress vine, native to Mexico and tropical America, which Thomas Jefferson grew) and *Ipomoea coccinea*, a red morning glory. For years I endeavored to grow *quamoclit*, for its truly star-shaped flowers (the cardinal climber's are more pentagon shaped) and finer-textured foliage. And almost every year I failed, because much of the nursery trade seems to have little regard for keeping these straight. I'd always only get cardinal climber, until I checked with longtime friend and heirloom flower collector Marilyn Barlow, founder of Select Seeds, who had a carefully guarded stash.

A few seedlings of any of these *Ipomoea* spaced a foot apart in sun will cover a garden arch or *tuteur*. Spanish flag grows lustily to 10 to 15 feet in a season; cypress vine and cardinal climber maybe more like 8 to 10 feet. Each takes 12 to 14 weeks from seed to bloom, so I start indoors at least 6 weeks before final frost. Treat them like other morning glories and soak the sometimes slow-to-germinate seed in warm water for a few hours before sowing, to soften the hard coat.

One more thought about annual vines and birds: Despite a shared common name, the northern cardinal takes no interest whatsoever in the cardinal climber, preferring not nectar, but a diet of seeds, fruit, and also insects. Regarding the latter menu item, you may be surprised to learn that the mostly nectivorous hummingbirds agree: delicious, yes, but make their bugs pint-size, such as gnats and mosquitoes and perhaps the occasional spider—not the crickets and beetles and moths that the much larger red bird can gobble up.

Tall Perennials

In the way that I crave the botanical extravagance of outsize leaves, I have a strong attraction for plants that attain a great height in a season. Though early on I would not have known what to do with a 6- to 8-foot perennial, today I can think of many uses: to back a perennial border; to punctuate the corners of a bed or the start of a path, the way a column might; to simply break up the monotony of a bed of so many lumpy 2- and 3-foot shapes with a giant exclamation point; or to create a seasonal living wall or screen.

A big bed I created of towering perennials is positioned perfectly to block the view of my compost heap and an extra vegetable-growing patch where asparagus and raspberries are tucked away. While all around them are losing their heads, the tallest perennials are just coming into their own. No need for deadheads; these big boys are fresh looking, a striking counterpoint to tattered earlier stars.

The ones I have a special affection for include some American natives that attract bees and butterflies; later in the year, birds investigate the seed heads, too. My first tall perennial was Joe Pye weed, *Eutrochium purpureum* (often still referred to as *Eupatorium*), which I had seen growing wild in moist wild spots and then at the garden center, too. Soon came *Rudbeckia* 'Herbstsonne', the autumn sun coneflower, thought to be a hybrid of *R. nitida* and *R. laciniata*. It rises to 7 feet with a wonderful linear, swaying quality. Then *R. submentosa* 'Henry Eilers', at maybe 5 feet with strangely quilled yellow rays. *Vernonia noveboracensis*, the New York ironweed, is another 7-footer, with magenta-purple fall flowers. The tallest herbaceous plant I grow, an Asian import, joins them in that big camouflage bed: *Miscanthus* 'Giganteus', which soars to 10 feet and in years with lots of rain tries to reach a dozen.

In a shadier location in July, I enjoyed my big stand of black cohosh or bugbane (*Actaea racemosa* or *Cimicifuga racemosa*), an eastern native plant whose creamy candelabras of bottlebrush flowers can top 8 feet and emit a distinctive sweet scent, calling in all manner of interested insects. Even its seed heads are charming, and I leave them standing into latest fall.

I have complained about plants I've had forever that I wish would simply go away. A counterpoint: *Thalictrum rochebrunianum*, a towering meadow rue, has been here more than 20 years, too, and I sincerely hope it never departs. This old friend is a Japanese native (there

These flowers adorn a 10-foot-tall *Thalictrum rochebrunianum*.

Rudbeckia 'Herbstsonne' tops 7 feet in the high-summer garden.

Rudbeckia submentosa 'Henry Eilers', which is 5 feet tall, has strange quilled ray flowers.

are American species, such as the charming little rue anemone, *T. thalictroides*, with white blooms in spring hugging the woodland floor).

My summertime companion, though, produces lavish lavender 3-foot-wide sprays of tiny flowers, each with showy yellow stamens, on 10-foot stems painted appropriately purple and dressed up with delicate, blue-green foliage reminiscent of columbine. No wonder, since the two are cousins in the Ranunculaceae or buttercup family (as are delphinium, clematis, and *Aconitum*). A note about the height of my stalwart giant: All the references say 6 or 7 feet when blooming, but I took a tape measure into the garden, and 10 feet it is.

Houttuynia, and Other Weeds I Planted

I have killed many plants, most of them unintentionally and many of them with regret. So why can't I kill *Houttuynia cordata*, the so-called chameleon plant, despite years of trying?

I bought it more than 20 years ago, for the showiness of its then-variegated red, green, and yellow foliage and its touted use as a ground cover in moist shade—even suited to plunging right in a pot in water, apparently. Certain that I had acquired a treasure, I was upset when it didn't return from underground after its first winter. Dead, I reported in my newspaper garden column at the time. Gone.

It was another year before the chameleon turned on me again, and resurfaced. Its resurrection was cause for celebration. Not dead, not gone!

I guess you know the rest of the story if you've ever grown an invasive disguised as an ornamental: It behaved for a moment or two, acting thoroughly charming, then proceeded to get thuggish (and also to lose its variegation, reverting to the stronger-willed green version).

The chameleon plant, *Houttuynia cordata*, is probably the worst weed I actually planted, thinking it was a treasured ornamental.

Not on your life, I said, as it overran *Pulmonaria* and goldenseal and trilliums. *Oh, no you don't.* Out came the spading fork, and after the seeming bulk was sent to the trash, out came the sheets of heavy plastic, as I tried to bake the remainder to death all summer, called solarizing. At first I used black plastic, but things get even hotter under clear, I read, so that was next.

By springtime, it was not gone. A year later (by then two years beneath plastic), still not gone, but it had spread farther sideways underground. Even if I wanted to use the herbicide glyphosate to stop it, friends reported that it didn't work on theirs—and it was insidiously tangled in plants I'd harm.

I tried lifting the plastic and sowing grass seed instead and mowing for a few seasons, to no effect, and then resorted back to the plastic, repeatedly digging out every emerging shoot and root. Mowing for a decade or so will probably kill whatever re-sprouts, I figured, right? Or not.

And so I ask again: Why won't this plant die? Ditto gooseneck loosestrife (*Lysimachia clethroides*), which is pretty enough, and nice in arrangements, but all I really want to say about it, too, is: *Go away.* Add the ground cover called yellow archangel (*Lamiastrum galeobdolon*) to the depressing list of weeds I planted and will never be rid of—though with that one I actually think digging for multiple years just might do it, and I recently embarked on that campaign.

Take this as commiseration, since I suspect you have your own such burdens. Take it also as a warning to all of us who shop for plants, since all of my invasive "ornamentals" are still for sale. These days every purchase I consider is preceded with a little online research about its reputation for bad behavior in my region—an essential cautionary step.

Senescence

SEPTEMBER & OCTOBER

NOTHING LASTS

I HAVE YET TO GROW a cherry tree, but by my way of thinking, that is just some pesky detail I cannot let weigh me down. In the spirit of how it's really the *spirit* of a thing that counts, I nevertheless observe *sakura matsuri*, the cherry blossom festival, pretty much weekly from late April through November, as I have for years.

Yes, it is a festival that traditionally marks the coming of spring—or in bigger-picture terms, of renewal—in the form of the *Prunus* blooms. But *sakura matsuri* is more than an "Oh, what pretty flowers" celebration, most poignantly reminding us to pay particular attention to the fact of the ephemeral nature of all living things. Cherry blossoms are beautiful, but fleeting; what might for a moment be full bloom is suddenly pink and white snow.

Nothing lasts. Need I say more to a bunch of gardeners? Not winter, nor spring; not the flower nor its pollinators. Not us.

However tight we hold, we cannot stop the petals from shattering.

I repeat: Nothing lasts. All these years of growing things has instilled a reverence for the winding-down side, and so my own derivative tradition is to mark each major passing in the garden, each fallen hero, and not just each arriving bloom. In April it was the magnolia by the kitchen window who could not hold on one moment longer. In June the giant rhododendron out back said farewell for at least another year. As if to make its point, it dropped its lavender flowers in the garden pool beneath, creating a serendipitous color play with the midribs of the Japanese painted ferns at the water's edge.

Now around me it is so many, many leaves, too many for one girl and her rake—and how can it be another autumn so soon?

Nothing lasts, which makes it all the more precious, no? Watching this over and again through so many seasons, how is it that I still defer or delay even a moment of a single day? And yet, so far at least, there are bulbs once again not ordered—as if I have an infinite number of falls ahead to plant them in the hopes of a spring show—and frankly, much bigger life-list items have been pushed back over and again, too. What am I waiting for?

A friend was talking just yesterday about a corollary: about things she had been saving for some special occasion—that perfume her father gave her that she never dares wear, as if she'd be wasting it; the favorite (but unworn) jeans. It brought up memories that trace, as many things do, to Grandma Marion, my mother's mother, the first gardener I ever knew.

Grandma always gave us treats—things like "homesick pills," as she called the red and white swirled peppermints that she'd dispense to me and her namesake, my sister, when our parents were away. Or the madcap gumdrop "faces" on our scoops of ice cream, and preposterous, home-baked birthday cakes, one shaped like a lamb, and flocked in shredded Baker's coconut.

There were beautiful, big cookies from Schrafft's shaped like ducks and chicks, colorfully frosted and carefully wrapped in clear cellophane so you could keep an eye on them. My cowgirl of a baby sister tore open and beheaded her pastry poultry before we could even say thank you, but not me. I kept a big tin box on the floor of my closet, and each new adoptee would be gently added to my secret Noah's Ark. I never ate a single cookie; everything stayed just so, and just in case—just like my friend, Miss Save It For a Rainy Day, and her perfume.

I never told her, but if I had, Grandma would have understood.

She repeated the same line, every Sunday at dinner: "I'm going to the old folk's home soon." A widow, she hinted in this way at financial insecurity, and fear.

It turned out that Grandma had her own treasure chest on her closet floor, a small safe my mother came upon when choosing a dress for her mother to be buried in. Inside was a stack of bankbooks that wouldn't have qualified Grandma as rich, but could have kept her in her beloved house and garden nearby—the one she "had to" sell, when into a gardenless apartment she dispatched herself.

The bankbooks represented the house proceeds and then some. The way I tally things, Grandma gave up 10 more seasons in her garden for the false security of a lockbox and some bankbooks.

I hope I can resist such emotionally costly parsimony, and just stay here and watch the succession of every passing, until it's my turn.

My friend is right: We need to light the candles, drink the "too-good-to-drink" gift wine, eat those damn animal cookies already. (Well, maybe the latter are many decades past their sell-by date.) We need to go ahead—to stop pretending that deferring will make the perishable persistent, or the now forever. No amount of magical thinking can make it otherwise: Nothing lasts.

The garden, the most ephemeral of art forms and rigorous of spiritual practices, is a constant reminder of why we mustn't wait. *Hurry; limited engagement only. Act now.* It's a vivid, perishable embodiment of how things live, and die.

Nothing lasts. (I say it all the time when I lecture to garden groups; the cry of carpe diem.)

Celebrate the passings, I say out loud, too—not just the full bloom on the crabapples, but the pink puddle of fallen petals beneath them.

Stop chasing just the "peak" moments, I invoke. Perfection, with everything "just so," is an illusion (and here comes an angry gust of wind or a pounding rain or ice storm to prove my point).

Savor every drop—not just the obvious. Yes, enjoy the big, insistent flower, but don't overlook the little things; the buds, the bugs, the bark.

Apparently I need to take a seat in the audience for one of my upcoming events, and really listen.

Leaves fall. A potted Japanese maple made quite a display this week on the paving stones around itself, and I am in no hurry whatsoever to rake things up. If I do adopt a cherry, perhaps it will be *Prunus subhirtella* 'Autumnalis', which if happy with its location and the conditions in a given year will flower not just in the spring, but again in fall—two more opportunities for a *sakura matsuri*, and with the correct genus both times, even.

'Scarlet Runner' bean pods, many years past harvest, fill a dish on the coffee table.

(above) These pods fell from an old Loebner hybrid magnolia tree called 'Ballerina'.

(left) Tender things like my various old *Clivia miniata* and *Alocasia ×amazonica* come indoors again after doing warm-season garden duty.

(opposite) The first hints of fall are taking hold, as seen from the upper bluestem meadow.

The perennial
chrysanthemum 'Will's
Wonderful' is not for the
faint of heart.

Fall Leaves and Pink Mums

We should all age so gracefully, assuming a glowing, honey-gold stage like the last breath of the most generous ferns and hostas in one of their finest moments, poised just before they fade in a glorious, violently colored decline to sleep awhile until the cycle begins again. The growing season may come alive in earliest spring in colors suited to a baby's layette, but when the end is near, the well-planted garden goes out in a blaze of glory. I like this bawdier, hot end of things. Don't clean up too soon.

As much as I love fall, it would be easier for me to list plants I've purchased that *don't* look good then than those that do. Maples in general are hot stuff, whether the giant native red and sugar maples at my boundaries, or the purchased "Japanese" maples, particularly *Acer pseudosieboldianum*, a Korean species about 15 to 20 feet high and wide and among the hardiest and most fiery.

Masses of fruit everywhere are extra-ornamental, until the cedar waxwings and robins have at it. Sumacs and blueberries, spicebush and bottlebrush buckeye all contribute, and panicle hydrangeas (*Hydrangea paniculata*) are a crazy mix of hot sauce and cotton candy, a twist on the usual fall palette.

Which gives me another idea: With all this flaming stuff, I wonder each fall why garden centers sell chrysanthemums that match the foliar display—flowers in rusty or maroon or gold tones? (I also wonder why we have such a passion for those pinched-into-submission pots of too-perfect mums, anyhow—like some kind of containerized throwback to Victorian carpet bedding—but apparently that's just me.) May I suggest pink mums instead, and specifically perennial ones? You won't toss these on the compost, but will instead divide them in spring– and yes, some pinching along the way will be required to make them manageable size and not too leggy at bloom time. If you are feeling very brave, look for 'Will's Wonderful', with small,

With larger, paler pink flowers, 'Sheffield Pink' is a more subtle choice of perennial mum.

Across the lawn, the big herbaceous perennial bush clover, *Lespedeza thunbergii*, is coming into bloom in front of a 10-foot wall of *Miscanthus* 'Giganteus'.

extra-hot pink flowers with oversize gold centers. More discreet would be the larger, pale pink choice of 'Sheffield Pink'.

A gardener wanting extra-good results must bone up on the following perennials and bulbs or bulb-like plants, at the very minimum: toad lily (*Tricyrtis*); yellow bells (*Kirengeshoma palmata*); asters; ironweed (*Vernonia*); autumn crocus (*Colchicum*); bush clover (*Lespedeza thunbergii*); hybrid Japanese anemones; goldenrod (*Solidago*)—and . . . oh, if only I had planted dahlias, too, in spring—specifically in every shade of pink.

Repeat After Me

Early fall allows another opportunity for divisions and transplanting, and so I have a little story to tell:

It was my first really rare plant, a plant so unusual that it wasn't even in the commercial nursery industry at the time (and still isn't widely sold). I had scored it at a botanical garden auction, and was very impressed with myself, as if this possession made me someone special. I had *Hylomecon* hybris.

Each April at its bloom time, I would go out to see my *Hylomecon japonicum*—which I regarded more like a shrine than a plant, really—patting myself on the back all the while. Then one cold, wet spring day there was a hole where my plant had been, and a very tall man in a yellow rain suit the color of its flowers was standing beside the hole, carving up the extracted plant with his pocketknife, as if he were eating an apple.

The man was my friend Charles, and I wanted to kill him. Screaming, door-slamming, and worse ensued.

"You are so selfish with this plant, you don't even share it with yourself," Charles said, still shouting, and then proceeded to go back outside and begin to deposit little divisions of *Hylomecon*—an Asian ephemeral in the poppy family—in potentially drift-like patterns around a few spots. "You love this plant," he pointed out, saying we should make it a signature of the garden—not just one lonely dot.

You know, of course, the outcome: Now my April-into-May garden is positively alive with sunny little yellow flowers, thousands of them in lavish sweeps all around. Do not be stingy with your beloveds; do not be afraid to share—to dig them and divide them and distribute them around, in the name of greater design good.

Put simply: Repeat, repeat, and repeat. (Do I sound like a broken record yet?)

Making Compost

The volume of yard waste (and to a lesser degree, kitchen scraps) will dictate what composting system you use. I create far too much raw material for a typical bin—either the commercially available metal or heavy plastic kind that is about as big as a garbage can, or an easy, inexpensive "pen" of chicken wire and rot-proof stakes, or a multicompartment unit fashioned of recycled shipping pallets joined into cubicles.

I once had a metal composter that shut tight and kept animals out of my vegetable food wastes, alternating them with layers of garden debris and a little soil or finished compost to get things activated and reduce unpleasant odors. Now I just dig a hole in my giant heap—a long, open pile called a windrow—and bury food scraps, topping them with a shovelful of compost or rotting debris, to deter pests when I dump my kitchen compost bucket.

My windrow is about 40 feet long and 6 or 8 feet wide, and in peak fall cleanup gets to more than 5 feet tall, too. But as the material begins to settle and eventually breaks down, it's usually more like 3 to 4 feet high. I also have a pile of shredded leaves only, about 20 feet long and a few feet high, that I age into mulch or soil-improving leaf mold.

If I hadn't allowed my precious clump of *Hylomecon japonicum* to be divided, I would not have rivers of gold in the garden in spring.

Hylomecon japonicum, an Asian ephemeral, is delightful when viewed up close.

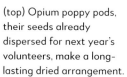

(top) Opium poppy pods, their seeds already dispersed for next year's volunteers, make a long-lasting dried arrangement.

(bottom) Faded *Boltonia asteroides* 'Nally's Lime Dot' lies down on the job beside a culinary sage.

(opposite) Blueberry bushes, besides their white flowers and blue fruit, boast hot-colored autumn foliage.

Yes, you can just make a pile in a corner of the yard, no enclosure required.

Don't site the heap in the shadows, though; a position in at least part-day sun is better, and also one near a water source, so the pile can be kept slightly moist but not sodden. There is no precise recipe, just a traditional formula of green plus brown equals black gold. Layer the two: green ingredients (nitrogen-rich materials such as grass clippings and leafy green plants) and brown ones (carbon-rich dry, brown leaves or twiggy bits). Too much of either will impede decomposition. Never add fats and oils, dairy products (eggshells are fine), meat, fish or bones, or pet manures. Also avoid manures from farm animals who have been fed crops treated with persistent herbicides, which can render your pile "killer compost" that thwarts plant growth.

I liken successful composting to the combustion that goes on when my car is running smoothly: to ignite, the car needs fuel, air, and a spark. The heap's spark is the nitrogen-rich green stuff; the fuel is the brown stuff; the air is supplied by occasional turning of the pile. Too much green stuff in one spot (particularly wet things like grass clippings) will produce a smelly heap; too much brown (like thick piles of orange rinds if you are into juicing) will just sit there. Chopping things up speeds decomposition; so does aerating the pile by turning, or adding more green.

For good measure, I inoculate the pile of fresh materials here and there with a shovelful of microbe-filled aged compost, or garden soil, and skip the store-bought inoculants.

Composting hot, between 120 and 160°F, will help kill weed seeds and most funky stuff. An 18-inch-long compost thermometer will help eliminate guesswork. If weeds are sprouting from finished compost, heat up the pile, or pre-kill weeds and weed seeds by bagging them in plastic with some green material (like lawn clippings) and leaving the bags in the sun for a few months, before returning the solarized material to the heap. The bagging idea is great—a sort of waste-not, want-not tactic for recycling weeds versus tossing them into the trash—and you can even reuse the same bags.

A Longer Clematis Season

With a strategy combining proper plant selection, timely cutbacks, feeding, and vigilant watering, we can stretch the blooming season of *Clematis*, Dan Long of Brushwood Nursery, a vine-mad friend, has got me thinking.

First, select a range of *Clematis*—not all spring bloomers If you have mostly large-flowered hybrids, which bloom in late spring, you won't have explored earlier and later moments. A rough sequence of some possibilities:

Extra-early varieties are being developed by breeders, and the *alpina*, *montana*, and *macropetala* species and their hybrids are all early. Even among the large-flower hybrids, which come after these, there are early and later selections to stretch your time with them.

The *viticella* hybrids don't have flowers as big, but are prolific and easy. *Clematis integrifolia*—which can bloom for a long time—behaves more like a herbaceous perennial, at maybe 3 feet, and there are hybrids with *integrifolia* that add those long-blooming genetics to slightly more scrambling or semiclimbing plants. Probably the best-known one of those would be *durandii*.

At the entry to the garden, *Clematis* 'Venosa Violacea' greets visitors, scrambling over a massive old *Corylopsis spicata*.

Some clematis, like the Tangutica Group, make extra-showy seed heads when bloom finishes.

By late summer and autumn you can enjoy the Orientalis Group, including *Clematis tangutica*, and the white-flowered native *C. virginiana* (less showy and fragrant than the long-popular sweet autumn clematis, *C. paniculata*, which is invasive in many places). I have vastly oversimplified, but you get the idea: Shop for a sequence of bloom (and for varieties with good seed heads, too). Then . . .

Feed the plants organic rose fertilizer; water regularly Good, steady fertilizing using an all-natural organic food rated for roses can bring on more blooms. How often and how much

The handsome caterpillar of the equally dramatic spotted black-and-white giant leopard moth rests on a colorful leaf.

depends on soil conditions and the specific product (follow label application rates). Top-dress each plant in spring or fall with compost.

A regular supply of water can make a critical difference between a plant surviving and thriving. These deep-rooted perennials can be set back by dry spells. Drip irrigation is ideal, but if not, plan to water thoroughly and frequently.

Some plants respond to a midseason cutback, too After their massive bloom, the large-flowered hybrids can look ratty. Cut back a third or half, feed and water well, promoting a flush of growth and possible rebloom. Some, like 'Jackmanii', may rebloom promptly; others later or not so much, but the cutback and TLC won't hurt. I cut my nonvining clematis like *Clematis recta* to the ground after bloom, too, and they respond with tidier, fresh foliage and perhaps even more flowers.

When Inner Conifer Needles Turn Brown

Don't panic: Nothing's wrong, and they're not all dying in unison. Though we commonly call them "evergreens," conifers such as pine, arborvitae, spruce, and Hinoki cypress lighten their load of old needles in late summer and fall, with a show of yellowing or browning that can scare a gardener.

This phenomenon should not be confused with browning at the tips or overall yellowing or browning that can happen at other times—such as from winter desiccation; from roadside salts; from pests and diseases (including *Diplodia* tip blight in some pines or *Phomopsis* in spruce and nonresistant junipers); or from drought. Do a web search to see what road-salt damage and winterburn look like on conifers, by comparison.

The browning I noticed in late July on my eastern red cedar (*Juniperus virginiana*) is suddenly showing up as gold or rusty-brown or a progression on other species. The eastern white pine (*Pinus strobus*), with its long needles, is always the most dramatic, turning what looks like mostly gold. It's hard to believe the plant will be O.K., but needle-drop is normal, though the rate varies by species, and can also accelerate from environmental stresses like dry conditions or pest infestation in a given season.

Before calling the arborist, examine a branch to identify where along it the fading foliage is. Losses should generally be from the inside out, not at the tips. Inner needles are the oldest, and as they age and get shaded by new growth farther out, they photosynthesize less effectively and are shed. The plant lightens its load—and good thing, since snow and ice on extra needles could be too much to bear.

All conifers drop their needles every couple of years to every 5 years or longer. The deciduous conifers, such as dawn redwood (*Metasequoia glyptostroboides*), bald cypress (*Taxodium distichum*), and larch (*Larix decidua*), do it thoroughly every year. But that's another story.

Putting Up a Year of Herbs

I hate paying a couple of dollars for a bunch of organic parsley in winter (or chives, or cilantro, or sage) and twice that for basil, if you can get it. As summer heats up, I start freezing herbs, and do big batches before they're gone—not a perfect substitute for fresh, but very good, and economical. I do it one of three ways:

* **as pesto** (using oil as the base, sometimes with extra ingredients)
* **as ice cubes** (whole or chopped, pressed into trays and covered in a tiny bit of water, or blended with just enough water to make a cube)
* **or stuffed tightly into freezer bags** (or small freezer jars)

THE HOW-TOs:

Pesto, flavored or plain Get out a food processor, or blender, and get creative. Purée virtually any green herb (from chives to parsley, basil, oregano, cilantro, arugula, sage, and even garlic scapes in season) in an olive oil base. Some cooks add garlic and/or nuts and grated cheese; some think the mixture doesn't store as well with extras. Freeze as cubes, knocked out of ice cube trays into freezer bags with air expressed.

Freeze herbs as ice cubes This method is preferable when an oil base doesn't suit, such as for lemon balm or other mints (or with other green herbs that might be used later in a recipe that does not call for olive oil). Wash herbs, pat dry, and remove from stems. Chop if needed, or simply press densely into ice cube trays and drizzle a little water over to fill, barely enough so a cube will form when frozen. Or process the herbs with a little water as the base, and then make cubes, and when frozen, pop them into freezer bags.

The asters and goldenrods have faded, but the upper meadow—and the crabapple trees that surround it—are a favorite destination for seed- and fruit-eating birds.

Earlier in the season, garlic scapes made a good base for pesto that is stashed in the freezer.

Freezing rosemary, thyme, or bay Some herbs are easiest to freeze right on the stems, including rosemary, thyme, and bay (if you are so lucky as to have a bay tree). Simply cut the twigs, spread out on a cookie sheet, and put into the freezer. Once frozen, pack twigs into freezer bags by variety, express the air, and simply pick off leaves from a twig anytime, returning unused twigs to the bag. Or, after they are thoroughly frozen (a week or more), you can un-bag the twigs briefly, detach the foliage by hand or with a rolling pin, then pack the frozen leaves quickly back into freezer jars or bags.

Freeze herbs in "logs" of leaves I use a lot of parsley, making logs of leaflets pressure-rolled tightly inside freezer bags. The log technique (so easy, and probably the only cooking Good Thing I contributed in my years at *Martha Stewart Living*, though my record with gardening ideas was better) goes like this: Wash and dry parsley in a salad spinner. Remove leaflets from stems, and press loads into the bottom of a quart freezer bag, until there is about the diameter of a half-dollar, densely packed, when you roll up the bag. Seal, expressing air, and surround the log with rubber bands for good measure. When you need some, you just slice a disc from one end of the log and return the rest to the bag, and freezer.

Chopped chives also freeze well this way (or in small freezer jars), and friends report doing this with various green herbs that I have not tried first-hand. Basil, because it blackens, is one I would not, but rather put up in oil or water as a cube. One year I had a big fall crop of dill and I just removed the thickest lower stem, then folded up the plants to fill a freezer bag like a thick mat, then gradually chopped off bits as needed from the frozen mass.

* as an ingredient in a soup or stew or sauce
* with pesto cubes, as a garnish for soups and stews
* again, with pestos, spread on crackers or bread, served as appetizers or to otherwise accompany a meal
* pestos on pasta or rice as a main dish or side
* to enliven a sandwich or an egg dish (I love them in frittatas and omelets, for example)
* plain frozen herb leaves are not great as a garnish on, say, a salad, because they can be limp, but mix them into the dressing instead

I Just Call Them Asters

I still recall the suspicious glare of the person beside me in the checkout line at the garden center a couple of dozen springs ago, when I was buying asters and she was buying azaleas. Her purchases were blooming. Mine looked dead. She was smug then, but come fall, it's pretty clear who got the better deal.

Because they flower so late and don't look like much earlier on, asters were for too long one of the lessons learned late in a gardener's career, after years of having things peter out by fall and scurrying to find solutions. With the increasing emphasis on native plants and especially on pollinator plantings—asters are especially loved by bees, syrphid flies, and butterflies—the message of their value is being heard sooner. I learned about them in two places: the former Heronswood Nursery catalog from Daniel Hinkley near Seattle, which listed more than 50 at one count, and outdoors all around me each fall.

Many wild asters, representing numerous native eastern species, pop up around the garden and the surrounding fields and roadsides, and even in the woods. The first aster to intentionally find a home with me, though, thanks to a mail order placed at Heronswood, was the hybrid 'Little Carlow', with dime-size violet-blue flowers produced over many weeks. Another winner in the genus that was *Aster* (but is now divided into various others) is what I first knew as *A. lateriflorus* var. *horizontalis*, with sprays of tiny flowers on wide-spreading branches that the *horizontalis* part gave away. Now the calico aster is called *Symphyotrichum lateriflorum*, and like many gardeners I like the cultivar 'Lady in Black' for its dark leaves and profusion of white daisies with rose-colored centers. It is one of the plants known as a weaver, as is the species *S. cordifolium*, or heart-leaved aster, another volunteer at my place.

Most asters bloom as autumn comes on, from late August to right up against hard frost, as late as November. Plan accordingly. Asters are generally sun-lovers, though *Eurybia divaricata* (formerly *Aster divaricatus*), the charming white wood aster, and inclined-to-be-thuggish big-leaved aster or *Eurybia macrophylla* (formerly *A. macrophyllus*), to name two, can handle shade and pop up at the woodland edge here and under big trees. There are an estimated 250 to 300 species of asters worldwide—even asters adapted to beach areas, or the wet. Each year I promise myself to track down an expert and learn the rest of my local natives and the best garden selections of each.

The trick is to learn to tolerate their early appearance, like the ones in my shopping cart that long-ago spring day, which ranges from nondescript to downright weedy. Conventional wisdom says to lift asters and divide them regularly, for most vigorous performance. With the taller ones, it's also advisable to pinch or prune them once or twice before letting them fill out and bloom, to insure bushier, more compact plants. The timing for this might be mid-June or even July 4, but probably no later. Whack them back to about 6 inches—something deer did for me before I had a fence, and rabbits or woodchucks do if I am not vigilant nowadays about keeping them away. Don't pinch the naturally compact ones like the arresting scaled-down New England aster cultivar called 'Purple Dome' or its raspberry-colored sport 'Vibrant Dome', or the nearly prostrate white one called *Symphyotrichum ericoides* 'Snow Flurry'.

Cover Crops: Feeding the Soil

A month or more before killing frost, the vegetable-garden soil that fed me gets a meal, or at least the promise of one. I sow soil-sustaining cover crops—always from non-GMO, organic seed—as my various food crops are harvested, gradually turning empty raised vegetable beds into minifields of winter cereal rye and mammoth red clover for the colder months, or maybe a mix of quick-to-grow, easy-to-manage, and beautiful field peas and oats.

Come spring, several weeks before I plant each area, I'll cut or mow or pull the so-called "green manure" down, then fork under the remains. It's like composting in place, with the foliage and underlying root systems decomposing to improve soil texture and fertility. If sowing then, I might use hairy vetch or oats or field peas; in summer, I could use annual ryegrass or buckwheat, among others.

Cover crops are a living mulch, protecting the soil from erosion and outcompeting weeds, making the management of fallow areas easier. They can serve other purposes—some specialized ones, like various brassicas, provide not just biomass but also pest and disease control. The subject is much wider than this simple explanation, but stated most briefly there are a few main types:

Grasses (like rye, sorghum-sudangrass crosses, and wheat) add organic matter to the soil very effectively. I didn't list buckwheat, another great, fast-growing cover crop that bees love, too, because that rhubarb and sorrel relative is not technically a grass or grain, though we think of it as such because of how we use it food-wise.

Legumes (clovers, cow and field peas, vetch) with their inherent nitrogen-fixing capability, enrich the soil. Many farmers and gardeners like to grow a heavy feeder like tomatoes where a legume cover crop was last. Field-pea bonus: eat some of the leafy tips and blooms and young pods in salad along the way.

Brassicas and mustards (rapeseed or canola; radish; mustard) have the extra benefit of proving effective against various nematodes, fungi, and insects.

Choosing the right one for your location and timing will take some homework, but once you do, keep a bag of organic seed or a mix of each of your chosen cover crops on hand so you're always ready, as each spot opens up.

Smarter Bulb Shopping and Planting

It's bulb-planting season—or more accurately, geophyte-planting season, because not all the dormant storage organs sold in bulb catalogs are technically bulbs. But all are clever stockpiles of water and carbohydrates stashed for when there's not a rainy day. Whether you use technical or generic terminology, tuck tubers and corms and tuberous roots and rhizomes and yes, even some true bulbs, into the soil now for years of enjoyment. But which ones, and how? Some miscellaneous advice for smarter shopping and planting:

Use animal-resistant bulbs Tired of waking up in spring to beheaded tulips and disappearing crocus? Shop for animal-resistant flower bulbs. If it's crocus you are losing specifically, try *Crocus tommasinianus*, the so-called Tommies, earlier to flower and more animal-resistant than the bigger Dutch crocus. If you can get the straight species of it, they will seed about, not just clump up as bulbs multiply underground.

Try bulbs for the shade garden Is your garden (like mine) a place of increasing shade as deciduous trees and shrubs mature? Some bulbs, including Spanish bluebells (*Hyacinthoides hispanica*), winter aconite (*Eranthis hyemalis*), snowdrops (*Galanthus*), and trout lily (*Erythronium americanum*), among others, can manage in that situation, doing their thing early, then shutting down as the leaves above fill in.

Add extra-early blooming bulbs Minor (mostly small) bulbs like winter aconite, snowdrops, and crocus can extend your garden bloom time weeks before the official start of spring.

Remember: early, middle, and late One of my mantras is "early, middle, late." Don't shop just for color or size in the tulip or daffodil or other bulb listings, but for bloom time, too, to have the longest possible succession of each genus.

For lastingness, look for the word "naturalizing" Generally speaking, daffodils (genus *Nar-cissus*) will be longer lived than, say, tulips. But even some daffodils will falter in the wrong climate, certain ones preferring the cooler or warmer ends of their hardiness range. Given the right conditions, lilies, Spanish bluebells, *Scilla*, *Camassia*, snowdrops, snowflakes (*Leucojum*), glory of the snow (*Chionodoxa*), winter aconite (*Eranthis hyemalis*), and trout lily are among others inclined to stick around. *Crocus* would, but are sometimes gobbled up. Scan catalogs for "bulbs for naturalizing" to find longer-lasting choices.

Make tulips live longer Though often used for a year or two of extra splashes of color, almost like annuals, certain tulips can offer more enduring beauty. The smaller species types, like *Tulipa tarda* and *batalinii* and *clusiana*, are recommended, and among larger tulips try Darwin hybrids for durability. Plant Darwins extra-deep—not just 6 or 8 inches but 10 or 12 inches—which insulates bulbs from moisture fluctuations during summer rains, since they like a dry dormant period. Extra benefit: animals intent on digging or gnawing may not bother with these.

Mix it up; be daring Go ahead: order a flowering bulb you've never grown before. I dare you—like a foxtail lily (*Eremurus*) or some oddball *Fritillaria*—and don't be stingy with the numbers; order more than you usually do for greater impact, like 5 not 1 or 10 not 5, not so many lonelyhearts. If we don't widen our palettes and plant more lavishly, how will we ever grow as gardeners?

Compare prices, but read the fine print Prices may vary widely by catalog, but don't be fooled. Some deals in mass-market catalogs are too good to be true. Read the fine print about what size bulb you'll be receiving. Another budget tip: Naturalizing mixtures (a blend of varieties, such as many different narcissus) can be good value if you want a less formal massed look.

Plan for plants to show bulbs off, then conceal them I am inspired by public gardens like Chanticleer in Pennsylvania where careful thought is given to every detail, like what other adjacent plant will provide a foil for bulb bloom (when the garden is mostly asleep still). Examples inspired by Chanticleer: *Sedum rupestre* 'Angelina', or the Mexican hair grass, *Nassella tenuissima*, left standing from last year through bulb bloom, then cut back as fresh growth begins. Also to consider: companions that emerge later to cover ripening foliage and the void the spent bulbs will leave.

Plan your spring bulb purchases now, too Remember: Some bulbs are only sold in spring, such as pineapple lilies (*Eucomis*). Make yourself a note now to order them then, so you leave room.

Eranthis, the Winter Aconite

You can count on *Eranthis hyemalis*, or winter aconite, for a couple of things: to be a pioneer each spring, blooming extra-early even among the early bulbs (they coincide with snowdrops), and to provoke consternation among gardeners who planted them without result. The disappointed toss about phrases like "slow to establish," and hope for a later ascension.

After some failed attempts, I've managed to establish a colony here, with two more recently planted areas now developing, too. Each year around mid-March I see more plants pushing up

The winter aconite, *Eranthis hyemalis*, is starting to sow itself around under an old magnolia, sometimes blooming as early as March here.

The sunny little flowers of *Eranthis hyemalis*, blooming even before crocus, are a welcome sight after a long winter.

than the year prior (though one recent nonwinter year, the showing began February 20). The best colonies I've seen were where the plants had sown themselves around over time. Grow these deciduous woodland natives from areas in the Balkans, Italy, and southern France under deciduous trees and shrubs where they have a place to arise, bloom, fade gradually until they're good and done before the canopy leafs out, and set seed at their own pace. Don't root around and pester them; vigorous cleanup, as with any such volunteer, or too-deep mulching, even, can prevent next-generation seedlings from settling in.

Plant tubers in early fall, when they are fresh and not dried out, soaking thoroughly beforehand in water, then burying them 1 inch deep and several inches apart. As with any fresh planting of small bulbs (or garden peas) squirrels may dig them up, so pinning down black plastic netting temporarily can help. If you have a friend that grows winter aconite, ask for a trowelful or two of the little plants when they are up and growing—my favorite way to spread all kinds of little things around successfully.

A Nectaroscordum by Any Name

Call it what you like, but plant it. Whether labeled as *Nectaroscordum siculum*—the way I first knew it—or *Allium siculum*, it's a wonderful oddball of a flowering bulb that always elicits inquiries from visitors at my June garden events, though some of its assets are not as obvious as its lovely dangling mauve and green bells.

This Mediterranean native is animal-proof, since nobody messes with onion relatives, and long-lasting, perennializing and even self-sowing. If you don't want more, simply pull the slender seedlings, or better yet, deadhead the parent plants before seed is set.

The allium relative *Nectaroscordum siculum* is easy, long-lived, and attractive to bees.

Bees love it, and hummingbirds are also inclined to investigate. They're curious, apparently—and that's a good word for this plant: curious. First come elongated, papery-covered buds on spear-like stems, before the odd-colored clustered bells held about 30 inches aloft. The foliage is not flat but 3-dimensional, madly twisted. The tan seedpods that follow the faded flowers seem to shift position from dangling toward vertical as they mature.

It is one of those plants, owing to its old-fashioned and subtle coloration in bloom—all creamy and plum and green, plus its gray-green foliage—that seems to be able to knit together other plants you might not at first think would make a match. One idea: a jumble of blue-leaved *Rosa glauca* and a purple smokebush (like *Cotinus* 'Grace') underplanted with blue-leaved sedums, dark-leaved *Heuchera*, and pink- and purple-flowering perennial geraniums.

Saving Seeds

Seeds are forming everywhere, a resource to be gathered in and preserved, a thread to tie together this year's garden and the next. Not all seeds will be worth saving, however, so I limit my efforts to species or open-pollinated (nonhybrid) plants that can be expected to come true from seed in subsequent generations.

Plants deliver their seeds in two basic ways: moist, or dry. With wet seeds—ones enclosed in a fruit (the part we might eat, such as tomatoes, tomatillos, eggplants, peppers, squash, and cucumbers)—the process involves first separating seeds from flesh.

Dry-seeded plants are simpler, the only tricky part getting them when they are ripe enough but have not been dispersed. Easy dry seeds to save include calendula, zinnia, opium poppies, and peas and beans.

With some wet-seeded crops, you could simply separate seeds from the pulp, smearing them on an unwaxed paper plate or paper toweling to dry—or better than that, soak the seedy pulp in water for 8 or 12 hours, then rinse off all the loose remaining flesh in a strainer before drying them. For cucumbers and tomatoes, though, the smelly-gooey part of the process serves a purpose, because the natural act of fermentation helps break down germination-inhibiting compounds such as the gel sac around tomato seeds, and can also reduce some seed-specific diseases.

The step-by-step procedure, using tomato as the example:

Choose a few of your best-looking, slightly past-mature fruits (but not decaying) from each of your healthiest plants The variety must be open-pollinated (not a hybrid), to insure consistency in the next generation. Though modern hybrid tomatoes rarely cross-pollinate, the old-time potato-leaf ones (like popular 'Brandywine') may; save from plants that were isolated from another tomato variety by at least 25 to 50 feet. Choose fully mature fruits that look like the variety is supposed to, from a vigorous plant. Keen seed-savers with any crop actually begin their selection process—to narrow things to their best genetics—from the moment they sow the seed in late winter, discarding any extra-small seeds from the packet, next rogueing out any slow-to-emerge seedlings, and continuing that process to eliminate runts all along.

Bean seeds, like peas, are among the easiest to save.

Fermenting tomato seeds is part of the process of saving them for use next year.

If the tomato is a little past peak ripeness, no worry Nature saves and resows her own seed when overripe fruit falls and rots in place, and in fact we're about to simulate that. (For cucumbers, the seeds at the stage we eat the fruit are not fully mature, so wait about six weeks after the edible stage, letting the fruit hang on the vine—or even longer, if possible, until just before frost.)

Quarter the tomatoes, squeezing seeds and pulp into a container, such as a large canning jar.

Reserve all the tomato flesh in a pot or your food processor bowl, to make sauce or soup or salsa or gazpacho (If seeding cucumbers, the past-prime flesh can be discarded.)

Add water to your seeds and pulp to create a concoction that's equal parts fruit and water, and set it aside (but not in the sun), covered with paper towel or cheesecloth to keep bugs away. Allow to ferment about three days.

Keep a close eye so that it doesn't go too far Stir daily, and observe. Depending on temperature, timing can vary batch to batch. The clue: Once a smelly scum or mold forms on the top of the mix, it's time to wash the seed.

Skim off the mold, in which will probably be floating some seeds. Discard those, too; floating seeds are nonviable; good ones will have sunk.

Put your mix in a strainer and wash thoroughly Empty clean seeds into an unwaxed paper plate (labeled as to variety) and allow to dry well. If it's humid, run a fan on low nearby.

Store thoroughly dry seed in a cool, dark spot in an airtight jar—and again, label them. Numerous breathable envelopes of seeds can be stashed together in large glass jars. Wicking materials put in the bottom of the jar can help draw moisture from the seeds, and range from silica gel to rice that has been dried in a 250°F oven, then cooled.

As with cucumbers, let summer squash fruit get overripe on the vine before saving seed, six weeks or even longer past good eating stage. Winter squash seeds may continue to develop inside the harvested fruit for a few months, and then processed. Melon and watermelon will have a higher percentage of fully mature seed if allowed to go a little way past ripe as well, though perhaps by a couple of weeks.

How to Grow Garlic

I grow hardneck garlic because I like the big heads with their extra-fat cloves, but also because of what happens around early June, when my plants send up their early bonus–a tasty flowering stalk, or scape. Softneck garlic, the more familiar kind in the grocery store, has a row of largish outer cloves and a row or two of inner small ones. It would keep better than what I grow (see storage ideas, following), but oh, those scapes. I prune each mildly garlicky curlicue off, grill it whole or cut it into pieces, and sauté or stir-fry it, or make a batch of scape pesto for the freezer.

There are many hardneck types, and also many softnecks, and selecting a variety that's well-suited to your conditions is where to start. Inquire through an organic garlic specialty catalog for help in making a good match for your soil and season.

Like any bulb, garlic prefers well-drained soil, and my raised beds that have been amended for years with compost are ideal. Though it's a tough plant that can adapt to less prime

Hardneck garlic has a woody flower stem that will hold the scape.

Hardneck garlic

After garlic plants cure for several weeks in a warm, dry spot out of the sun, they are ready for the stems and roots to be cut back.

conditions, I think It's worth preparing the soil by adding organic matter, and also incorporating a good source of nitrogen—whether composted manure or an organic fertilizer. You only get one chance a year to plant garlic, so do it well.

The target time for planting in fall is 3 to 5 weeks before the ground freezes hard (or if you are in a no-freeze zone, around Thanksgiving or early December). Separate the heads into individual cloves, leaving the bulb wrappers intact, and plant each clove 2 to 3 inches deep and spaced about 6 to 8 inches apart in each direction. Watering at planting time is critical to getting root growth started before the ground freezes. Since I am in a cold-winter zone I also mulch the bed with a couple of inches of chopped, rotted leaves, straw, or another mulch.

There is not much more to it except patience (and regular attention to weeding and watering), since garlic is in the ground from around November to the next July sometime. I know the garlic is ready when it tells me so: when several of the lower leaves go brown, but five or six up top are still green. With garlic, unlike its cousin the onion, waiting until all the leaves go brown will promote overripe bulbs whose cloves are starting to separate, and the resulting heads won't store as long, since each brown leaf is one fewer potential bulb wrapper. Harvesting too soon can also diminish storage life, and may limit bulbs reaching full size.

Harvesting garlic couldn't be easier. However tempting, don't pull the bulbs out by the aboveground stems, or at least without first loosening the soil alongside each row with a spading fork well away from the heads.

Another difference between garlic and onion: Assuming it's a dry day when harvest comes, onions can be left out to dry right beside the rows you dug them from. Not so with garlic, which should be moved out of direct sunlight immediately once unearthed. Cure the harvest for several weeks in an airy, warm spot (about 80°F is ideal) out of the sunlight—such as by hanging plants in the back of the garage, or spreading them on wire racks there. I have used old window screens stretched between sawhorses, for instance. Once cured, the tops are cut off, roots trimmed, and the cured bulbs stored.

Storing and Preserving Garlic

My homegrown garlic crop gets me to almost February, and then it's just not what it used to be. You know how it goes—you've bought late-winter cloves that start to sprout and just don't feel as firm or weigh what they did before time took its toll. I don't have a perfect storage spot, which would be 40 to 55°F with 60 to 70 percent humidity, but with a few tricks—including freezing some as whole, peeled cloves—I do quite well.

A barely heated room above my barn, which stays around 40, is the best I can offer for fresh storage of a portion of the yield. You may have a pantry closet on an exterior wall that stays cool. A spot that's too humid (including the refrigerator) may foster mold; too dry and the garlic will dehydrate quickly. Don't put all your harvest in one place if you're not sure how it will fare; experiment with two or three best possible locations.

Not all garlic stores equally well, I learned years ago from Alley Swiss, who operates the venerable Northern California organic garlic operation called Filaree Farm. Softneck varieties, especially Artichoke and Silverskin types, generally keep longest, often remaining firm

I freeze peeled whole cloves from about half my harvest so I have some of my own garlic year-round.

10 months after harvest. With hardnecks, some store better than others; Porcelains like 'Romanian Red' are among the best. Rocamboles have very good flavor, but often dehydrate within a few months. His strategy: Grow multiple kinds and eat the shorter-storing varieties first.

After using some to put up tomato sauce, pestos and soups for the year, I freeze about half the remaining garlic, following safe, sane methods—and no, you cannot just pack it in oil. Even at below 40 degrees, such as in the refrigerator, harmful bacteria may form after about a week, including spores of *Clostridium botulinum*, the cause of botulism. The low-oxygen conditions that bacteria loves are ideal, thanks to the oil packing. Oil-packed, peeled garlic sold in the market contains a preservative, such as citric acid. Achieving safe preservation this way is best left to commercial packers. (Ditto with sun- or oven-dried tomatoes. Dry them, pack them crisp in airtight bags, then soften a week's worth at a time in oil before using. Herb-infused oils, particularly those with garlic, run the same risk.)

I freeze some whole, peeled cloves by the first method following, and I also offer other tactics gathered from university extension services and preserving books:

Whole, unpeeled cloves can be frozen as-is at harvest time or slightly later, then used as needed I prefer to separate and peel each clove, toss them very lightly in olive oil, and freeze them in freezer bags or canning jars. I don't thaw the cloves before cooking, but roast or slowly sauté them, or drop them into recipes like soups while cooking, then locate and mash them against the side of the pot with a fork or back of a spoon once they soften.

Some people prefer the convenience of making logs or small bricks of chopped garlic— not unlike my parsley logs (page 240)—and slicing off just what is needed for a recipe.

Likewise, a purée of garlic and olive oil can be frozen like other pestos in cubes or small containers The University of California at Davis recommends 1 part garlic to 2 parts oil, for a sauté mixture that remains safely frozen but soft enough to scrape the needed amount off.

With all freezer methods, freeze immediately after preparation Do not refrigerate or store at room temperature even briefly first.

Around January, if I see that I still have a lot garlic left in storage and worry it won't last, I freeze more Onions starting to sprout in storage also can be rescued if caught in time, and sliced or chopped and frozen in airtight plastic ziplock bags.

A Saner Fall Cleanup

When we say, "fall garden cleanup," just how clean do we mean? I don't clean up as if I'm vacuuming the living room, from one corner to the opposite and hitting every inch between, but rather selectively—leaving anything that might look good to me or the birds, teasing the place apart gradually.

The more I learn about the life cycles of birds, other animals, and especially beneficial insects, the messier I am getting—if not right in front of the house, then at least in all the less-conspicuous spots where a looser style makes for more supportive, high-quality off-season habitat.

I have always saved all my leaves, never bagging them but rather using them as mulch or soil amendment once they were composted. Now I am careful to let any that I can lie where they fell, such as under all the big trees at the garden's periphery. I learned why this matters from experts at The Habitat Network (www.yardmap.org), a joint project of Cornell Lab of Ornithology and The Nature Conservancy.

The ecology of leaf litter is surprising: Various Lepidoptera—butterflies and moths—deposit their eggs on leaves of trees of their host species in early fall, presuming that when those leaves

Someone is getting a head start on the leaf cleanup.

A few of the 179 moth species I have identified in my garden so far are (left to right, top to bottom): variable antepione (summer female); giant cecropia; tolype; twin-spotted sphinx; luna; twin-spotted sphinx, in profile; clymene; waved sphinx; and variable antepione (summer male).

drop beneath it, the emerging caterpillars will be near their needed food source. Some butterflies, like the mourning cloak and eastern comma, even overwinter as adults in thick layers of leaf litter, and still others remain in their chrysalis or as larvae rolled in a leaf cocoon in a similarly protected spot. Other beneficial insects and spiders overwinter in such places, too.

All of our leaf blowing and mowing and raking is disastrous to such insect strategies.

Leaving faded flowers standing encourages offseason foraging by birds, who can feast on seed heads (and even on galls of spent goldenrod, which may be filled with protein-rich larvae that can sustain a goldfinch). Nature is intricate, and I love learning what I can do—and just as important *not* do—to support it.

More ideas: I create a lot of woody debris, and though some must go, I always keep a brushpile—another wildlife-supporting mechanism. At the other end of winter, I learned from

The Habitat Network to wait until after several 50°F days to start my spring cleanup. Getting aggressive out there any earlier will destroy nesting sites of bumblebees and other critically important arthropods. I can wait in the name of the greater good.

As a gardener, I do make some exceptions to the nature focus, specifically with diseased plants, and those with a serious insect infestation or those prone to insect pests, like brassicas are to imported cabbage worms. Good garden sanitation in the fall to remove delicious overwintering places for these non-native pests can help. Hoping to minimize squash bugs, cucumber beetles, those cabbage worms, and more, I don't leave spent troubled or vulnerable plants standing. If I had any serious fungal diseases, such as with peonies or roses, I'd clean up extra carefully under those and discard the spore-covered debris, too.

Mad Stash: Overwintering Tender Plants

I am asked two questions over and again by visitors: "Where did you get that plant?" (referring to whatever looks showiest on the day of their visit) and, "Where do you put all those big pots of tender things in winter?" My reply to the second part begins with a question: Are you ready for an adventure?

Unless you operate a climate-controlled greenhouse—and even then, if the power fails—matching nonhardy plants to the possibilities of our domestic winter environment, especially in a northern location, is indeed an exploration.

I have been experimenting for years with stashing tender plants in the cellar, garage, house, mudroom—wherever I can—to try to turn each purchase into an investment plant. Before I go attempting any real heroics, though (and have to move to a hotel because the house is full), I ask if there is a way to carry over a piece of each instead, as seeds or by taking late-summer cuttings of, say, *Coleus* or *Pelargonium,* and rooting them—or simply by digging up tubers or bulbs and stashing those (some of the easiest of all, like cannas or callas)?

My adventure begins with this kind of thinking about the candidates:

Is the plant evergreen, or deciduous? The ones with leaves (say, rosemary, citrus, or a bay tree) will require light even in winter and can be trickier to accommodate here; the leafless, dormant ones (like a fig tree in a big pot) do not.

Where did the plant originate? (That is, where were its ancestors native?) This piece of information will reveal the lowest temperature a plant might withstand, and also whether it might expect a dry, dormant period—a common phase of the life cycle in some Zone 8 or 9 or warmer places. Plants willing to rest completely are easier for me to carry over than ones wanting bright light and cool or mild temperatures in my low-light winters and dry, heated home.

With those first two considerations, I'm trying to categorize my wish list into rough buckets of winter storage conditions like "cool, bright," or "dark, dry, above freezing," or "try as a houseplant."

Next I give my home, garage, cellar, and shed the same good, hard look As with the plant analysis, I'm evaluating both offseason temperature range (and is it fairly constant or fluctuating?) and amount of light, if any. No two cellars (or sunrooms, or garages) are alike.

The Rex begonia vine, *Cissus discolor*, is my latest experiment in overwintering.

Then I try to make good matchups between plants and places
Sometimes I get it right, but often the first time out, I don't. Typically I learn something, though, so I can fine-tune my next try—going cooler, or warmer, or brighter, maybe, within the limits of my available spots. And sometimes I surrender, acknowledging I lack a welcoming location for certain things without a greenhouse, or at least without setting up supplemental lighting in one spot that's currently the right temperature but too dark.

Whatever I plan to do with a plant, I try to ease the pain of making the transition from outdoors to in. This is important: Don't wait till it's 38°F and damp outside and the drying heat is blasting 68°F indoors to do an instant relocation, then expect your houseplants or potted Meyer lemon not to drop their leaves in shock. Anticipate the eventual move in stages over a couple of weeks, perhaps moving them first to a protected porch or garage to dry off before heading inside.

Another tip, with plants that retain their leaves and want the conditions I have the least of, bright and cool: Though it will look insane, stage your pots near windows so that the tallest ones are farther from the light than the small ones (which would otherwise be shaded). I know, *ugh*, but it makes a big difference by efficiently allocating limited light resources.

Banana canna lily, *Canna* 'Musifolia' or 'Grande'.

Some plants that I have overwintered for multiple (or many) years in Zone 5B:

Bulbs and bulb-like things: Easiest of all are the cannas. Dig the tubers (cutting back the frost-blackened foliage) and stash them in the dark, dry cellar or a garage that's frost-free, and even 45 to 50°F; unpotted is fine. My one and only canna is the giant called the banana canna, *Canna* 'Musifolia' or 'Grande'. Also easy dark and dry, potted or unpotted: calla lilies (*Zantedeschia*).

I do likewise with the old-style shiny-leaved green elephant ears in the genus *Alocasia* that make a big bulb. The newer, irresistible matte-leaved *Colocasia* like 'Mojito', 'Black Magic' or 'Black Coral', don't bulb up, so they are trickier. Try leaving them potted and actively growing in good light at 60°F (at least), or semidormant at 45 to 50°F and fairly dry (light is not critical therefore).

Amorphophallus or voodoo lily tubers, and *Eucomis* or pineapple lily bulbs are both easy. Store them dry and dark, such as in your basement. I don't even unpot mine, but you can.

Store tuberous begonias (including *B. boliviensis* types) after just a light frost—not a hard freeze—tells them to slow down; these I do not unpot.

I find dahlias a bit more hit and miss. First, wait two weeks after a hard frost before cutting stems to 6 inches and digging carefully, because tubers are easily damaged. Store layered in boxes or crates (but not in plastic) in sand, peat, wood shavings, or vermiculite at 40 to 50°F, checking for decay once or twice during storage.

I overwintered an angel's trumpet or *Brugmansia* until it got so big I could not drag it down the stairs to the dark cellar that hovers around 40°F or slightly warmer, where I had to lay the pot down since the ceiling was too low. Same with a potted banana (*Musa*). Both can be cut back before storage if need be, but don't top-prune a banana that's been dug from the ground, which would mean stress at both ends and might prove too much.

I have a couple of "hardy" fig trees, Zone 6-ish plants like 'Brown Turkey' and 'Chicago Hardy', that I grow in giant pots. Once they are dormant, I roll the pots on a handcart into my insulated but unheated barn, where it gets very cold but they are spared wind and ice. The cellar would also be a possibility. Ideally I'd keep them just above freezing all winter, like mid- to high 30s.

Rosemary stumped me nearly forever. I'd get it to late January in my 60°F bright mudroom and then it would start to stretch pitifully before going crisp. I finally succeeded in a barely heated shed with windows, keeping it much cooler—at about 45°F—and watering only very occasionally, like monthly, if the soil felt quite dry.

My latest adventure is with *Cissus discolor*, or Rex begonia vine, a Zone 9- or 10-hardy member of the grape family that can grow 8 to 10 feet in a season—far too big to lug indoors. I have purchased large plants from a specialty source every year for a decade because I love it so much, but each year I have killed them in winter (except ones I donated to nearby public gardens with greenhouses). I finally called for reinforcements to help get a very large clay pot, bamboo tripod supports and all, into my back mudroom in fall, and it looked good all winter, then went dormant as spring arrived but took till midsummer to resprout. Next time I will cut it back halfway or so before the mudroom treatment. Who knows?

Taking the Year's Inventory

With shears and rake in hand and a clipboard and pen beside me, I tease the garden apart. Cleanup is not all about sanitation, but a bit of a forensic exercise, really, a time of sober analysis before all remnants of the growing season that was are erased from memory, or masked by a blanket of snow. Normal types may make resolutions at New Year's, but for a gardener that is no time for such important business.

After spring, this is when the garden-journal entries should be most frequent, notations of which plants didn't fare well (with suspicions why); which are too crowded; which look too isolated (add some more of the same) or too overpowering (subtract) for the garden's good. If there were pest or disease issues, the coming dormant season is a good time to research tactics for outwitting them—not next summer in the midst of a repeat outbreak.

Yes, we must ask: How many times did we run to the garden center to try to shop our way out of an outbreak of something, or a weak performance by some plant? Such "remedies" aren't remedies at all, really, and no substitute for time spent building your soil (as in: compost, compost, compost), and practicing vigilant garden hygiene methods.

Fall is the best time to evaluate and record your own issues, too. Did you expect too much of yourself by shopping too often? (Tipoff: a small army of plants in nursery pots still sitting in

Fruit of 'Winter Gold' winterberry holly and *Sorbus rufoferruginea* 'Longwood Sunset' seem to have escaped the earlybirds.

'September Charm'
Japanese anemone and
gone-by *Astilbe chinensis*
reach around the small
gate to a shady area of the
garden in fall.

the driveway.) Was there simply too much deadheading, watering, weeding to manage—has the garden gotten too big, or too complex in some places? Perhaps such troubles can be alleviated by budgeting for a few hours with a helper, or better use of mulch, or by a drip-irrigation system you could install now—or maybe by changing out the underplantings in some areas to a simpler ground cover palette. Should you find someone to mow next year to free up more time for real gardening? Were there too many tomatoes and cucumbers to eat or can (or worse, too few), or not enough basil or dill to accompany them—or no flowers to cut for indoor use?

My resolves by the time my rounds are through will range from "test soil in vegetable beds" (now, not spring, is the time, because the labs will be backed up then), to "turn compost an additional time and moisten more often" (hoping to heat the pile and reduce weed seeds in finished material), to much loftier matters. I offer this semigeneric list of resolutions for you to cull a few from and customize as you reflect during your own year's review:

Mow more creatively Can you "unmow" a spot to add diversity, or eliminate a lawn area completely?

Make better use of self-sowns, with alert editing and moving around of what the garden offers up spontaneously—admittedly sometimes in too great concentration or the wrong spot entirely.

Dig up "onesies" and either eliminate or replicate them Unless a plant is a stunner that can stand alone, onesies are usually the recipe for a polka-dot garden.

Repeat successes (the yang to the previous resolution's yin).

Add more vines, both annual and perennial.

Grow (fill in the blank) next year This is where you get to insert that thing you always want to try but don't—whether some rarity, or just a massive bed full of every last kind of zinnia or sunflower.

Rethink and fine-tune vegetable supports, and while you're at it, what else was under-supported where a better job could have been done?

Grow more herbs

Compost better than ever

More mulch, less sprays

Be a more ruthless pruner Not a butcher, but extending a firmer hand to that shrub over-taking the path, for instance. There is no cure for too-stingy spacing, but certain things can be kept in check with a firmer resolve, before it's too late.

Remember to go back inside before it's all erased and look out the window, where the biggest decisions about design begin.

Death and Afterlife

NOVEMBER & DECEMBER

DEAR FRIEND (LOVE, MARGARET)

DEAR OLD FRIEND,

Ouch! Little wonder that you are craving getting all tucked in, my dear, and staying put. Me too, though I have no acute cause like your recent surgery to point the finger at. I can only explain the urgent instinct to hunker like this:

I am an animal.

The longer I live in Nowheresville, with its intimate window on the natural world, the better I grasp my kindredness with other local species. Yes, I boast a bigger brain; the ability to walk upright; opposable thumbs. (Though I suppose I'm not alone in that last one, since the local Virginia opossum has them, albeit on his hind feet—and a tail designed to do some grabbing, used for stability while hanging from my suet feeder, gorging, each cold evening.)

Apparently furlessness and the mechanism to sweat (since cooling down efficiently can boost endurance) are other evolutionary advancements on the human side of the ledger. Right now, though, some fur sounds welcome, and getting overheated inconceivable. *Brrrrr.*

The furbearers and the rest apparently regard the garden as a wildlife park, and inspired by their example I'm getting in touch with my animalness. No time of year is it more pronounced than at the seasonal cusps, exaggerated in response to the most extreme pull of natural forces. Like everyone in this habitat, I'm behaving as dwindling daylength, temperature, and resources dictate, going about seasonally appropriate business to insure food, shelter, and safety—or else. (Note to self: Check batch of homegrown apples, sliced and drying in oven.)

Which animal I'm most like, I am not certain—perhaps it's some interspecific hybrid of bird, frog, mammal—some ×*hybridus* creature like my hellebores? Once inclined to constant anthropomorphizing, in my rural years, I've become more inclined toward seeing the animal in me. (Is that sense of identification called *zoomorphism*, or what?)

I can't stop repeating what I know I have quoted to you before, human-behavior wisdom gleaned in a course on bird behavior, from Cornell ornithologist Kevin McGowan: "Thinking of animals like people is misleading and unhelpful, and offers no assistance in understanding animal behavior. Thinking of people as animals with the same survival goals can provide profound insights into what we do."

And so, like many birds, I am diurnal, punching the mirror-image time clock from the nocturnal mice in my wall lately who scuttle around as their shift starts at 4 p.m. or so, with the arriving darkness, and again when settling back into their nests after maybe 12 hours. Each afternoon around 4 o'clock I'm about done for the day this time of year; at 4-something in the morning, I stir toward starting another.

I am resident, like a woodpecker or turkey, not migrant like brilliant forest-breeding rose-breasted grosbeaks, scarlet tanagers, or indigo buntings, which visit in the milder months. I never wander far from where I nest.

I do not scatter-hoard my store of food for the duration—placing the equivalent of an acorn here and another there and another somewhere else, the way a squirrel does, or a tufted titmouse or blue jay with their sunflower seeds tucked under bits of bark or siding. I've

Many gardeners consider gray squirrels a nuisance. I gave this one and his colleagues a discarded jack-o'-lantern to feast on.

spent the fall larder-hoarding instead, like the mice or adult eastern chipmunks, stashing all my provisions in one central pantry: back and forth, back and forth, load after load.

Exciting: A bobcat lately is paying regular visits. The handsome feline is by nature solitary—I am no pack animal, either, as you well know. He is a sometime-hoarder: If a deer is scored in winter, such a cache lasts weeks—a lucky thing when snow is deep and hunting rodents or rabbits challenging. I am no carnivore, but am guarding three freezers stocked with what the garden offered, brewed into soups and stews and sauces, jewel-colored bricks of suspended-animation sustenance.

A disappointing divergence: Nobody out there seems to reciprocate the delight I get from their presence, appearing either indifferent or occasionally disturbed by mine. I find my outdoor neighbors endlessly fascinating, even two acrobatic black-morph individuals of the eastern gray squirrel who have made the garden home. Perhaps they don't have a *Peterson Field Guide to Eastern Humans* to read up on all my most riveting aspects, the way I have my reference books depicting each of theirs.

"Now what?" you asked in your recent letter. Here, there is still the last yard cleanup to complete (I know, but the *leaves*—they held on and on this fall, lacking the proper weather triggers to the abscission layer that say "let go," and even now keep descending, so onward I do rake). There are more apples to be processed into sauce; the water gardens to winterize. And then there is surrender to a sober rhythm; then we are resting, but not completely down for the count. I liked how you put it: "Lying fallow is different from doing nothing."

Not just some abandoned or neglected bed or field, a fallow one is a deliberate stage in a scheme of successful crop rotation, perhaps sown with green manure awhile so that it may

Various local animals hoard acorns in mast years, fueling successful overwintering.

be more bountiful at another time. It may look like nothing is happening, but good soil health is being intentionally cultivated. What's going on here, you ask? Everything, if all unseen.

We are not alone in our hunkering instinct, nor is there total stillness even on the quietest approaching days. I think of the female black bear, who though still in hibernation rouses just after the New Year to give birth to her young, then naps again while they take sustenance from their sleepy mother.

I think of the tadpoles in my garden ponds, waiting for their chance to move on up. Apparently the green frog species will wait longer than a year if conditions so require—holding on, half-baked, even through a hard winter, before letting go of their heavy, unneeded, but familiar tails. Metamorphosis is no instant karma, baby. (And we all shine on.)

I think of the mated female bumblebees—the only members of last season's colonies who even survive winter. Bumblebees, like annual plants, do everything by the end of summer, and then die out. All the males and workers and even the founding queen of the colony: gone.

At our senescent life stage we're not fecund like they are, or like those mama bears, but we are full in our own ways, no? (Please say yes.)

In March, weather willing, I'll see those gravid female bees hovering low among the earliest flowers, seeking nectar for themselves and pollen, too. It is only then, not in fall, that the queen-to-be provisions a nest by stashing the pollen. Unlike honeybees, who rely on honey inside the hive all winter, bumblebees have no need to store resources because they're hibernating or already gone on to their reward, having lived a good short life.

Me?

"I'm hungry all the time," I told a doctor friend last winter when the deep-freeze descended, my tone implying it was symptom of something amiss. "I can't stop eating."

"Have you watched the squirrels and birds at your feeders lately?" he said, rhetorically, fully aware that I do just that nonstop, between trips in search of yet another snack, and then back under the duvet to study the latest catalogs.

Love,

Margaret

Shiny little red peppers pinned up and drying on the dining room wall will yield seed for next year's transplants, or spice for a chili.

The trunks of *Stewartia pseudocamellia* are starting to shape up and exfoliate.

The bark of native paper birch is, like most trees here, festooned with lichen.

The camouflage pattern of the lacebark pine, *Pinus parviflora*, is very handsome—if you don't have sapsuckers to destroy it.

The Asset of Bark

A 1947 article, "Woody Plants with Interesting Bark in Winter" in *Arnoldia*, the bulletin of the Arnold Arboretum, stated the case simply: "The more color in the winter landscape, the more interesting the garden," wrote the great plantsman Donald Wyman, whose *Wyman's Garden Encyclopedia* was for many years my most-used volume. From a winter walk on the Arboretum grounds, Wyman listed many dozens of plants with twigs of red, gray, yellow, green, or white, or colorful trunks or branches, and others with patterned or texturally appealing bark.

Too often, though, we seem not to notice. Maybe that's because it's always right in front of us, 365 days a year on every tree and shrub. Perhaps we just take bark for granted, instead of seeking it out specifically as we shop for plants, distracted in the warmer months by flowers and leaves.

The various white-skinned birches, so often illustrated against a snowy backdrop as the stuff of Christmas cards, are not the only example. The native river birch (*Betula nigra*) has better resistance to birch borer and other insect pests, and peeling bark of various pinkish salmon to reddish brown shades. The compact 'Little King' is ideal for a home garden, at under 15 feet. Nuthatches, brown creepers, and oh so many squirrels share my gratitude toward whomever planted the now-towering, triple-trunked arborvitae of some kind perhaps a century ago just beyond the kitchen door, with its peeling cinnamon bark.

I am intrigued by the distinctive bark of a massive *Thuja* I inherited from the house's original owners.

Besides good bark and fall color, *Stewartia* has camellia-like flowers in July.

The kousa dogwoods offer flowers, fruit, fall color—and great peeling bark.

Exfoliating bark that lets go in patches with age to reveal a camouflage pattern is an endearing trait of Japanese stewartia (*Stewartia pseudocamellia*) and the kousa dogwood (*Cornus kousa*), another Asian import. With not just the bark to recommend them but also vivid fall foliage and showy flowers (the stewartia's in July, when they are so unexpected), I am happy to greet these trees every day. In the case of the kousa, there is even fruit—like giant raspberries—that every chipmunk in the county seems to know about by now.

The lacebark pine (*Pinus bungeana*) has vivid camouflage-pattern bark, but members of the ample local population of yellow-bellied sapsuckers did mine in with incessant drilling of sapwells. Thin-skinned trees like that and the magnolias—many have smooth, handsome gray bark—are targets here for that woodpecker, and even if the tree survives, it defeats the purpose to have it gridded out in pockmarks. (I have to stifle my anger, because it's all part of a bigger coevolutionary plan, apparently: Ruby-throated hummingbirds east of the Mississippi find sustenance at the sap wells when few flowers are blooming at spring migration time.)

With all such trees, choose the individual you adopt carefully for its structure, since good bark and a good silhouette are the most powerful combination of all in the winter landscape. I am inclined toward multistemmed specimens that branch low, rather than waiting till a substantial distance up the trunk to begin breaking.

A number of maples promise color and texture in the winter garden, including the paperbark maple (*Acer griseum*), from China, with cinnamon-colored bark that exfoliates. Among so-called Japanese maples is the coralbark maple (*Acer palmatum* 'Sango-kaku'), startling against the winter sky. There are Japanese maples with gold winter bark (like 'Bihou') and also green, which remind me of the native moosewood (*Acer pensylvanicum*), with its green trunk striped in white that makes up a component of the woodland edge encircling my garden. Such chlorophyll-containing bark can even trap light energy and conduct photosynthesis, including in winter, so it's not just window dressing.

Generally younger wood will have the best color in all of these, as with blueberries (*Vaccinium*) and even some roses, and the shrubby twig willows and dogwoods that I enjoy so much. I placed a red-twig dogwood, *Cornus sericea* 'Sunshine' (with gold foliage in season) just beyond the window through which I glimpse my first bit of garden when I come downstairs each morning. A true 365-day garden plant, and tolerant of damp soils, it is a mass of gold spring-into-fall, and then a vivid arrangement of bright red stems the rest of the year. Among the "red-twig" dogwoods are gold-stemmed possibilities, including *Cornus sericea* 'Silver and Gold', a fine selection of this native species with white-variegated leaves. 'Cardinal', which I use in more naturalistic plantings on the hillside, has plain green leaves and vivid red stems. All are exceptional pollinator attractants, and produce white fruit that birds go mad for.

Maybe the best-known willows for this trait of hot-colored winter stems are *Salix alba* 'Britzensis' and *S.* ×*fragilis* 'Chermesina', which are easily confused.

Dogwood and willow twig color will be most vibrant if they are rejuvenated—either by removing a quarter or so of the oldest stems at the base each late winter, or cutting the whole plant to maybe 8 inches (called coppicing or stooling) every other or third year. The prunings make great architectural arrangements, and with the willows, you can even stick them in the ground and probably get another shrub.

These examples are just a few with "good bark" that I grow. As a bonus, I am likewise delighted by intricate patterns of various lichen species further adorning tree bark here, too, especially vivid against the somber off-season palette. Taking a cue from that 70-plus-year-old article: Perhaps a walk in a local arboretum or botanical garden this time of year is called for?

Cultivating Snags, or Wildlife Trees

Snag. Not as in my pantyhose, which I haven't worn since departing the corporate world in 2007 for an existence where fashion has zero status. Snag as in wildlife tree—a place to nest or den; a source of food for insects, who are in turn food for many other creatures; a perch for lookout, and more. If a tree on your property is dying or dead, or if a healthy tree must be lowered for safety or other reasons, you have the opportunity to cultivate a snag.

In 2014, I had to finally reckon with a 40-foot-tall twin-trunk birch that was in decline, dropping massive portions of its crown on two small outbuildings. To the arborist's surprise, I didn't let them take it all down, or even cart away most of what had to be cut, but rather simply let the carcass lie beside the remaining trunk to rot. Here's why:

Biomass.

Removing all that living or recently living mass of organic material would be a big loss, biologically speaking, for the complex organism I call my garden. The National Wildlife Federation estimates that the removal of dead material from forests "can mean a loss of habitat for up to one-fifth of the animals in the ecosystem."

Some experts recommend an ideal snag population to be about three dead standing trees per acre—that's how important they are. Never remove any more of a dying or damaged tree than is required for safety reasons. Even a high stump can support a lot of wildlife action, compared to a clean cut at ground level, or worse, a ground-out stump.

Lowering the larger, cut-down limbs and trunk portions to the ground, and allowing them to rot there as if they had fallen naturally, is also better ecologically than carting them away. Make like the tree fell beside where it once grew (even if logistics require you to do it in big pieces, rather than whole). Who will thank you?

* **Cavity nesters**, from pileated woodpeckers who can actually excavate, to secondary cavity nesters such as flying squirrels, wood ducks, and even bluebirds.
* **Any creature that is at least partly insectivorous**, since insects and other small invertebrates will show up to feast on the tree's carcass.
* **Birds such as hawks and owls**, who want a good vantage point to survey the area for prey.
* **Animals as small as salamanders and snakes or as large as bears**, who may enjoy the hiding place a fallen tree provides. One of my most beloved birds, the shy little brown creeper, will nest beneath loose bark, for instance, and other animals cache foodstuffs for later use there, too. The list is long.

Years ago, when one trunk of a multistemmed century-old apple tree here lost its crown in a storm, I simply stabilized that snapped-off trunk by taking off anything that was hanging, and left it otherwise intact. I've spent more than 15 years since watching who shows up to enjoy it along with me, and the distinctive evolving character of the elderly tree.

My newest snag, the birch, isn't perfect: Ideally, there would have been some lower branches to leave intact, to make it a more attractive destination to wildlife, but the giant twin trunks were already naked until past 20 feet, where the die-off had set in. I could have had the arborist create jagged tops to each trunk to make it more naturalistic and also speed decay. If the tree had not already had plenty of cavities, we could have started some, but it was already a condo complex.

And this: I should have cut the trunks down even lower, because they could still potentially fall on one shed. I think that's unlikely for many more years, though, so I was happy with the risk-reward ratio in leaving the snag as big as could be. I expect the birch to host a lot of happy visitors between now and then.

A twin-trunk birch was declining, so I topped it and made it a snag, or wildlife tree.

It didn't take long for woodpeckers to explore the snag and start excavations.

and how long it holds on the plant (not counting bird intervention). Since I crave gold-leaved plants, when I learned that both winterberry and gold foliage came in one package, there was probably no chance I'd escape heading to the cash register without at least one *Ilex verticillata* 'Sunsplash' in my cart, a Broken Arrow Nursery introduction of a female clone with orange-red fruit and gold-variegated leaves.

Only one problem: The birds know me by now, and get a little greedy. Normally they start eating in late October, after the winterberry leaves drop, and a mixed flock of cedar waxwings and robins attack one or two plantings and then move on—or not. If they are out in forceful numbers and stay a couple of days, I'll be fruitless. One tip: Normally birds start with red fruits, and don't eat the paler orange and golden ones till much later, so to (hopefully) extend your visual enjoyment, include some nonred ones.

The years when it's "all gone" so early, I worry about both of us. Maybe the birds have discovered another trove of winter food nearby and staked it out for later sustenance. I hope so, but I have no personal backup plan, although some long outdoor extension cords and several-dozen strings of those tiny twinkly Christmas lights not in white but red might do the trick.

Willing Houseplants

The ultimate 365-day plants are the ones we label houseplants, a term that wants to diminish their actual versatility. In fact, my collection of "houseplants"—some of which, like several very big pots of *Clivia miniata*, have been with me for more than 40 years—are happy to keep company together indoors when the weather forbids anything more daring, and then just as capably relocate and dress up semishady spots in the garden through the frost-free months.

Workhorse houseplants reduce the need to buy anywhere near the number of tender annuals each spring to stage lavish vignettes of pots leading up to the house, in areas of bright shade beneath trees, as a sort of "welcome to the garden" message. Because I use more indoor-outdoor foliage stars than bedding flowers, the effect hints at what you'll see elsewhere around the place, too: good foliage first and foremost, in color, texture, and scale.

I have the random oddballs that stay inside year-round to stave off loneliness—a *Pilea peperomiodes*, the Chinese money plant, and the biggest *Clivia*. Far odder still are a couple of very old plants with caudices (singular: caudex, a specialized swollen base and water-storage organ). The bombax (*Pseusobombax ellipticum*) and climbing onion (*Bowiea volubilis*) stay put as well; everyone else goes out. When I say "everyone else," mostly I bank on fancy-leaf begonias, the clivias, and an odd assortment of bromeliads for years of year-round trusted service.

The clivias, divisions of family hand-me-downs, are easy, provided they're given well-drained potting soil, bright light but not direct sun, and most of all are rested below 50°F (but above 35°F) for about 40 days, starting late fall. I don't water while they literally chill out. The idea is that about two months after you raise the temperature to over 60°F, ending their rest, flower spikes will start to form, for bloom in March or April. Without the cold period, they would probably bloom in June, or even summer, and the flower stalk may not elongate fully (so the orange or yellow blooms will be hidden). With their shrubby scale, they make a big statement, indoors or out, in bloom or not, and no doubt will outlive me as they did my forebears.

Begonias and other houseplants join annuals and tropicals outdoors, alongside the seasonal trough water gardens.

Vriesea is among the bromeliads that do indoor-outdoor duty alongside fancy-leaf begonias and *Clivia*.

Begonia 'Autumn Ember', a recent introduction from Logee's Greenhouses, holds its striking orange color even in winter.

I can't really claim to make the bromeliads ideally happy without more indoor humidity in winter. I find that I can get about 5 years from them, anyhow, by offering regular showers in the bathtub as an imperfect substitute, and diligently keeping the cups of each rosette of leaves filled with water. It seems worth the investment to have their sculptural, multicolored foliage and the occasional tropical bloom in the mix in my staged pot groupings, even if they are not forever friends.

If you select the right begonias, they will be around a long time. I just call them all fancy-leaf begonias, but they divide into several structural groups. I do best with some of the fibrous-rooted cane types (like hybrid 'Little Brother Montgomery', which can achieve shrubby proportion) and most of all the rhizomatous ones—skipping the extra-flashy rex ones among those, which don't seem to like me. Reliable rhizomatous 'Marmaduke', 'Autumn Ember', 'Kit Kat', 'Palomar Prince', and 'Black Fancy' are among the many I recommend.

By midwinter, the begonias are not thrilled with our shared digs and looking worse for wear. Supplemental fluorescent lighting, and perhaps a humidifier, would make them happier, but we've managed well enough for years. They dislike low humidity, especially when it's warm (indoors or out). They dislike cold. I try not to subject them to anything below about 55°F, but my brightest winter spots are in the too-cool-for-comfort mudroom. Like virtually every houseplant, they hate wet feet or soggy soil, so avoid watering before dry and don't let them stand in saucers of water. In winter I barely water once a week. Feed weakly, weekly, in periods of active growth, and not at all from about October to February.

I think the fancy-leaf begonias spend winter dreaming of their escape to the outdoor months of high humidity, where they grow happily in the filtered light under trees. I remind them that such better days are just ahead when they're sulking and starting to look pretty sparse. Blessedly, unlike a bromeliad you pushed too far, many of the best begonias resurrect miraculously when they are set free to serve in the garden once again.

Conifers I Have Known

What I do *not* know about conifers could fill a book almost as big and weighty as the *Royal Horticultural Society Encyclopedia of Conifers*, which is 1,507 pages and crammed with more than 8,000 cultivars representing the world's 615 species. Funny, then, that the first thing I planted here was a conifer—and a rare one at that. I carried a Japanese umbrella pine (which isn't a pine at all, a hint at why I have trouble learning my conifers) out of the moving van, dug a hole, and that was the start of a garden.

I knew nothing at all when I heaved the then-very-unusual, chest-high young *Sciadopitys verticillata* out of the ground in the borough of Queens in New York City, two zones to the south, and plopped it unceremoniously into a bushel basket for the trip several hours north. Of course I didn't know then that where the Japanese umbrella pine and I were headed was two zones colder, because I didn't know anything about zones then. There was nothing but one giant rhododendron alone behind the house, and I made the umbrella pine its companion, hoping they would get along.

The twin-trunked Japanese umbrella pine, which I carried with me in the moving van from my first garden more than 30 years ago, enjoys a late afternoon.

Young green frogs from the little garden pools spend summer days nestled up in the limbs of dwarf white pine beside the water.

No tree has better cones than the Korean fir, *Abies koreana*.

The fine-textured gold Hinoki cypress, *Chamaecyparis obtusa* 'Crippsii', reaches out above *Angelica* foliage.

No conifer is more graceful than the weeping Alaska cedar, *Xanthocyparis nootkatensis* 'Pendula'.

The wonderful drapey foliage of the weeping Alaska cedar deserves a close look.

There was no back porch then; there was nothing but high grass and invasive wild blackberries tangled throughout it, and my youthful enthusiasm. The house was a wreck; about 15 feet from where the tree now stands about 25 feet tall was a giant crater, where the back foundation had collapsed.

Today the umbrella pine is the most asked-about plant on my website and in my garden, mostly for its unusual appearance. Its needles are arranged in whorls, like the spokes in an umbrella, hence the name, and everyone wants to know more about the "tree over there with the plastic-looking needles," since they're so thick and lustrous. (Technically, it also has another kind of leaf, the tiny scale leaves on the stems, but nobody notices those.)

I thank the *Sciadopitys* every day for holding up to 30-plus winters of uneasy snow loads and countless ice storms, not suffering winterburn in the spot I chose, and settling in without so much as losing a needle. Umbrella pines hail from cloud forests in Japan, where rainfall and humidity are both high, so it won't cooperate with drought and wants babying in the first year or two after transplanting, plus, in the warmer end of its range (Zones 5 to 7 or 8), protection from the midday sun. Oh, and one more "expert" tip: Skip the stupid moving-van caper I somehow got away with.

None of the conifers in the following list arrived in a moving van, but all have made themselves at home. In addition, for fastest screening I use *Thuja plicata* (western red cedar, and—surprise again!—not a cedar). For greatest wildlife value, I recommend the native-to-me eastern red cedar (except it's a juniper, *Juniperus virginiana*). Other standbys, trees and shrubs:

concolor fir, *Abies concolor* (the bluest of all blues, nearly turquoise, and soft needles)
dwarf eastern white pine, *Pinus strobus* 'Nana' (white pines that don't grow into trees, but rather a mounded, bonsai-like shape; there are many newer named cultivars with a slow-growing habit)

golden spreading yew, *Taxus baccata* 'Repandens Aurea' (gleaming gold in spring through fall, and a sideways, eventually thigh-high habit)

Korean fir, *Abies koreana* (pyramidal tree with purple cones, no less)

lacebark pine, *Pinus bungeana* (mottled, camouflage-pattern bark on a long-needled pine)

Japanese white pine, *Pinus parviflora* (pyramidal when young then flat-topped and spreading; twisty green or blue needles)

prostrate Japanese plum yew, *Cephalotaxus harringtonia* 'Prostrata' (great for ground cover in semishade, with yew-like texture but deer resistance; I would grow the upright form, too, but it splays open in my snowy winters)

Russian arborvitae, *Microbiota decussata* (lacey texture and a ground cover habit in semishade—and not an arborvitae, which is actually in the genus *Thuja*, and commonly called a cedar)

'Skylands' Oriental spruce, *Picea orientalis* 'Skylands' (a pyramidal golden conifer that likes afternoon shade in hot zones).

weeping Alaska cedar, *Xanthocyparis* (or *Chamaecyparis*) *nootkatensis* 'Pendula' (maybe the most graceful conifer)

My Seed-Shopping Rules

I'm mad about seed, so mad that I require "rules" for seed shopping. Some are simple and practical to-dos, like I must restrain myself before binging in the new catalogs until a careful inventory of leftover seed is undertaken, to see what I really need. It doesn't always stop me from ordering just one more (*fill in the blank*), but at least I tried.

Most of my rules are a bit more textured, and some even political, because not all seed is created equal, either genetically or ethically. In a country where we increasingly ask where our food came from, fostering the growth of farm stands and CSAs and the sales of more organic brands, why don't we ask where our seed comes from? After all, seed is the source of virtually all our food, whether we actually eat the plant or we feed it to animals who then provide meat, milk, eggs, and even honey.

All my rules are really about making the best possible match between the seed I order and the place, and way, I garden. The first two guidelines are uttered in the hopes of best garden success, since seed is alive and I want to make it feel at home here. Like any living organism, seed adapts genetically over generations to the conditions it is bred and grown in, and my kind of growing season and cultural practices should suit the seed I order as closely as possible. My rules:

I buy organic seed when available, because I am an organic gardener—and also because I don't want to contribute my dollars to upstream pollution. I use my seed dollars in support of organic farming, as I do with food purchases. Conventional seed farming can be a particularly dirty business, and no surprise: Each crop isn't grown for a mere few weeks or months, like we grow lettuce or broccoli, but instead through its entire life cycle to reproduction age and beyond, meaning that it may encounter more pests and diseases and other pressures along

Beets sown thickly can offer multiple cuttings as baby beet greens.

the way. Conventional farmers would potentially intervene with pesticide or fungicide at each such juncture—and also supplement the soil with chemical fertilizers that I don't use but the seed might have come to expect.

I seek out regionally appropriate varieties, too, reading the fine print not just for days to harvest to suit my season length, but also for whether it was developed for Northern growers in particular—always a bonus. I use the example of a cattle farmer in Minnesota. He wouldn't go to Texas to purchase livestock—Texas cattle are adapted to thriving in a hotter and drier world. A cold-hardier breed would be more suitable, no?

This doesn't mean I don't try regional specialties from elsewhere Southern greasy beans or an heirloom pepper from the desert Southwest are definitely on my wish list. I just don't rely on them for my main crop, in case they don't like it here.

I have a strong preference for supporting seed companies that have on-farm breeding or growing operations and offer either an entire or a substantial selection of seed grown by organic or sustainable practices. Many seed companies are merely resellers, not breeders or even farmers, and I try to avoid those.

I am delighted, and reassured, when it is revealed right up front exactly where the seed in a catalog comes from (besides the company's own farm, since even most of my favorite sources don't grow everything they sell). It shouldn't be a secret; they should be proud to show off the exceptional stashes of genetics they have tracked down, and to shine a light on those growers. If nothing is mentioned, I often email to ask; I am suspicious if there is still no clear answer, and figure that's because they buy from conventional (not organic) giant seed farms in places like China, Mexico, or who knows where—places nothing like my garden.

A corollary: I admire seed companies that have taken a special interest in a particular crop, or to reinvigorating old-time open-pollinated (nonhybrid) varieties that were almost forgotten or in sorry shape, and are working through the long, rigorous process of selection to do it.

Speaking of which: "hybrid or heirloom?" isn't an either-or debate I happily grow both.

I'm not content with merely the claim of "non-GMO" seed, which I'd expect from a home-garden seed catalog since transgenic hybrid seed for cotton or corn or canola or soy, for instance, is an *agricultural* product. GMOs are licensed to farmers for one season's use (the way we license computer software but don't own the intellectual property of it); they're not sold outright in little packets to us. I understand why seed companies must put that on the packets and catalog covers—to reassure so many shoppers worried about that topic—but I want to have more relevant information. I want to know where the seed came from, is it organic or grown sustainably—again, all aimed at answering whether it's a good match for my garden and ethics, seeds I will be comfortable with and that will be at home with me.

A Wheelbarrowful of Prevention

As one recent year wound down, I made a single garden resolution:

"Be thoughtful, keep weeding."

I was reminding myself: to remain focused, always and forever, on prevention—the sharpest tool an organic gardener has—of pests, weeds, and other general chaos in the coming year. Nowhere is this more the case than with plants that insist on growing in the wrong place, our personal palette of weeds. Right until the ground freezes and refuses my advances, I'm pulling more patches of garlic mustard (*Alliaria petiolata*) from the moist soil, and uprooting yards of vine-like ground ivy (*Glechoma hederacea*) that apparently intends to keep disrespecting the lawn-meets-bed edge I'd cut. Against my will, that wily, wiry thing keeps creeping ever inward, overstepping the boundary and then some, and though I will never overcome it, I can at least enforce the line of demarcation. Also on the hit list: deadheading anything noxious that's seed- or fruit-laden.

No, I won't be hosting any garden tours anytime soon, so these last skirmishes are not about an aesthetic payoff. It's about being able to head into my own semidormancy, knowing that I did my best. There is no illusion: I will never have the upper hand in this delightful but labor-intensive contrivance called a garden—this momentary imposition I have imprinted upon nature. But I know better than to let everyone run totally amok because, very simply, I will hate it and be driven madder when, come spring, those outlaws have occupied even wider territories and emerged in bigger gangs. I will blame myself.

So as the year began, it closes: with Margaret bending, to pull more weeds. And if I am blessed to garden another year, I know the next one will start and end just exactly the same way (with the in-between part heavily punctuated by weeding, too).

Inside-out: A view of the old copper beech above the meadow is framed by a windowsill vignette of a bit of Japanese maple, 'Nest Egg' gourds, and discarded snake skins.

Nothing lasts: Deadheading the pansies will keep them blooming and creates festive debris.

References and Sources

Hardly a day passes that I do not page through a field guide or its online equivalent, seeking answers to the endless natural history questions the garden poses. Having a well-stocked shelf of field guides (or knowing the url of related websites) has enriched my relationship with the outdoors, making me a better gardener. Likewise garden catalogs, my first points of reference decades ago when I began experimenting with plants, continue to be a source of inspiration and learning. Here, then, are some favorites from each category.

Field Guides

Bradley, Richard A. *Common Spiders of North America.*

Brock, Jim P., and Kenn Kaufman. *Kaufman Field Guide to Butterflies of North America.*

Cranshaw, Whitney, and David Shetlar. *Garden Insects of North America.*

Dickinson, Richard, and France Royer. *Weeds of North America.*

Eiseman, Charley, and Noah Charney. *Tracks and Sign of Insects and Other Invertebrates.*

Evans, Arthur V. *Beetles of Eastern North America.*

Faust, Lynn Frierson. *Fireflies, Glow-Worms, and Lightning Bugs.*

Glassberg, Jeffrey. *A Swift Guide to Butterflies.*

Golden Guide, *Spiders and Their Kin.*

Kays, Roland W., and Don E. Wilson. *Mammals of North America.*

Leckie, Seabrooke, and David Beadle. *Peterson Field Guide to Moths,* northeastern and southeastern North America editions.

Paulson, Dennis. *Dragonflies and Damselflies.* Princeton Field Guides series, East and West editions.

Pieplow, Nathan. *Peterson Field Guide to Bird Sounds of Eastern North America.*

Shunk, Stephen A. *Peterson Reference Guide to Woodpeckers of North America.*

Sibley, David Allen. *The Sibley Field Guide to Birds,* eastern North America and western North America editions.

Wagner, David. *Caterpillars of Eastern North America.*

Wheelwright, Nathaniel, and Bernd Heinrich. *The Naturalist's Notebook.*

Williams, Paul, and Robbin Thorp, Leif Richardson, and Sheila Colla. *Bumble Bees of North America.*

An amphibian face appears in the duckweed.

Websites

All About Birds, Cornell Lab of Ornithology

allaboutbirds.org

> Species-by-species guide to birds, plus articles, and interactive learning features like All About Feathers, Bird Song Hero, and more. Join and support their work; get their e-newsletters.

BirdCast migration reports

birdcast.info

> Who's flying by your location when? Migration reports in real time, from Cornell Lab.

BirdNote

birdnote.org

> A two-minute daily National Public Radio show and podcast about birds.

eBird

ebird.org

> Record your sightings in this online checklist application while contributing to a citizen science database; browse your area for recent or historical sightings.

NestWatch, All About Bird Houses

nestwatch.org

> From Cornell, including a "Right Bird, Right House" tool to identify birds in your area that might benefit from nest boxes and precisely which nest box design they prefer.

Sialis bluebird site

sialis.org

> Everything bluebird, from nest box protocols and plans and how to monitor them, to bluebird biology and predator prevention information.

Yardmap (Habitat Network)

yardmap.org

> Map your yard, and in the process get connected with tools to foster better decisions about how to manage landscapes sustainably. From Cornell and The Nature Conservancy.

BugGuide insect identification

bugguide.net

> An online community of professional and amateur naturalists. Browse for help identifying insects, or even upload a photo of your own insects for expert identification.

Xerces Society

xerces.org

> An invertebrate-focused nonprofit with downloadable Pollinator Conservation Resources reports, including region-specific pollinator plant lists.

Mail-Order Sources

SEED CATALOGS

Adaptive Seeds

adaptiveseeds.com

> A Northwest-based grower of organic, open-pollinated seed, with kale and peppers among the many specialties.

Fedco Seeds

fedcoseeds.com

> A longtime Maine cooperative selling Northern-focused organic and sustainable seed, potatoes, fruit trees, and more.

High Mowing Organic Seeds

highmowingseeds.com

> 600-plus varieties of open-pollinated and hybrid certified-organic seed, including many bred or grown on their Vermont farmland.

Hudson Valley Seed

hudsonvalleyseed.com

> Open-pollinated seed grown on their certified-organic New York farm and those of like-minded sources.

J. L. Hudson, Seedsman

jlhudsonseeds.net

> "A public-access seed bank—established 1911" is how this packed list of everything describes itself.

Johnny's Selected Seeds

johnnyseeds.com

> A comprehensive catalog including supplies, tools, and many farm-bred seed varieties, including open-pollinated and hybrid organic choices.

Native Seeds/SEARCH

nativeseeds.org

> A nonprofit seed conservation entity offering traditional Native American varieties and Southwest-adapted vegetables.

Peace Seedlings

peaceseedlings.blogspot.com

> Open-pollinated organically grown seed, including many favorite peas, marigolds, and more bred by Alan Kapuler, plus edible Andean tubers.

Prairie Road Organic Seed

prarieroadorganic.co

> Two generations of the Podoll family have been breeding and raising seed on their certified-organic North Dakota farmland.

Sandhill Preservation Center

sandhillpreservation.com

> Glenn Drowns's unparalleled, preservation-focused collection, including 275 beans, 100+ squash and pumpkins, and 225 sweet potatoes (plus heirloom poultry).

Seed Savers Exchange

seedsavers.org

> A nonprofit preservation organization focusing on heirlooms, including seed and antique apple varieties, since 1975.

Select Seeds

selectseeds.com

> Unusual and heirloom flowering seeds and plants, including annual vines, fragrant annuals and perennials, and pollinator favorites.

Siskiyou Seeds

siskiyouseeds.com

> An organic, farm-based seed breeder and grower in Oregon, offering open-pollinated vegetables and flowers.

Southern Exposure Seed Exchange

southernexposure.com

A longtime cooperative offering organic vegetable, herb, and flower seeds, including Southern heirloom specialties like greasy beans and okra.

Sow True Seed

sowtrueseed.com

Asheville, NC–based source for open-pollinated, sustainable, and organic seeds, including regional specialties, plus sweet potato starts.

Strictly Medicinal Seeds

strictlymedicinalseeds.com

The former Horizon Herb catalog, herbalist Richo Cech and family's trove of everything herbal—medicinal and culinary seeds, plants, roots—plus vegetable seeds.

Turtle Tree Seed

turtletreeseed.org

A nonprofit based at Camphill Village, Copake, NY, selling biodynamic and organically grown open-pollinated seed, including from their own gardens.

Uprising Seeds

uprisingorganics.com

Open-pollinated, certified organic growers of seed for vegetables, flowers, and herbs, including fine selections of beets and North-friendly tomatoes.

Wild Garden Seed

wildgardenseed.com

Breeder Frank Morton, famed for his farm-original, certified organic lettuces, calendulas, and greens, grows everything he sells and supplies other seed companies.

EDIBLE BULBS AND TUBERS

Filaree Farm

filareefarm.com

Nearly 30 years farming organic garlic, potatoes, shallots; the largest privately held garlic collection in the U.S.

Potato Garden

potatogarden.com

Seed potatoes naturally grown according to organic practices (plus garlic, onions, shallots, and Jerusalem artichokes).

FLOWER BULBS

B&D Lilies

bdlilies.com

Brent and Becky's Bulbs

brentandbeckysbulbs.com

John Scheepers Bulbs

johnscheepers.com

Old House Gardens (heirlooms)

oldhousegardens.com

Swan Island Dahlias

dahlias.com

Van Engelen Bulbs

vanengelen.com

PLANTS, CANADA

Botanus

botanus.com

Perennials and a bulb assortment deep in dahlias, lilies, and begonias, plus some roses and other shrubs.

Fernwood Plant Nursery

fernwoodplantnursery.ca

A specialty nursery focused on the best hardy ferns for Canadian gardens, offering more than 60 kinds.

Fraser's Thimble Farms

thimblefarms.com

Unusual perennials, shrubs, and vines, including ferns, hardy orchids, hepaticas, and hellebores.

Harbour Breezes Daylilies and Japanese Iris

harbourbreezes.ca

A staggering selection of daylilies (including some nursery-bred originals) and of Japanese iris varieties.

Phoenix Perennials

mailorder.phoenixperennials.com

A large selection of distinctive perennials, plus unusual fruits, subtropicals, and succulents.

Wildflower Farm

wildflowerfarm.com

Seed, including mixes, for North American wildflowers and grasses, including ecological lawn alternatives.

PLANTS, UNITED KINGDOM

Ashwood Nurseries

ashwoodnurseries.com

An extensive collection, with specialties in *Hellebore, Hepatica, Lewisia, Cyclamen,* and *Hydrangea.*

Beth Chatto Gardens

bethchatto.co.uk

The favorites of plantswoman and author Beth Chatto, most propagated right from her famed garden.

Binny's Plants

binnyplants.co.uk

Exceptional perennials, climbers, and woody plants, including the U.K.'s largest offering of peonies.

Jekka's Herb Farm

jekkasherbfarm.com

Herbs, including the most comprehensive collection of culinary ones in the U.K, from expert and author Jekka McVicar.

Woottens of Wenhaston

woottensplants.co.uk

Perennials, with particular depth in bearded iris, daylilies, *Auricula, Pelargonium,* and hardy geraniums.

PLANTS, UNITED STATES

Annie's Annuals and Perennials

anniesannuals.com

Unusual things, many old-time cottage-gardenish or California natives, from Bay Area–based Annie Hayes.

Avant Gardens

avantgardensne.com

A source for the distinctive plants that owners Kathy and Chris Tracey rely on in the dramatic gardens they create for clients.

Bluestone Perennials

bluestoneperennials.com

A big list of workhorse perennials, ground covers, and shrubs.

Broken Arrow Nursery

brokenarrownursery.com

Outstanding woody plants and perennials, with a particular focus on great foliage.

Brushwood Nursery

brushwoodnursery.com

Dan Long's collection of hundreds of species and varieties of *Clematis*.

Fancy Fronds

fancyfrondsnursery.com

A small family Northwest nursery from longtime world-class fern expert Judith Jones.

Four Winds Growers

fourwindsgrowers.com

Dwarf citrus, perfect for containers, in all its many variations is the specialty here.

Klehm's Song Sparrow Farm

songsparrow.com

Specialists in peonies, hostas, daylilies, plus exceptional woody plants, including many Roy Klehm introductions.

Logee's

logees.com

Fancy-leaf begonias, flowering vines, fruiting plants, and other special things for windowsills, containers, and gardens.

Plant Delights Nursery

plantdelights.com

For more than 30 years, plant explorer Tony Avent's unrivaled collection of rare and unique perennials.

Prairie Moon Nursery

prairiemoon.com

Plants and seeds for 700-plus native species, emphasizing the Midwest.

Seed-filled spent heads of garlic chives, and some *Rudbeckia* for good measure.

Acknowledgments

I had barely welcomed my first hundred garden visitors when I wrote the original *A Way to Garden*. The many thousands of people who have walked through the evolving landscape since then have my particular gratitude, because they are part of the reason it evolved at all.

There is nothing so informative, and sometimes humbling or downright hilarious, as watching strangers move through the garden you thought you knew intimately, stopping to take photos from vantage points you never assumed—of "moments" you didn't intend. There is also nothing so motivating as knowing people are coming, to make you do your chores. *Uh-oh*.

Thanks to those visitors and also readers and radio and podcast listeners alike for making me a better gardener with your often-provocative observations, and years of Urgent Garden Questions.

Likewise, I am grateful to those many world-class experts—ornithologists, entomologists, botanists and horticulturists, geneticists, plant pathologists, you name which other *-ists*—who over the decades have made time to fulfill my interview requests so I could ask them my own Urgent Garden Questions, and ones about birds, bugs, and everything my curiosity drew me toward.

Some people I met that way—by requesting an interview—have become longtime mentors, and the prize for exceptional patience over the long haul probably goes to Marco Polo Stufano. (Runner-up mentions go to Ken Druse, John Trexler, Bob Hyland, Glenn Withey, and Charles Price.)

Martha Stewart sent me off to see America's great gardens (to produce stories for her magazine and television program), and that changed me. My friends at Broken Arrow Nursery in Connecticut have helped me grow my open garden days and workshops; Windy Hill Farm in Massachusetts has been there since the start with the right plant and the help needed to learn to care for it.

The rest of you know who you are, and many of you are mentioned anecdotally in these pages, with some tidbit of the wisdom you have shared. Thanks most recently to Aaron Bertelsen of Great Dixter garden in England and Canadian garden writer Niki Jabbour for their recommended nurseries to add to the book's sources list.

Though I was bereft when my friend and former colleague and neighbor Andrew Beckman headed west to head up Timber Press, it is thanks to him and his welcoming and expert team that there is a new edition of *A Way to Garden* to share now with you. My agent Kris Dahl facilitated, as ever, and photographer Mick Hales showed up at a garden tour right in time to get drafted to visit again and again to help illustrate the latest version.

May we all keep handing down pieces of wisdom (and plants) to one another over many more growing seasons to come.

Zinnias are one of the first plants I ever grew from seed, and they still are a sentimental favorite.

Photo Credits

Mick Hales, pages 1, 5, 10, 11, 13, 18, 21, 24, 25, 26, 27, 28, 42 top, 63 bottom right, 69, 73, 74, 77 bottom, 78 top, 79, 102 bottom right, 107, 135, 146, 149 top, 160, 163, 166 top, 170, 172, 176, 177, 186, 188 top, 191, 192 bottom, 194, 196–197, 200–201, 203 bottom, 204, 208, 209 top, 211 top and bottom left, 219 bottom left, 226, 227 top and bottom left, 233 bottom, 235 top, 258, 267, 268 left and middle, 269, 272, 276, 278 top, 281 bottom, 286, and 299

All other photos are by the author.

Index

A

Tiny, curiously shaped cones found under the dawn redwood, *Metasquoia glyptostroboides*, which can grow to 100 feet tall.

MARGARET ROACH, one of America's best-known garden writers, creates awaytogarden.com and the public radio show by the same name, which has been called a "top-5 garden podcast" by *The Guardian*, and winner of multiple Garden Writers of America medals. She was the first garden editor of *Martha Stewart Living* magazine, where she also co-hosted a weekly call-in radio show on Sirius for several years. She lives in rural New York State, and her garden has been open for Garden Conservancy Open Days for more than 20 years. She is the author of two other books, including *The Backyard Parables*.